odern

ove

THREE RIVERS PRESS | NEW YORK

Modern Love

50 TRUE AND EXTRAORDINARY TALES OF DESIRE, DECEIT, AND DEVOTION

With Story Updates and an Introduction by the Editor

EDITED BY DANIEL JONES

Published in the United States by Three Rivers Press,
an imprint of the Crown Publishing Group,
a division of Random House, Inc., New York.

www.crownpublishing.com
Three Rivers Press and the Tugboat design are registered
trademarks of Random House, Inc.

The essays in this work were originally published in
the "Modern Love" column of the *New York Times*.

Due to space limitations, permissions credits appear at the end of the book.

Inquiries concerning permission to reprint any column (or portion thereof)
which originally appeared in *The New York Times* newspaper should be
directed to The New York Times Company, News Services Division,
The Times Agency, Ninth Floor, 229 West 43rd Street, New York,
New York, 10036 or rights@nytimes.com.

LIBRARY OF CONGRESS CATALOGING-IN-PUBLICATION DATA
Modern love : 50 true and extraordinary tales of desire,
deceit, and devotion / edited by Daniel Jones.—1st ed.
1. Love—Miscellanea. I. Jones, Daniel, 1962–

BF575.L8M564 2007

306.7—dc22   2006029412

ISBN: 978-0-307-35104-3

Printed in the United States of America

Design by Barbara M. Bachman

10 9 8 7 6 5 4 3 2 1

FIRST EDITION

ontents

PART THREE

Breeding: What to Expect That You're Least Expecting

PART FOUR

Staying: The Ties That Bind

PART FIVE

Leaving: The Ties That Fray

PART SIX

*B*ound: Family Ties

Introduction

ONLINE DATING. GAY MARRIAGE. NO-FAULT DIVORCE. Viagra. Sperm banks. Text-messaging. Internet adoption. Blogging. MySpace. YouTube. Psychopharmacology. Cyberpornography. Trophy husbands. Breadwinner wives. Microchipped children. Cellular-linked lives . . .

Welcome to love in the new millennium. No more sock hops or mixers, drive-ins or love-ins. Goodbye to sweaty palms and missed phone calls. With our electronic gadgetry, prescription libidos, sophisticated emotional vocabulary, and 24/7 communication, we're finally getting this whole dating and mating thing under control.

Or are we? Look just beneath the shimmering surface of our technology and you'll find that we're still muddling along with the same doubts, disappointments, miscommunications, and thwarted desires that Shakespeare plumbed so brilliantly four hundred years ago. Sure, there's been social progress, scientific breakthroughs, revolutionary changes in our understanding of our world and ourselves. But when it comes to realizing that someone is just not that into us, we're still at a bit of a loss.

Marriage, it seems, only gets more puzzling every year. The befuddling angst of adolescence rages on. Human sexuality, relentlessly explored, never ceases to surprise, shame, and mystify.

We all want to know what we're supposed to feel, how we're supposed to connect. And if we can't know, we at least want to empathize with others who are in the same leaky boat. Some of us—admit it—may even take solace in knowing that others are in a boat more leaky than ours.

If such empathy and solace is what you're looking for, you've come to the right place. This collection of essays, culled from the first eighteen months' worth of "Modern Love" columns in the *New York Times,* invites you into the hearts, minds, kitchens, and bedrooms of real people facing real relationship struggles. The writers here range in age from eighteen to nearly seventy and find themselves in very different predicaments, but they have one trait in common: When facing hard truths, they don't look away—whether they're trying to understand how a single date imploded or to comprehend and convey, in the space of only a few pages, the most important story of their lives.

As a whole, this collection also serves as a kind of literary time capsule of early twenty-first-century love with contributors exploring how technological and social changes have transformed the way we fall for one another, stay in touch, conceive children, define a family, express our desires or satisfy them.

Particularly striking is the degree to which electronic communication allows people to misrepresent themselves and stumble into bad relationships more rapidly and more often than ever before. When it comes to meeting and getting to know someone, the medium that has been maligned as one of "too much information" might more rightly be criticized as revealing not nearly enough as secrecy, evasiveness, and outright lies seem to rule the day.

And when it comes to having children, today's remarkable medical advances prove to be both blessing and curse, as couples wonder about playing God by choosing a father from a sperm bank or avoiding a genetic disease through in vitro fertilization. Science aside, our notions of what constitutes family and marriage also continue to evolve, as gay couples form families, raise children, and wrestle with how to apply traditional (or untraditional) roles to their increasingly mainstream (and in some cases legal) unions, while the ever-rising earning power of women similarly forces heterosexual couples to rethink the roles of husband and wife.

Taken alone, each story marks only a moment, a glimpse behind the curtain of one person's most pressing romantic or familial drama. Cumulatively, however, they form the arc of a more complex and far richer story: how we seek, find, lose, and hold on to love over the course of a lifetime.

Where better to begin such a story than with the doubts, bravado, fakery, and thrill of those seeking love? Part One, Seeking, features tales of dating delirium and disaster, with such headliners as the woman who zips through all the phases of a relationship solely via text-messaging, the Casanova who is baffled at having been dumped for the first time, and the blogger who learns far more than she'd like to about her boyfriend's other woman when she unwittingly stumbles upon *her* blog after following a link from *his* (yes, hurt feelings ensue).

But for the lucky among them, this oft-torturous process actually leads to The One. And in Part Two, Finding, sometimes this is good news, resulting in happiness, marriage, children, growing old together, reserving side-by-side burial plots, and so on. But other times it's not such good news, as in the account of the woman who falls in love with an attractive single man when she's pregnant and engaged to be married to someone else. Or the man whose new female love happens to be both married and already involved with another extramarital boyfriend. (The fact that her husband is on board for this trio of lovers doesn't simplify matters.)

Part Three, Breeding, tackles the complicated emotions of having and raising children. One happily married mother of two, her family seemingly complete, finds herself transfixed by photographs of children on adoption Web sites until she finally, surprisingly, yields to her passion and takes in a young girl from Russia. Some struggle with conception, trying everything medicine can provide, while others battle the children they have, searching for the once loveable child inside of their now unruly adolescent. No stories in the book are more poignant and powerful than these anguished confessions of maternal and paternal desire fulfilled, postponed, surrendered, or lost.

Part Four, Staying, explores the hows and whys of relationships that survive and thrive, whether as a result of lasting sexual passion or a recovery from alcoholism. In one notorious essay, a woman explains how she has kept her husband at the center of her passionate universe even as all of her peers have redirected their passion to their small children. She professes guilt over this inclination of hers, yet she can't help but wonder if this isn't why her marriage stays hot while others do not.

Which leads us to Part Five, Leaving, about the nearly 50 percent of unions that fade away or blow up, despite, in some cases, decades of marriage, children young or old, cherished memories, and often lingering feelings of affection. In these trying accounts, the break is often swift but never clean. One essay startles us with the story of a wife and mother who puts a chicken in the oven for that evening's dinner, and discovers by the time she takes it out that her marriage is over, her husband gone for good, leaving her stunned and grieving along with her bewildered small daughters. For her and others, the end of marriage is usually the beginning of a whole new phase of struggle—one that can last a lifetime.

These lifetimes are what form the core of Part Six, Bound, which examines the multigenerational family ties that fray but don't break, those riddles of devotion and frustration that we often spend our whole lives trying to understand. A young widower finds himself in the curious position of loving two women at once, his new partner and his deceased wife. A daughter, now grown, tries to understand the dark, complicated love of her abusive and alcoholic father.

Some tales make the commonplace seem new again, while others allow us to glimpse lives rarely written about, much less so openly: A former Moonie laments her arranged marriage and its ultimate deterioration; a female sergeant in the Missouri National Guard, fresh from Iraq and possibly headed there again, confesses what she is not supposed to confess about the woman she is not allowed to love.

And miracles happen. A mother meets the son she gave up for adoption twenty-one years before. A daughter grows close to her emotionally remote father after he gets Alzheimer's. On Valentine's Day, a house explodes and burns to the ground, yet the occupants—a longtime married couple—escape with their lives and a new appreciation for each other.

These tales shock and instruct. They provoke outrage and laughter and tears. Occasionally (it's true) they aren't even very modern. Always they pry open the oyster shell of human love to reveal the dark beauty within.

—Daniel Jones

Modern Love

Part One

Seeking

R WE D8ING?

No? No? No?
Let Me Read Between the Lines

Steve Friedman

SHE DUMPED ME. WHAT'S IMPORTANT ARE NOT THE DE-
tails but the pronoun placement, she preceding me. But
there is no villain here. My therapist suggests I repeat this
mantra to myself. So I do. THERE IS NO VILLAIN HERE.

There is no green-eyed, wasp-waisted, pillow-breasted,
sneering-queen-of-the-damned villain who dumped me
so swiftly and with such imperious, frigid beauty that I experienced chest pains and
shortness of breath, leading to something called
a Cardiolyte stress test,
which I've just discov-
ered my insurance com-
pany may not pay for and
which has left me not
only miserable and lonely

> *Romantic rejection
> offers us opportunities
> to behave with grace
> and courage and self-
> respect. It also offers
> the opportunity to do
> what I did.*

and occasionally sobbing in public bathrooms but also
about six thousand dollars in debt. But no one is to
blame here. My therapist suggests I repeat this phrase,
too. *No one is to blame here.*

Did she have her reasons? Could I have been a better
boyfriend? Is it telling that I was forty-eight when we
met and never married, that I had spent the better part of

three decades shedding wedding-happy sweethearts as a tailback dances away from fiendish linebackers, and that I had recently looked in the mirror and seen, staring back, male-pattern baldness and the egregious folly of my broken-field-running brand of romance? No good can come from dwelling on such questions.

So let's assume she had her reasons. What's important is not what she did or why. What's important is how I handled it. Personal setbacks and romantic rejection, according to authorities ranging from the Dalai Lama to the editors of *CosmoGirl,* offer us all opportunities to behave with grace and courage and self-respect. They also offer the opportunity to do what I did.

First, a day after she dumped me, I sent an e-mail message. An affectionate, graceful nondesperate note of about two hundred words that I worked on for three hours.

"I remember how wonderful and sweet things felt with you," I wrote.

That was good, I thought. Bold yet sensitive.

"From laughing and kissing on the tennis court to drifting in the ocean to holding each other and feeling so lucky and grateful. I just wanted to let you know that."

Not bad. Heartfelt but not clinging.

"And I wanted to own up to the toxic stuff I brought to the relationship. And to tell you how much you meant/mean to me, and to acknowledge the enormous amount of effort and kindness and love you brought to me and to our relationship."

I wanted her back so bad it gave me a stomachache. But I remembered with distress the times she had accused me of whining. I struggled over the last line for twenty minutes. I decided on "Write back if you want, but you don't need to feel obliged."

She didn't feel obliged. Which made me want to call her. Which made me want to have sex with her. Which made me want to wake up next to her, to grow old with her. Or to see her age and grow fat and ugly very quickly.

"She's dead to me," I told my friends. "I was mentally ill to have dated her," I told my friends. "Obviously a borderline personality," I told my friends.

"Why did I throw away the best thing I ever had?" I wrote in my journal. "Please, God, bring her back."

A week later I received an e-mail message. She thanked me for mine, apologized for not getting back to me sooner, admitted she was sad about how things had ended. Then came the key line: "I just hope we can have some sort of friendship going forward."

I decided this was her way of widening the dialogue. I decided this was her way of signaling that she was open to romance. I decided to ignore the advice of every single one of my friends. Not to mention my therapist. I telephoned her and suggested we try again.

She laughed. I persisted. She might have used the phrase "just friends," but I have not been able to locate those words in the detailed notes I kept of our conversation. Besides, are the details really that important? Didn't the fact that we had loved each other unconditionally and fully and intensely for four weeks and three days and nine hours and twenty-six and a half minutes mean more than mere words?

We made a date to see a movie. On the afternoon of, she canceled, pleading fatigue and an impending sore throat. She said she would rather make it another night. Was that okay?

But of course it was okay. I'm an adult, after all, not a child. *I am not a child.* She couldn't possibly suspect that I would be bothered by a postponed date, could she? Or hurt, suspicious, or deeply wounded, or reminded with a throbbing emptiness in my gut and sticking pain behind my eyes that when we were making out on tennis courts and drifting in ocean currents and discussing plans to hike in New Zealand together and holding each other in bed, nothing like a sore throat—excuse me, an *impending* sore throat—would ever keep us apart.

Feel better, I offered majestically. Call or write when you're on the mend and we'll celebrate your return to health, I suggested, manfully, powerfully. With confidence. No neediness there. No rage. No desperate, Cardiolyte-test-inducing words.

Almost a week later, on my birthday, as I was finishing a magazine profile, I received another e-mail note:

HOPE YOU'RE HAVING A V. SPECIAL DAY!
IS THE STORY DONE??
XOXO

I spent that afternoon and evening deconstructing the text. Two lines—not good. Eleven words on my birthday—not good. The "v." instead of *very*—not so good. But perhaps I was misreading. Perhaps I was bringing my own insecurities to bear on a sweet, loving signal from cyberspace. I cross-referenced her word usage with all her other e-mail, which I had saved in a special file, and made a startling discovery. She had used the v. abbreviation before! Obviously it was a literary affectation or just a communicative tic. I had been entirely too eager to see in it proof of withered feelings. And it would be blind, and horribly unfair, would it not, to ignore the "xoxo," a clear, unambiguous indication that she was ready to drift with me in the ocean currents again?

I called her to clear things up. I didn't want to misunderstand her, I said. Did she want to date or not?

She suggested I not call again.

Oh yeah? Well then, I suggested *she* not call again. And that she lose my e-mail address. And furthermore, if she ever saw me on the street, she had better . . .

She hung up.

I stewed. I composed bitter letters about how she was incapable of love, how she didn't recognize the gifts I had given her. I did not send the letters. (Thank you, ten years of therapy.) I did not technically stalk her. I did ride my bike by her apartment building one evening, but I didn't stay for any legally significant amount of time. I drifted through the photos of her in my computerized slideshow, accompanied by Rebecca Luker singing, " 'Till There Was You" over and over and over again. I lost ten pounds in two weeks.

Then, a blinding epiphany. I shouldn't have snapped at her on the phone. Of course she had recoiled. Who wouldn't? With the insight came a great sense of calm. With the calm, a sense of hope. With the hope, a plan. If I made her understand how much I loved her, how I in no way blamed her, and how I had changed and was now neither needy nor angry, but just a man filled with love and affection and magnificent intentions, then she might take me back, and we could get back to the ocean currents and tennis courts.

This time I stayed away from the phone. Spoken language was so easily misconstrued.

"I'm sorry," I wrote. "I'm really, really sorry." Then, I elaborated. "You have no idea how sorry I am." Other literary high points included: "I was such an idiot. You don't know how much I miss you. I wish you'd give us another chance, on whatever terms you want."

A week later she wrote back. She appreciated the apology. She didn't trust me. She wished me well.

Didn't trust me? No *wonder* she didn't want us to travel to New Zealand together. Surely if she knew about the chest pains and shortness of breath, her doubts about my sincerity would vanish. Surely if I told her about the way I listened to *The Music Man* while mooning over her digital photos, she would come back.

So I did. I told her. One more e-mail message. I told her all that. I also cited lines from *Casablanca* and *Malcolm in the Middle.* I mentioned my prayers.

That was almost a month ago. In that time I have reflected on and marveled at the chilly and dignified silence that has been maintained by the women I myself have dumped over the years. I have thought of the pathetic old professor in *The Blue Angel,* whom Marlene Dietrich compels to cluck like a chicken, of the poor bastard in *Endless Love,* of every mopey mope whom Frank Sinatra immortalized in his greatest loser anthems. I have considered the Dalai Lama and the *CosmoGirl* way of life, and realized that I behaved with all the dignity of a furious and heartsick and grievously wronged Teletubby.

But I'm getting better and, finally, getting it. I know this because two weeks ago, for the first time in a long time, when a woman smiled in my direction on the subway, possibilities occurred to me. I know this because, for the first time in a long time, I'm not racing to check my e-mail every day or gazing at photos of her.

I haven't destroyed those photos, or the letters and e-mail, as friends have advised. But I don't need to. This time she's really dead to me. Really. I mean it.

UPDATE: *Steve never heard from his ex again, nor she from him.*

Traveling the Too-Much-Information Highway

Heather L. Hunter

I AM A BLOGGER. AN EMOTIONAL EXHIBITIONIST. ON A DAILY basis I make my Dear Diary entries available online to the general public. A few years ago, I began writing my Web log to vent about a particularly difficult relationship.

> *And then, I saw it: the Musician's name—my musician—mentioned as her date for the previous evening. Oh, I thought. I see.*

It was therapeutic, relatively safe, and vastly preferable to, say, slashing my boyfriend's tires. To my faceless Internet audience, I could express raw, sometimes grossly undignified aspects of my day-to-day life without fear of being judged, misunderstood, or rejected (at least not to my face).

Love-scorned and willing to share every gory detail, albeit anonymously, I had, within my first year of blogging, effectively vilified my ex-boyfriend to the Web-surfing masses (two thousand daily readers, at last count). Sex sells. Apparently, so does angst. But these days, while I am hardly shy about revealing juicy details of romantic encounters with foreign tourists, I have become much less inclined to tell the whole, sordid truth. I have learned the hard way that there can be such a thing as too much information.

My story begins in the fall of 2003, when I met the Musician—or, I should say, I met his blog. I was immediately drawn to the openness of his writing, and we soon developed a close friendship through e-mail and instant messages. Long before we met in person, he knew about my compulsive housecleaning, trust issues, and addiction to Ben & Jerry's cookie dough ice cream. In turn, I knew about his fears of flying and commitment, and his grand passion for aviator sunglasses.

When we finally got together, one cold night in late November, the resulting romance became an intriguing addition to my blog. From our snowy weekend at a cozy Connecticut inn to our frenzied moments in the bathroom stall of a seedy Brooklyn bar, I taunted readers with the details of our spicy affair.

During the summer, I began to see less of him. In fact, weeks and then months passed when I did not see him at all, unless I happened to pay the cover charge to attend one of his performances. He was always glad to see me and was as charming and affectionate as ever, but he hadn't asked me to meet for coffee, catch a movie, or take one of our walks by the river in ages.

He said he was busy, and I empathized. After all, his blog looked like an extraordinarily complex to-do list: documentaries, marathon training, concerts, family obligations. Rather than appear needy, and knowing quite well that pushing for "face time" would send him reeling in the opposite direction, I settled for keeping up via hasty instant messages and the occasional e-mail, and by checking his blog.

One afternoon, after finding his entry to be nothing more than a dull account of rehearsal schedules and late-night dinners ("Healthy Choice turkey, potatoes, and vegetables"), I started clicking through some of the newer blog links on his site and quickly found myself caught up with one in particular, the diary of a young photographer. Accompanied by striking photos of its pretty Web mistress were scandalous tales of her Manhattan dating life: bizarre one-night stands, the indiscretions of B-list celebrities, hot and steamy cab rides. I was immediately hooked. I was also struck by an odd feeling of familiarity while reading about this girl's social engagements. And then, I saw it: the Musician's name—*my* musician— mentioned as her date for the previous evening.

Oh. I see.

While I'd known he was dating other people (I hadn't exactly turned a blind eye to the mascara smudge I'd seen on the collar of his jacket one night), I never expected to be privy to the actual play-by-play. My face grew warm as I read about their candlelit dinner (lamb was on the menu) and night out at swanky clubs in the meatpacking district (she had worn falsies). My God, he'd even kissed her good night in full view of her doorman—this, the same guy who had told me of his fierce objection to public displays of affection. Kissing! In front of her doorman! I had to fight the overwhelming urge to flee to the ladies' room and hurl my Starbucks iced mocha.

Because the Musician and I had met through our respective Web logs—and thus always understood that oversharing was an inherent risk—our relationship had never been terribly traditional. We didn't seem to spend time wondering what the other person was thinking. In my case, I figured I'd just write about it anyway.

But unlike me, the Musician rarely wrote about his dating habits. He had conspicuously failed to blog about our own relationship, and so I was blissfully ignorant of other women in his life. Suddenly, with the discovery of the Young Photographer's blog, that bliss was gone. Gone also were the days when I assumed that night-vision goggles would be necessary to stalk a lover. All I had to do was open my Internet Explorer. Although good sense told me that blog-stalking my lover's lover wasn't the healthiest approach to the situation, compulsion trumped reason, and I stalked freely.

It wasn't long before I knew about her preferred sexual position (her toes had to be pointed), her birth control (the pill), and her bra size (34C). And the more I read, the more I was convinced that she was more stylish, more intelligent, and more charming than I could ever be. If she wrote about applying a "contouring duo" eye shadow before one of her dates with the Musician, my mind raced: Did I even *own* a contouring duo, much less know how to use one? If she mentioned wearing vintage Chanel to a press junket, I became painfully aware of the conspicuous lack of silk, vintage or otherwise, in my wardrobe. I bought more silk.

Still, it remained: my shoes weren't expensive enough, my social engagements not nearly as glamorous, and my freckles not half as lovable. Despite knowing that he didn't expose his love life in his blog, I began combing through the Musician's daily entries for any mention of her and for any unthinkable indication that he might like her more than me.

I had been in nonexclusive relationships before and had demonstrated my ability to share perfectly well with others. In fact, I had found that I preferred being the *other* woman to being *the* woman in most cases. But idly wondering what the object of my affection was up to, and *knowing* what he was up to, were two different matters. I did not get on well with the second.

Despite my earlier instincts not to crowd the Musician, I began lobbying for more time together, and soon we were sharing a dinner or two and a few nights on the town, but I remained on edge. His behavior toward me had changed, or so it seemed, in subtle ways that perhaps only I noticed. If he neglected to take my arm while crossing the street, I was painfully aware. I found myself snapping at him, baiting him, and getting upset over the smallest miscommunications. I wrote long, pouting posts on my blog, blaming work or other stresses for my anxiety.

The Musician, perhaps sensing that my bout of unhappiness was not work-related, and maybe even suspecting his own role in my mood, appeared at my apartment early one evening and offered to buy me a drink. A few minutes later, sitting in the dim light of an Upper East Side pub, he asked, "Should I be worried about you?"

"No, it's just stress."

He sipped at his pint of Stella. "Is there more to it?"

"No."

"Would you tell me if there was?"

"No." That was as honest as I would get that night.

Maybe I was waiting for him to ask the right question, or maybe I was hoping the wine would make me bold enough to tell the truth. But neither happened, and it was very clear that our relationship colored by too much information had suddenly become one of not nearly enough. I didn't know what he was thinking, and he didn't know what had been obsessing me. We were reaping all of the consequences of a blogging relationship and none of the benefits.

And then, a few weeks later, I was jolted by a new entry in the Young Photographer's blog: she'd broken off her relationship with the Musician, after learning about his complex love life through his links to other blogs— maybe mine, maybe even another girl's. "I hate the incestuous nature of blogs," the Photographer wrote. "I hate learning things about people in blogs, reading about someone I know in a blog."

It turns out the Photographer didn't like stumbling upon details of the Musician's racy exploits any more than I did. All this time I'd thought she and I were adversaries. Now I felt a sense of solidarity with her.

Only after time had dulled the agony of my own experience did I finally find the nerve to tell the Musician the true nature of my insecurities. And once I'd done so, our relationship began to improve. Our e-mails became friendly and flirtatious again, and our time together was tension-free. My confidence was restored. The Musician even became a regular character in my writing again.

So when I received a bitter, anonymous e-mail message one day from SmugontheUWS, calling me out as "nothing more than the Musician's groupie," I had the uneasy but not altogether unpleasant feeling that I had come full circle. Instinct told me that it was from someone he was dating and that the same insecurities that had driven me were now driving her.

I also knew that if she was anything like me—and let's face it, she probably was—she had her own blog. But there was also a major difference between us; I had never sent a nasty e-mail to the Young Photographer. I'd never sent her *any* e-mail, nor would I. I had to wonder: Who was this smug Upper West Sider whose bitterness knew no bounds?

I was tempted to ferret her out, to learn her story. Very tempted. It would take only the click of a mouse and a simple Google search to satisfy my curiosity. But this time, I'm happy to report, reason trumped compulsion—I knew I had to close and permanently delete the e-mail, and I did. My sanity required it.

A Prince Charming for the Prom
(Not Ever After, Though)

Frank Paiva

LATELY I'VE BECOME WARY OF THE QUESTION "FRANK, what are you doing next Saturday night?" In the month of May it can only mean one thing: I'm going to yet another prom. And no, I'm not doing a favor for a cousin. Cousins are out. I'm this century's new answer to the last-minute prom date: the gay best friend.

By the end of June I'll have worn the tuxedo I swiped from the school drama department three or four times. While most eighteen-year-old guys are

I'm supposed to be straight, so I do my best. Am I ever worried about being found out? Not really.

preparing for their one big night, I'm whipping up more magical evenings than Lance Burton or David Copperfield.

I am also swimming in corsages. I went to the florist today for the second time this week, and she gave me a suspicious look. Does she know what I'm up to? After all, I can't be the only one who understands that gay is the new cousin.

Until recently this wasn't really possible, because most gay men postponed coming out until college or later, if they came out at all. But now more and more young men are coming out in high school. I knew I was gay in sixth grade and came out in eighth. Originally I didn't plan to tell anyone until ninth grade, when I would enroll in a new school, but I decided I needed to let people know who I really was.

My decision had a traumatic aftermath. How is a school supposed to handle the coming-out of an eighth grader? My middle school also contained an elementary school, and alarmed parents feared for their little children, worried, I suppose, that I might convert them or something.

I endured a set of excruciating meetings with school administrators, during which parameters for my behavior were discussed. That and the cruelty of my classmates left me feeling isolated and scared, and I found myself turning mostly to girls for support and friendship.

Although things improved in high school, I still found myself relying primarily on friendships with girls, some of whom I met at summer drama camps and who attended different schools.

As I see it, these girls saved me, and now it's my turn to save them. Dancing a few steps in a beautified gymnasium is the least I can do to thank the girls who helped me become who I am.

I don't even have to go broke doing this. Any girl who's progressive enough to go to her prom with a gay guy understands that it's no longer the 1950s and that I shouldn't have to pay for everything. They also understand I won't turn into a drunken, groping creep in the middle of the evening, so I figure it's an even trade.

And unlike the goofy cousin who might arrive in a ruffled, powder-blue tux and tell embarrassing stories about computer camp, I'm a safe, chic choice. Neither of us will blush with sexual tension when it comes time to attach corsage to bosom. I won't make a fool of my date or myself with awkward straight-boy dancing. And I'll help her figure out the details of her dress and hairstyle. After all, we wouldn't want anyone committing social suicide on the biggest night of our tender young lives.

As the gay date, I also make one of the evening's most unpleasant moments a breeze. I have no problem meeting the girl's parents, a typical sticking point for most guys, because I know that wise and open-minded parents are smart enough to realize that a gay guy is their daughter's best and safest prom bet.

If I were a worried mother of a dateless daughter, I would scour the hip coffee shops of my town waving a rainbow flag in search of recruits. It might cause my daughter to die of embarrassment, but at least she would have a fabulous night out and wouldn't make me a grandmother anytime soon.

At the proms themselves, though, I'm supposed to be straight, so I do my best. Am I ever worried about being found out? Not really. My friend Katie goes to a Catholic high school, and at her prom I even passed rigid nun interrogation.

On our way through the lineup of nun inspectors, they shook my hand and eyed me up and down before pronouncing me a fit suitor. So what do I have to worry about? Then again, maybe nuns aren't known for their finely tuned gaydar.

One thing I've discovered in my brief barrage of proms is that they're all pretty much the same. There's that sense of finality, of going out with a bang.

Gay or not, there's still that stomach-churning feeling of anticipation as you and your date see each other in your formal dress for the first time. There's the poor couple wearing the absolutely wrong ensemble. There's that burned-out feeling in the early morning from so much fun packed into so little time. Rest assured that the onset of horror from wondering what the pictures will look like decades from now is there every time as well.

But sometimes our expectations get the better of us, and the prom's real purpose is lost. It's one of the last times to be together and have fun as a class before everyone scatters and comes back to the reunion ten years later balding, divorced, wildly successful, or exactly, pathetically the same.

Whether you loved your own prom, hated it, missed it, only made it to the parking lot, or were too drunk to remember, there's no denying it's a milestone that happens only once. Or, in my case, several times.

The one thing I can't understand is why many of my female friends, who are charming, attractive, and fun to be with, don't have straight male suitors to accompany them. Surely the school halls aren't filled with date-snatching floozies offering the one thing no teenage guy, except the gay best friend, can say no to. So I've got to believe I see things in these girls that straight guys can't, because with me the element of sexual attraction was never there to begin with.

Many young gay men make friends with the cool girls who fly under the radar because they don't possess conventional good looks and they don't put out. We get to know these girls for the things about them that matter.

Sometimes I want to hold up a sign that says, HERE! DATE THIS GIRL, YOU IDIOT! Of course if they aren't smart enough to figure out that a girl is worth dating, they probably aren't worthy of the girl in the first place.

Perhaps this is why certain girls and certain gay guys become such good friends in high school. They're waiting for an environment that isn't based on popularity or games, an atmosphere where they can thrive. While I've had an excellent time in high school these past four years, I have to believe there is something better out there for me in years to come. I know many of my friends feel the same way.

We've all heard famous women talk about how they were ostracized in high school or unpopular with the boys, only later to become gorgeous and desired. Even though they ended up successful, they never had that high school experience of the prom, that one magical time that can never be taken away. I'm here to provide this to many future famous women, even if I don't get it for myself.

As much as I'd like to, I will not be attending my own school's prom with a guy. My florist must know this because each time I walk in, she always flips past the boutonniere section of her prom accessories book.

I wish this weren't the case. I wish I could take someone with me, because I've got prom dreams of my own. They involve buying expensive ingredients at the gourmet food store and spending the entire day making dinner with my date. We would enjoy the food even more knowing we put all the effort into making it ourselves.

When we walked into the dance, the two of us would initially stun people, not because we were two guys but just because we looked great. I wouldn't care if I had to learn to make clothes myself if it meant avoiding that awkward "I rented this, and it doesn't quite fit" look. I would be able to hold his hand all night without feeling weird or attracting attention. By the time it was over, we would be so tired we wouldn't even care.

Right now, however, my prom dream is just that. My school is a great place, but out of about five hundred students, there are only a few other openly gay kids. (There are also a handful of openly bisexual girls, but that's considered trendy, so they don't count.)

I'm pretty brave, but, sorry, I just don't feel ready to take a boy to prom. I once tried to take a boy to a school dance, and it was just too weird. It felt like every eye was focused on us for all the wrong reasons.

Maybe things will be better for younger guys. I hope so.

At my school, attending the prom in groups of friends is normal and acceptable, so that's what I'm doing. Time to drag out that tuxedo again. But I'm looking forward to it. I will thank my friends for the great times and try not to focus on the thing I cannot yet have. I'll walk in feeling sad and knowing that, for better or worse, I'll be leaving these people in the fall. We'll all go off to our own lives. Who knows what'll happen in mine?

All proms have their cheesy themes, and ours is no exception. "Let the Dreams Begin!" cries out from invitations and prom updates throughout our school.

My dream began a long time ago. I'm just waiting for it to come true.

R We D8ing?

Sandra Barron

THE ORANGE MESSAGE LIGHT ON MY CELL PHONE STARTED blinking as I was getting ready for bed. Barely an hour had passed since our quick kiss good night at the subway, and I was surprised to see the screen light up with the initials I'd just entered into my phone. It wasn't voice mail; it was a text message, and it made me smile.

U miss me? ;-)

I'd met him a week before at my usual Wednesday night hangout. He was alone but gregarious, and he seemed to be pals with the female bartender—a tacit vote of confidence. He chatted with my friends and me and then left early with a wave from the door, and when my friend Kate and I ordered our next drinks, the bartender said this round was on the guy we'd been talking to. Surprised, we debated his motivations. I insisted that perfectly normal people sometimes buy strangers drinks just to be nice. Kate thought he was way too aggressive.

> *That orange light flashed on and, sure enough, it was him. "Miss me now?"*

When I saw him at the bar the next Wednesday, I thanked him for the drink. He asked if he could take me out to dinner sometime; I said I'd think about it. He walked me to the subway, and we exchanged numbers, but I thought it would be days before I heard from him, if ever, making this late-night text message all the more unexpected.

I like text messages. They fill an ever-narrowing gap in modern communication tools, combining the immediacy of a phone call with the convenience of an answering machine message and the premeditation of an e-mail. And if they happen to be from a crush and they pop up late at night, they have the giddy re-readability of a note left on a pillow.

So did I miss him? Certainly not yet. But I was flying from New York to West Virginia in the morning for work; maybe I'd miss him while I was away? I could already hear my friends citing his enthusiasm as evidence that he was coming on too strong, but I'd had enough of aloof. I found his boldness refreshing.

Before I turned out the light and snapped the phone into its charger, I allowed myself one more grin at his message and grimace at his middle-school style. ("U"? A winking smiley face?) Then I deleted it.

He called the next afternoon while I was grounded in Pittsburgh between flights. He kept me company while I ambled down moving walkways and wandered through a loop of food courts. We talked about work for the first time; he said he worked intense hours as a freelancer so he could take months off at a time to travel, and he showed he'd been paying attention by asking me about things we'd discussed at the bar. He asked if we could have dinner when I got back to town, and I said sure.

A few hours later, as the prop-plane taxied toward the

gate in West Virginia, I turned on my phone and an animated lighthouse beacon indicated that it was searching
for a signal. For three days, the light swept the dark cartoon sea in vain. Every time I saw NO SIGNAL on the
screen, I felt unmoored and isolated. But as soon as the
signal bars sprang to life on my trip home Monday, that
orange light flashed on, and sure enough, it was him.

Miss me now?

I'd missed having cell phone service, and my mind
had indeed wandered at times to our airport conversation. But that degree of nuance was too much for the
twelve-button keypad, so I wrote, *Hi! Sure. Talk when
I get back.*

This set off a volley of texts. Where did I live? What
day is good? What about tonight? Tomorrow? We decided
on dinner that Thursday, and I finally signed off, my
thumb sore and eyes tired.

At the office on Tuesday, as the light blinked on again
(*Din in SoHo then drinks in the E vil, and maybe a kiss ;-)*),
I wondered, *Just who is this guy?*

Google failed me. One time, armed only with a guy's
first name and the fact that he sold sneakers, I'd found his
full details and photos online. But all I had here was a cell
phone number and initials, and Friendster, MySpace, and
Technorati—the entire digital detective squad of the
modern dater—were stumped.

I'd actually have to learn about him the old-fashioned
way, in person. Which is partly why, on a slushy, windy
Wednesday afternoon, I liked his next message:

Dinner @ Raoul's 2morrow, I just made reservations 4 7:30.

I couldn't remember the last time I'd gone out with someone who'd made reservations.

Sounds good! I replied.

A message came back as I was leaving the office: *Its better than good—u r with me! Maybe I'll stop by the bar 2nite.*

So he remembered I usually went on Wednesdays.

On the way over, feet soaked and fingers numb, I knew that I didn't want him to brave the sleet just to see me, especially since it would be awkward trying to get to know him better while hanging out with people he'd never met. And after all, we had reservations for the very next night.

Don't come out in this weather! I wrote. *Can't really hang out anyway, see you tomorrow.*

His reply was impossibly swift for its length: *I live 45 seconds from there and I would be doing my own thing. I am not leechy. Very independent boy, I am. I may or may not, depends where the wind takes me.*

Was it just me, or had things just taken a hairpin turn for the hostile? My message was meant to be friendly. Had it come out that way? Or was I reading him wrong? I needed to find a way to respond that was light, in case I was only imagining he was angry, but not flippant, in case he actually was.

I swallowed my distaste for cutesy abbreviations and tried: *LOL! As you like, then. :-)* I cringed slightly as I hit Send; this suddenly seemed like a dangerously clumsy way of communicating.

Minutes later: *Would u like me 2 stay away?*

Oh, dear. At this point, yes. Wires were crossing that would probably be best untangled in person, the next day.

Entering the bar, I waved to my friends in their booth and, before joining them, whipped off a quick response, attempting to be both polite and clear: *Yeah, I guess that'd be better . . . you'd distract me if you were here.*

A minute later, after I'd settled in with my friends, the orange light looked like a warning: *2 late, im here.*

I looked up. Sure enough, there he was, talking to two girls at the bar. He drifted closer and hovered nearby but didn't make eye contact. By the time he came over and sat down, a full hour had passed.

He'd clearly had a few drinks, and our conversation went downhill as fast as it had on our phone screens. He said that I'd tried to "control" him by saying he shouldn't come to the bar and added that he hadn't come to see me but to see other people. After going on in this vein for a while, he suddenly softened and asked me to "promise one thing": a kiss before the night was over.

I stammered that I couldn't make any promises. He shook his head and stormed off, sloshing the beers on the table and sending a pool cue clattering to the floor.

Before I could process what had happened, he looked over from his perch on a nearby barstool, and smiled, winked, and waved over his shoulder like we'd never met. My friends, wide-eyed, asked what was going on. I wasn't sure, but I did know one thing: reservations or not, tomorrow's date was off.

Not so that evil blinking light. Only half an hour later, with both of us still in the bar . . . no, was it possible? Another message?

What was that all about? he'd written. *R we still on 4 2morrow?*

I deleted the message and put my phone away, hoping to erase the whole encounter. Soon he seemed to have left, and as long as my phone stayed in the dark recesses of my purse, I felt that he was powerless to bother me.

But suddenly there he was again, standing a few feet from our booth, smiling and crooking his finger at me.

I shook my head.

"I need to talk to you," he said.

I told him we had nothing to talk about.

Turns out I wasn't the only person who found him menacing: within minutes the bartender took the stocky wineglass out of his hand and told him to leave.

I hoped he'd be so embarrassed he wouldn't dream of contacting me again. But the next morning the blinking orange light seemed louder than my bleating alarm clock. Three new messages, mailbox full.

From 6:30 a.m.: *I am done boozing for a while!! ;-)*

From 6:38 a.m.: *What did I do 2 upset u? Do u not want to have dinner?*

At 6:45, as if he'd waited long enough for a reply: *Anyway, 2 bad, I would have liked 2 have gotten 2 know u.*

I liked the finality of that one. But had he really given up, or was there simply no more room in the in-box? I deleted those three and got on the subway. I emerged to find: *Pls forgive me and join me 4 dinner. ;-(*

We are not going out, I wrote.

What did I do?

I'm at work and we're not discussing this.

Whatever, he wrote. *U don't have 2 b ignorant. Peace.*

I turned off the phone, wrung out and dumb-founded. How had this happened? How had we managed to speed through all the stages of an actual relationship almost solely via text message? I'd gone from butterflies to doubt to anger at his name on the screen, before we had even gotten to know each other.

That was it, I decided: no more text-message flirtations for me. From now on I'd stick to more old-fashioned ways of getting to know a new guy. Like e-mail.

UPDATE: *According to the bartender, Sandra's text-messaging partner returned to the bar a few weeks later and was again asked to leave, after which he was barred permanently from that bar as well as several others in the neighborhood.*

Who's That Lady in the Bedroom, Daddy?

Trey Ellis

I HEAR THEM BEFORE THEY COME IN, ALL THUMPS AND frantic whispers in the hall outside my bedroom. Then the door opens just enough for their shoulders and elbows to jostle through as they compete to be first, followed by the melody of my own personal alarm clock: "Daddy, it's seven o'clock."

That's my daughter, who's six. She climbs onto the bed and presses her face next to mine.

> *I prayed my date would climb out the window and down the bougainvillea.*

I open one eye and see hers, huge. Then my son climbs onto the bed and across the landscape of the comforter, hammering my shins with his knobby little knees. "Daddy, it's seven o'clock," he parrots. He's three and a half.

And just like that, most every morning for the three years since my wife moved out, my big bed's emptiness is full again.

My bed is a vast California king made of Swedish memory foam developed by NASA. Both my son and daughter were conceived on this space-age polymer, and their first pushes from the womb took place here before the urgency of the situation hurried us to the hospital.

But only seven months after my son was born, I found myself alone on the springy expanse. My son was sleeping in his crib. My daughter was in her toddler bed. And my wife was in her bohemian studio on Venice Beach.

She wanted her freedom. I wanted stability for our kids. So she left, and I stayed, but I was a mess. Shocked and needy, I was desperate for solace.

Most of my male friends and all of my female ones cautioned me against rushing into another relationship, but I was convinced that what I most needed to help heal my heart was the smell of new skin. I threw myself into every singles bar in my area code, but always left as alone as I'd entered, and for months my personal real estate languished on the market.

Finally a veteran divorcé gave me this advice: "Think about all the women you wanted to sleep with when you were married, and call them."

A few days later I was driving home, top down, wind blowing the tears straight back to my ears, when I shouted to myself the name of a girl I'd always liked, a thirtysomething Nigerian who'd come by way of Liverpool.

When I got home I scavenged my oldest address books, found a number, dialed it, and amazingly, she answered. Sputtering, I told her my wife and I had divorced and I was calling to ask her out.

After a long silence she said, "I don't think so. You're still married."

True, the Dissolution of Marriage paperwork had been filed with the court only recently, and it would take another six months to be finalized. Luckily my soon-to-be ex-wife happened to be in the house at the time, watching the kids. We had always shared parenting duties, and our hours didn't change much after she moved out.

"Look, I'll put her on the phone, and you can ask her yourself."

I held my hand over the receiver and briefed my soon-to-be ex on the problem at hand. She took the phone into the other room.

What an odd life mine has become, I remember thinking.

Finally she returned and handed me the phone.

"Well, that's a first, Ellis," the Nigerian purred. "You must really want to go out with me."

Going out was one thing, but introducing new women to my kids was another. I was determined not to be one of those fathers who presented his kids with a new potential stepmother every few months. My ex and I even codified a waiting period into our Dissolution of Marriage agreement requiring us to wait six months before introducing to the children anyone we'd gotten serious about.

Since I'm the one still living with the kids, that deal is a whole lot easier for her than for me. It's a good plan, and it's been my fervent intention to abide by it. But navigating a new girlfriend into and out of my California king without my son or daughter noticing is sometimes a nerve-racking exercise in intrafamilial spycraft.

On my third date with the Nigerian, we'd gone back to my house after dinner. It was getting late, and hope was rising in me almost as quickly as terror. Would I break down and sob in the middle of it all? During those twelve years with the same woman had all my techniques become as clunky and unfashionable as Phil Collins and boxy suits?

But the next morning, I awoke alongside her in my bed both amazed and relieved—then terrified. My clock said 6:59. I jumped into my sweatpants, intercepted the kids on the stairs, and deftly steered them downstairs with a bribe: "French toast! Who wants French toast?"

I stuffed them with half a loaf and flooded each piece with syrup, hoping they'd pass out from the sugar buzz so I could sneak the Nigerian out of my house. Alternately, I was praying she would somehow take it upon herself to climb out the window and scale down the bougainvillea. Instead she flounced down the stairs and joined us in the breakfast nook—wearing my robe. My heart convulsed, but luckily the kids, who were only four years and eighteen months at the time, just giggled.

After that experience, during those agonizingly rare yet wonderful moments when a woman did find her way into my bed, I would have to explain to her up front that in my house checkout was sometime before dawn.

And then came the French woman. (I know—I go for international types. I can't help it.) She was twenty-seven. I was forty-one. Of course it was a cliché. Of course my friends threatened to schedule an intervention. And of course I didn't listen.

She and I had known each other for a year, e-mailing sporadically. Then one weekend, in Paris, we fell in love. Two weeks later, I was meeting her at LAX with a rose, so nervous I could hardly stand.

I explained to my ex that our six-month rule couldn't possibly apply to overseas lovers, could it? Who could afford three weeks in a Los Angeles hotel? So Frenchie stayed with me and the kids, but we didn't kiss in front of them, determined to take it slow. Then, somehow, our jokes about marriage became more serious. Less than two months after that first weekend, we were engaged. Instead of being petrified or repulsed by the idea of becoming an instant mother, she said she craved it. She loved my kids, photographing them incessantly, teaching them to bake fondant au chocolat.

When my little boy claimed he was too tired to walk to the car, and I declined to carry him, it was she who hauled him up against her chest, where he clung like a contented monkey. She even said she wanted us to start trying for our own child in the fall. I'd thought I was done with diapers, and yet the idea of having a child with her made me smile.

We planned a midsummer civil ceremony, to be held at her parents' fairy-tale village in Bordeaux. We pictured our families settled around one of those impossibly long tables in the middle of a golden field, a band of old French drunkards crooning with accordions and such. Then in January she returned to Paris for a month and only sent an e-mail back. A long one.

I made the mistake of opening it in the middle of a typical morning of crazed parenting. My son was not quite out of diapers, and I found myself changing him on the washing machine while my heart battered my insides like an unbalanced load. I swallowed hard and explained to my kids that plans had changed and that Frenchie wasn't coming back. Ever. It's been over a year and a half, and sometimes my son still says he misses her.

Over the following months I finally came to peace with my fate, and I told myself I didn't need to look any farther for love than the little ones I had helped create. I figured if I was kind to them and didn't damage them with scolding or indifference, their love for me wouldn't dissolve like the two great romances of my life. I decided that even if the rest of my life did proceed without a mate, I'd already been served a greedy helping of love.

And once I came to that conclusion, of course, I met a woman, Cris, an Italian who's not just lovely but closer to my age. It's now been five months, and she's flown in three times, and the kids haven't even seen us hold hands. During each of her visits she's stayed in a hotel down the street, and I've been setting the alarm for six to sneak her out. We want to be sure. We want to be surer than sure. But how can you ever be sure enough?

She arrives again in three weeks, our six-month anniversary, and we've decided it's time she be allowed to stay in my bed past the bewitching hour. We know each other well, though she can't yet really comprehend the entire package. She also has survived divorce but has no children of her own, so we'll see how she accepts my extremely cute and talkative baggage.

I was prepping the kids for this great shift when my son gave me a troubled look. "Will we still be able to cuddle in the morning?"

I cuddled him right then and said, "Of course, it's a California king. There's room for everyone."

And it's true: there is room for everyone in that big, comfy bed.

If only it were that simple.

UPDATE: *Trey and Cris have been together for more than a year, but they still live in different countries. On Trey's next trip to Milan, he plans to bring his children with him.*

I Seemed Plucky and Game, Even to Myself

Mindy Hung

I AM A GOOD, PRACTICAL GIRL. I EAT MY VEGETABLES. I GO to bed early. In fact, at thirty-one, I'm not just good, I'm an apprehensive priss—and I hate it.

> *I had decided to abandon the carefree adventurer. I was going to be a great big flirt.*

In a recent attempt to invent a brave new me, I contacted Tom on an online dating Web site. Something had to change. *I* had to change. On free evenings, I tend to gravitate toward bookstores rather than bar stools. I walk with my head plunged forward and my eyes down. I'm hardly a hermit; I have plenty of friends, take solo trips to Europe (with my agenda fussily planned out, of course), and fill my weekends with brunches and shows. But my romantic life has been tepid at best, usually stalled out by my caution and timidity.

Friends urged me to try Internet dating, and at first I was wary, but soon I realized I'd found the perfect medium. I could be an extrovert without the exertion. And suddenly I was popular: I seemed to appeal to males from Hawaii to Virginia. Musicians, marathoners, soldiers, brokers, a man who claimed to own five "Rolix" watches, a Hollywood dentist—all these men and more wrote to me and professed their interest. Their attention gave me a shot of bravery—or bravado, at least. They didn't know about my anxious, twittering self. They thought I was exciting. Maybe I was.

Tom's profile began unremarkably: he loved Australia, clean sheets, and orange juice. But midway through, he charmed me by confessing that he'd deleted an entire paragraph because he feared his was sounding like the kind of rambling and often incoherent messages that he sometimes left on people's answering machines.

I looked at this wry, sheepish admission, and I understood completely. What's more, I knew exactly how to respond.

"You seem very good at the charming, self-deprecating schtick," I teased in my introductory e-mail. "Do you blush and stutter in person?" I gave him my number, unasked.

A few days later he called, and as we bantered on the phone I surprised myself by asking him out. I chose the time (Saturday at 3:00 p.m.) and the place (Cha-An teahouse, on East Ninth Street). I forwarded him instructions on which train to take, which direction to walk in when he left the station, and where to meet me in case it rained. I tried to sound nonchalant and in control, like I asked men out all the time.

Heading out for our date, I wore a silk skirt, a low-cut shirt, and I brought a backpack. I was bound for Connecticut later that night with plans to go kayaking on Sunday. I seemed plucky and game, even to myself.

As I approached Cha-An, I saw Tom waiting out front—I recognized those long eyelashes and easy smile from his picture. But in person he was disconcertingly self-assured. He didn't stutter or blush as I'd imagined. And he was apparently bold in other ways, too: he told me he'd once quit his job to become a professional gambler. When I told him about my kayaking plans, he instructed me on how to turn my clothing into a flotation device in case my kayak overturned.

All the while, for three hours, I remained confident, engaged, decidedly unprissy. My only slip came when he stopped and said, "You have two very deep dimples." There was a pause. "And now you're blushing."

I recovered and held up for the rest of the date, but the damage had been done, and my poise—or my pose—didn't last long. But, worse, instead of maintaining my cool, venturesome, see-what-happens demeanor, I promptly plunged into fantasizing about our future together: Tom and me playing Frisbee in the park, sharing a cupcake with chocolate frosting, running along the Hudson. I would slap his behind and take off giggling.

By the second date, I'd decided to abandon the carefree adventurer. I was going to be a great big flirt. I would bat my eyelashes, stroke his wrist, and work some coquettish magic.

We had agreed to go out for Indian food in Curry Hill. I brought him two Aero bars because he'd told me that he liked English chocolates. His eyes lit up when I pulled out the candy. "You might be the perfect woman for me," he said. Or maybe not. Because then he talked about Nicole Kidman and other blondes he had crushes on. I concentrated on cooing and nodding my decidedly unblond head.

I was too focused on trying to secure my vision to realize that I was acting like a fool. If I'd been using my head, I would have noticed the warning signs: all the talk about ex-girlfriends and his complaints about the terrible women on the dating Web site . . . Tom was not interested—or not interested enough.

After dinner, I invited him to my apartment, where I made tea. He stretched out on the sofa and put his feet on the coffee table. I scooted up close to him. He pulled away.

He was nervous, he said. Women were unpredictable. He wanted to be honest. "I find you attractive," he said, "but I don't see this being long-term." Then he gave me a sideways glance and added, "I wouldn't be opposed to a fling."

I felt numb. Bold me might have asked what the hell gave him the right to make up his mind so quickly. But I wasn't a spunky fighter after all, was I?

Instead, I slumped on the couch. I wanted more; I'd acted like an agreeable, love-struck half-wit all evening in order to get it. I had no poses left.

Tom seemed a little sad, but nonetheless he guided me into the bedroom where he laid me down and put his arms around me. "I feel like a jerk," he said, touching the skin of my stomach. "We could always just be friends. We don't need to have a fling at all."

I blinked twice and propped myself up on one elbow. "Oh no, I'd like to have the sex," I said crisply, "but I don't see how we could ever be friends. The sex thing would always get in the way."

There was a pause. Apparently, this was rather original of me. This was also rather insane of me. Tom laughed.

For the first time that evening, he eyed me with what seemed like admiration. "That's usually my line," he said.

I'd gotten my game back. In one audacious move, I had regained my self-respect and control of my brain— or so I thought. We batted the idea around some more and decided that I should think it over. I walked Tom to the subway station. As we parted, I told him I would call him. He said that would be best and kissed me on the forehead.

The next morning, I got up and ran four miles. Then I went back to bed and curled up in a fetal position.

I could still be an adventurous me, I reasoned from the safety of my covers. I thought about Tom's eyes peering at me from under his long lashes. The more I brooded about it, the more a fling seemed like a good idea: I had a healthy libido, a year's supply of birth control pills, and several changes of sheets. If I could detach myself from the disappointment over the lack of long-term interest in me, I might have fun. Never mind that I'd spent the day in bed moping over a boy like a decidedly undetached and unfun girl.

I fired off an e-mail:

OK, SO I'VE THOUGHT THIS THROUGH. FLING IS FINE. IFFY ABOUT THE FRIENDS THING, THOUGH. I'M NOT SURE THAT I LIKE YOU VERY MUCH RIGHT NOW. PLUS, ALTHOUGH I AM FAMILIAR WITH THE GENERAL CONCEPT, I AM NOT SURE HOW THIS PARTICULAR SPECIFIC FRIENDSHIP WOULD PLAY OUT IN REAL LIFE. WHAT WOULD WE DO? PLAY

CATCH IN THE PARK? GET MANICURES TOGETHER?
ANYWAY, BARBARA EHRENREICH IS READING AT
BARNES AND NOBLE UNION SQUARE ON WEDNES-
DAY AT 7. INTERESTED IN GOING?

I read my note. It seemed casual. It conveyed some
anger, yes, yet I seemed detached, frank, witty, intelligent.

I was, of course, just confusing.

"I'm confused by your message," Tom wrote. "If you
don't like me very much, why do you want to keep seeing
me? I don't very much like not being liked very much!"

Okay, perhaps I hadn't come across as the adventurous, ready-for-trouble woman I'd intended. Perhaps I'd
come across as a bitter, scary nutcase.

I can fix this, I thought, rubbing my hands together.
But I wasn't sure what I wanted to repair: The potential
fling? Or the potential friendship?

I started typing. I explained that although I was drawn
to him, I couldn't possibly like him. I had to remain cold
in order to avoid being hurt. Surely, he would understand. "I'd like to see how this experiment turns out,"
I wrote in conclusion. "The question is, do you?"

I reread the e-mail: it was honest, vulnerable, and
realistic, with no obvious spelling mistakes. I hit Send.

This time, it only took me two hours to understand
that I'd written another crazy message. I wasn't a bold
explorer in the sea of love. I was the same timid girl I'd
always been, just working a little harder this time to
avoid heartbreak.

Tom never replied.

My friend Dwight tells me that craziness is what ensues when two clear and opposing visions collide. He is referring to Tom's fling plans versus my dewy vignettes of the future. Dwight is married. He can be objective. He says that my wild responses were a natural reaction to an unfair proposition.

I don't know. Perhaps my expectations—for a relationship, and for myself—were as unreasonable as Tom's. Based on one date and a phone call, I had envisioned a future of endless summers: green lawns, cupcakes, and Tom running beside a blithe, smiling me. The only thing less real than Tom's presence in my idyll was the brassy yet carefree version of myself I saw bounding along beside him.

Misery Loves Fried Chicken, Too

Mark McDevitt

NATE WAS MY BREAKUP BUDDY. WE WERE INTRODUCED at Scruffy Murphy's Irish Pub by a mutual friend who thought we'd like each other. And I liked Nate instantly. With his tight crew cut and animated features, he seemed transplanted from another generation. You could easily imagine him as a bit player in a fifties war movie, yelling out lines like "Hey, Sarge! Over here. He's inna hole!" or "They shot me, Ma! I'm bleedin'!"

We hung out that summer evening in support of a favorite local band. But when our mutual friend left Florida for Boston,

> **We bonded like shipwreck survivors on a bobbing raft.**

and Nate started seeing a woman, our fledgling friendship stalled out.

I was in a relationship then, too. She and I had been together for more than two years and had even begun to talk about marriage, which both excited and terrified us. We were approaching our thirties, so it seemed like the logical next step. And then it all unraveled rather suddenly, leaving me angry and bewildered.

It was during this aftermath that I bumped into Nate again. At first I didn't quite recognize him. In the year since I'd seen him, he'd packed on a good twenty pounds and grown a scruffy beard. Gone were the once-animated features and zippy one-liners. Something about his hollowed-out stare and shellshocked appearance told me his relationship hadn't worked out, either. No surprise, then, that the place we ran into each other was the Self-help section of Barnes & Noble.

This time our bonding was instantaneous and absolute, the kind shared between shipwreck survivors on a bobbing yellow life raft. While no model of mental health myself, I at least had a couple of months' head start on Nate. For him, only weeks after his breakup, the world was still a minefield of painful associative memories: a sudden whiff of jasmine or an innocent radio jingle was apt to produce in him bouts of demented laughter or uncontrollable crying.

Over the next couple of months our friendship flourished. Favorite recipes for chili were exchanged, along with Patsy Cline records. We swapped our many self-help books, which we referred to with titles like *Men Are from Mars, Women Are for the Birds* and *Cohabitating No More*. I gave Nate the entire collector's edition of the Three Stooges; he gave me a cactus.

"These prickly little bastards is some tough hombres," he explained. "Just like you and me. We may be in the desert right now, but I'm here to tell ya that we'll get through this."

Over time our anger and despair gave way to confusion. Just what had happened anyway? Where did we go wrong?

Like a crack team of FAA investigators we scoured the crash sites of our respective disasters looking for clues.

Details and timelines were relentlessly hashed over. But the cause of Nate's midair explosion remained as mysterious to us as the forces that had caused my own relationship to belly flop into the Everglades like a jumbo jet with the wings sheared off.

Our futile search for answers only deepened our depression, but the great thing about depression is that it's not one size fits all but, rather, comes tailor-made to suit one's particular personality. For me it's about insomnia, skewed priorities, and loss of interest.

Food, work, correspondence, even the Three Stooges: all lose their luster. The big picture fades as minor details assume gargantuan proportions. CDs will suddenly beckon to be rearranged, from alphabetical to reverse chronological order and back again. I simply have no choice.

The only real consolation is found in pop music. Leonard Cohen, Elvis Costello, the Smiths: a never-ending cycle of misery and heartache providing grist for our mill of self-pity. Pop music has the amazing ability to make you feel depressed and hopeful at the same time: depressed that you identify with the sentiment, and hopeful because someone feels more miserable than you.

For me that someone was Nate. The only brightness to my day was seeing my breakup buddy and feeling marginally better that he was even more depressed than I. He'd show up at my door carrying a family-size bucket of chicken drumsticks. If I'd lost all interest in food, Nate had gone in the opposite direction; he gobbled up anything that wasn't fastened to the floor. Even so, he couldn't figure out his weight gain.

"I just don't get it," he'd say, wolfing down his third cheeseburger. "I mean, where did it all come from? It's like you turn thirty and *boom!* You're a pumpkin."

I suggested a little exercise. There were tennis courts near his apartment, and so it became our habit to play once or twice a week. Neither of us played well, but with a lot of sweating and grunting, it proved therapeutic.

When I aggravated an old shoulder injury, our tennis came to an end. After that I didn't hear from Nate for a couple of weeks, and I assumed he'd found another tennis partner or become busy at work. But when my phone calls and e-mail messages went unanswered, I decided to drive over to his apartment and check up on him. His car was there, but the blinds of his place were drawn. After I pounded on the door for a good fifteen minutes, Nate finally poked his head outside, like a giant mastodon awakened from a thousand-year slumber. Something about his glassy-eyed stare and the greenish-orange hue of his skin told me he'd taken a turn for the worse.

Walking into his darkened lair, I understood that Nate had not found another tennis partner. Instead he had crossed over into Joseph Conrad territory; he'd journeyed up the Nang River into the "Heart of Darkness."

Without air-conditioning, the apartment was a good ten degrees hotter than the ninety degrees it was outside. The fetid hum of sweat, unwashed clothing, and rotting food hung heavy in the air. A chicken carcass lay on the kitchen floor, stripped to the bone as if by piranha.

Walking to open a window, I noticed there were vegetable peelings all over the floor. Nate appeared moments later from the kitchen, mechanically shaving a carrot.

When he finished, he chomped on the carrot and started peeling another.

"What's with the carrots?" I asked.

"Oh nothing," he said. "I just quit smoking."

"And you took up carrots?"

"Gives me something to do with my hands."

I filled three garbage bags with chicken bones and pizza boxes and took them out to the Dumpster.

Smack in the middle of the living room, directly in front of the television, was a shiny new bench press and giant barbell. Glossy brochures and bright plastic folders about how to become a real estate millionaire in ten easy steps littered the floor. Gradually a picture began to emerge of a man who hadn't slept or washed in days, spending his time alternately lifting weights, watching late-night infomercials, and eating fried chicken.

Alarmed and anxious to get out of there, I suggested we go see a movie. He was game, and after stopping for two bags of carrots, we pulled into the theater.

The event movie of the summer was *Cast Away*, starring Tom Hanks as Chuck Noland, a clever chap who washes ashore on a desert island after his plane goes down in the Pacific. As his hope of rescue fades, he begins the long battle for survival and, more important, his sanity. Something about the story spoke directly to Nate and me.

While I don't think *Cast Away* was intended as a comedy, we never laughed so hard in all our lives. It was like watching ourselves up there on-screen. People in the audience glared disapprovingly as we laughed in all the wrong places. We howled when Chuck knocked out his tooth with an ice skate. While the rest of the audience sniffled as he selected the tree from which to hang himself, we clenched our sides with hilarity.

Hopelessly isolated and lonely, Chuck develops a relationship with a volleyball, giving the ball a face, even a name: Wilson. It is Wilson, more than anything, that helps preserve his sanity, allowing him to mount a last desperate bid to escape his island prison.

I thought about the strange set of circumstances and coincidence that had brought Nate and me together. I told myself he was fortunate to have me as a friend. And while keeping an eye on him had allowed me to feel charitable and magnanimous, I knew my impulse had been anything but altruistic.

In truth, Nate was the yardstick by which I measured my own progress, helping me to feel good about myself and preserve my own sanity. Nate, I realized, had become my Wilson. This overweight, slightly addled person munching carrots next to me was my life raft.

When the movie ended, we shuffled outside with the rest of the Saturday night date crowd: handsome boys and coltish girls dressed in shorts and T-shirts. They wandered outside, laughing and smiling, blissfully unaware of the dangers they courted.

Would they still be happy and smiling in a year's time, knowing as we did that to love is to risk great unhappiness? For them the movie was over, forgotten like the too-large buckets of popcorn left under their seats. For us the movie clung like a lingering dream state. It followed us into the parking lot and beyond.

After getting ice cream, Nate and I sat outside admiring the clear night sky, each happy to have company but secretly wishing that he was somewhere else, with someone else. I couldn't even recognize it for the glorious time it was.

Six months later I finally managed to escape my own desert island by moving to New York. And though I've since lost touch with Nate, I often think about him. When I do, it's not the grief of my horrible breakup I remember but the laughter and friendship that followed.

Don't believe me? Just ask Chuck Noland. I'm sure he feels the same way about Wilson.

So He Looked Like Dad.
It Was Just Dinner, Right?

Abby Sher

THERE WAS THIS PROFESSOR NAMED ANDREW WHO STUDIED artificial intelligence. He was very handsome, in a professorial way. He wore gray turtleneck sweaters and smelled like mint aftershave and old books. He was fifty-five and recently divorced for the second time. He was my father.

He wasn't really my father. My father died when I was eleven. But Andrew was handsome like my father. He whistled like my father. He had sideburns with little touches of silver, like my father. And he was the only other person besides my father who ever called me by my full name, Abigail. It means father's joy. People usually just call me Abby.

> *We sort of spooned. He had a gray comforter. He was a gray comforter.*

The first time I saw Andrew was at a staff meeting. I don't know exactly why I was at the meeting. I was working for the university's research lab as a "content specialist." My job was mostly copying papers about studies on brain activity. On busy days I collated and stapled.

During the meeting I watched Andrew lean back in

his chair. His eyes were dark gray, like his sweater. He was biting his lower lip and listening intently. He looked like a little boy and a grown man at the same time. He glanced up and caught me staring at him. He smiled.

The next day I saw him by the copy machine. He was walking back into his office. His door was open, and there was classical music playing softly, because he was a professor. The light that spilled from his doorway was warm, and I could hear him humming along with a violin. I wanted a reason to go inside, to see his desk, his books. Maybe he had a potted plant? Framed pictures of his past?

Later that week I saw him at the coffee shop in the basement of our office building. He had a large coffee and large hands. I said hello.

He said, "Abigail, right?"

"Yes."

We just stared at each other. He looked like he might leave, so I said, "Oh wow! You like coffee? I like coffee, too."

He laughed. He had a soft laugh. His teeth were strong-looking.

Pretty soon I was going to that copier by Andrew's office all the time. Often I had nothing to copy, so I would make copies of my driver's license, and then make copies of the copy. By the fifth copy my face was just two eyes peeking out of a blizzard.

One day, while I was standing by his door, copying my hand, Andrew came out and stood next to me.

"Do you like duck?" he asked.

"Hmmm, duck," I said. "Who doesn't like duck?"

"So would you like to have dinner sometime?"

We made plans for the next Tuesday.

Tuesday afternoon I went into his office when he was out and wrote my address on a scrap of paper. I left it by his daily planner. Notes are cute when you still have braces and are just discovering lip gloss and boys. Notes are different when you're leaving them on a mahogany desk with an ashtray and a glass paperweight. I folded my note tightly and wrote "Andrew" in script on the front. Then I made sure the hall was empty before I walked out of his office.

I was living with my best friend, Tami. We lived above an all-night diner and had plans to write a movie together. We were supposed to tell each other everything. That's what best friends do. But I didn't want to tell her about Andrew. I thought there was something ugly about it.

I had told her vaguely about having had an interesting conversation with an older professor at work who studied robots. She said he sounded cool. Then I told her I might get dinner with him sometime. She said that sounded creepy. So when I got home from work on Tuesday, I tried to get changed and out the door before Tami came home.

I put on my blue velour pants and picked out an eggshell-colored sweater that clung to my chest. My father had never seen me developed. The summer he died I was still confused and embarrassed by my new tufts of hair and the sour smell in my armpits. Now I stared at my reflection in the mirror. The whole thing didn't make much more sense to me at twenty-one.

The door opened as I was putting on eye shadow.

"I got all the leftover pastries," Tami said. She worked at a coffee shop. That's where our movie would probably take place, so we thought of it as a research position. She looked at me. "What are you doing, Abby?"

"I told you. I'm having dinner with that professor guy."

"You said you *might* go out *sometime*. You didn't say you *were* going out."

"It's nothing big."

"It's a date."

"It is not."

"Then why are you wearing eye shadow?"

"I'm starting a new habit."

"It's a date, Abby."

"It's not a date. It's a Tuesday night."

Her voice got high and loud: "He's thirty years older than you. He could be your dad."

I got even louder: "Shut up! We're just going to have duck."

Andrew picked me up in his navy blue Saab. It had leather seats with coils that warmed you in the winter. He asked if I was warm enough, and I said yes. He dodged every pothole, swinging through a series of turns with only one palm on the wheel. We stopped at a light. He turned and looked at me. I did a fake sneeze to avoid making eye contact.

"You look sensational," he hollered over the classical music. He patted my knee. It didn't matter that it was a Tuesday night. This was a date.

We arrived at Andrew's building and got in the elevator. There were mirrors on all sides, so I decided to look at my feet. Andrew lived on the fourteenth floor in a beautiful apartment with tulips rising from tall, clear vases and the lights of the city blinking through the windows. Everything was on but turned down low, so the violins playing and the duck sizzling and the tulips tuliping would all mind their own business while we got to know each other.

I hopped up on one of his marble counters as those cute girls do in sitcoms. Andrew handed me a cracker with Brie on it. He lifted it to my lips and leaned in so close that my breath got caught under my ribs. I didn't want him that close, so I shoved the cracker into my mouth and said, "Mmmm. So what are we having besides duck?" Pieces of cracker flew out of my mouth.

Andrew laughed. "You'll see." He kissed my neck quickly. Then he went back to stirring something in a pot.

We had slim glasses of chilled white wine, and I stayed on the counter while Andrew cooked. I watched the back of his neck where his dark hair faded into his pink skin. He turned around and had me taste the orange-honey glaze. His eyes focused on my mouth as my lips covered the spoon, and I knew we were here in this moment for completely different reasons. I vowed to eat dinner and then ask him to take me home.

We had duck with steamed broccoli and creamy risotto that melted on my tongue. We talked about artificial intelligence and the role of pattern recognition in early education. When I stood up to clear the table, the floor wobbled. I concentrated on walking carefully to the sink and started rinsing off the dishes. That had always been my job at home. But Andrew shut off the water and asked me if I wanted dessert.

He had an espresso machine and said he wanted to show off. So I said I'd take a cappuccino, and then I excused myself to go to the bathroom.

I looked at the girl in the mirror and said, "Calm down. I'm going home."

Then I heard Andrew: "Come here! I want you to hear this CD."

He wasn't making coffee after all. He was in the bedroom, lying on the bed. He'd taken his shoes off and wore tan old-man's socks that were embroidered with tiny golf clubs. He was looking at the ceiling and listening to something so sad on his stereo. It sounded like a cello crying.

"Schumann wrote this for his wife before he went mad," he said. Then he held out his hand.

I stayed in the doorway. "I need to go home now."

"Really?"

"Yes."

"I promise I'll take you home," he said. "Just listen to this one piece."

He waited for me to take his hand. I did.

I lay on the bed next to him; he put his arm over me and we sort of spooned. He had a gray comforter. He was a gray comforter. He was my father. And we listened to that piece Schumann wrote for his wife. The whole thing. I loved being pressed into that moment, with his breath tickling my ear, still sweet with wine and orange and honey. I stared out his window at the lights from the downtown YMCA and I tried to hear only that moaning cello and to see only the light and dark of the night sky.

When the music stopped, Andrew whispered into my hair, "What do you want to do now?"

I wanted to have him hold me and count all the faces in the moon. Or tell me the story of how I first learned to use chopsticks when we ate noodle soup at Rockefeller Center. I closed my eyes and imagined him sitting in his maroon easy chair, his potbelly almost touching his knee. I listened for his *boom-skedada-boom-skedada* one-man jazz band.

But that moment had already happened ten years before. And Andrew didn't have my dad's potbelly and didn't smell like cocktail onions and Tums, and I wasn't his little girl, and this wasn't my home.

I was twenty-one years old. Not a little girl at all.

So I said, "Please take me home now."

I felt him sigh as he rolled away from me and put his feet on the floor.

"Okey-doke," he said. He stood up and turned his stereo off. There was nothing more to say.

And so Andrew took me home.

Like New! (With a Few Broken Parts)

Irene Sherlock

DUMP DAY IS ALMOST HERE, THE DAY WHEN WE GET TO clear out all the stuff we've been harboring in our basements, garages, and attics and drag it to the curb to be hauled off, free of charge. But typically, most of those things never make it to the dump. Someone comes along and decides that despite the stains and rips, there are still a few good years left in your old La-Z-Boy. Before you know it, the brass coat rack your ex-husband bent at its top has been bundled into somebody's station wagon and driven off to a new home.

I didn't tell the professor I'd been divorced twice. You don't say that on your first date.

At least two weeks before Dump Day, refrigerators, dishes, board games, record collections—things we used to call "belongings"—begin to line the road like orphans waiting to be claimed. Some residents attach notes to encourage adoption: "Humidifier—Works" or "Sturdy Lawn Mower—Just Needs Starter."

It's like my dating world lately, post divorce. In this neighborhood, we all attach notes to our e-chests and plop ourselves on our virtual curbs, hoping to be claimed. So far I've been picky. I haven't called any smokers or anyone who said he loves motorcycles, flying, bullfights, golf, race car rallies, or amusement parks. I avoid those who describe themselves as "intellectual" or "Mr. Right," or who want to start a family. I especially eschew men who claim to be a "White Knight for Hire." At fifty-three, I'm not hiring white knights anymore.

Most ads seem unoriginal and banal, and probably are not representative of the person at all. "I like sunsets, dining out, and good times." Is there anyone who doesn't?

Humble is nice. One fifty-five-year-old carpenter described himself as "not tall, not handsome—regular guy looking for regular gal." I'm sure he was swamped with responses. Most men, like Ron, see themselves as Adonis in pursuit of Aphrodite. "Attractive, well-built, intelligent, creative guy" his ad began. The wish list followed. "Seeks fit, slender, petite, nice figure, well-built, not chunky, not overweight." This is how most men's ads read.

I actually called Ron, a Brit, because he said in his ad he was a "book lover." On the phone, he assured me he was "incredibly good looking" and went on to describe his character in glowing terms. After giving my vitals, I revealed, a little too weakly, that I was . . . well, attractive. I must not have sounded convincing, because he wanted me to elaborate, to sell myself over the phone as he had. Sorry, Ron, I finally told him, we're not on the same page. I put him back on the curb.

Since my divorce, I have probably e-mailed hundreds of men and spoken with dozens of them. I've had drinks and/or dinner with a handful and a coffee date with a very sweet plumber who is also an aspiring poet. He sees plumbing as indoor art, an intriguing idea that we discussed through several phone conversations. The danger of personal ads, I realize, is that you become seduced by the ease a telephone situation can provide.

But you can't know if the chemistry is there until you meet, and when I met the poet plumber on the steps of the restaurant, even though I wanted us to be a perfect fit—if only so my plumbing problems would be solved forever—I quickly realized that was not to be. He had the annoying habit of wiping his hands on his napkin after every bite of his toast, which he chewed noisily. But we did have a nice chat, and after a while it felt like it did when we were on the phone. He told me about his successful business, about his children, who worked for him. I could tell he was smitten and already writing his next love poem.

Give him a chance, my head said. *A good man. A decent man.*

I don't want to kiss him, my heart said.

And then there was the professor, a Ph.D. who taught college chemistry at a private university and had joint custody of his two small boys.

"I don't want to get married again," he announced as we stood in line at the movie theater on our first date.

I led him down the darkened aisle and found two seats for us. "Don't worry," I whispered. "You're safe with me."

What I didn't tell the professor was that I've been divorced twice. This is something you don't tell people on your first date—not if you want to see them again. One divorce almost everyone understands. Two divorces is another story; and no matter how good that story is ("It was the sixties; I was a kid"), the fact remains that twice I stood before God and everyone and swore it would last, and twice it has not.

A colleague once said that he'd stopped seeing a woman when he discovered she had been divorced twice. "She was a bad bet," he said. "Why bother?"

It's true: statistically, we *are* bad bets. And it doesn't take a therapist to figure out that I'm terrified of yet another failure. Then again, there are days when I think I actually may have learned enough these past few years to be a better mate this time around. I might pick the right guy. Or at least I might be able to avoid the Mr. Wrongs of the world.

Which is what happened with the professor. Maybe he wasn't exactly Mr. Wrong, but it took only four dates to figure out that we had little in common except for the fact that we both worked in higher education.

On that fateful fourth date, we were hiking the blue trail at Steep Rock Park, the path rated "slightly difficult" according to the map near the entrance. We'd been discussing the financial fallout from our respective divorces, which included the legacy of a couple of bad real estate investments for me.

"That's why I'm broke now," I said, and then paused to catch my breath. It was a crisp autumn day with cottony clouds dotting the sky. Just ahead, the trail widened to a needle-strewn passage under a canopy of evergreens.

The professor adjusted his baseball cap. "You're broke?"

I inhaled, then smiled. "Well, maybe not quite broke." I explained about my college loans and the 401(k) that had tanked with the stock market. "Fortunately I have the house," I added modestly. "Mortgage and all."

A shadow registered on his face. Was he reassessing my potential value to him? He knew I was smart and could cook, but was he wondering if I would ever be able to join him on his annual Bermuda vacation unless he paid my way? The professor, it seemed to me, was done paying anyone else's way. He had children to support, but he clearly liked his hard-won, single-professional's lifestyle.

Little did he know that I'd grown up poor, that I'd paid my own way for quite some time, and that my whole adult focus had been on acquiring the trappings of middle-class life. Things he took for granted, like education and owning your own home, were the constant drivers of my life. I'd never been to Bermuda.

Three days later, the professor called to say that he was going to be busy with the boys for a while and that he'd be in touch. We played telephone tag for a while before we officially broke up via e-mail (if you can even call it "breaking up" after only four dates).

"You're a really nice person," his e-mail began, "but I'm not sure I want to be to be dating anyone right now."

'I don't buy that," I wrote back. "Just tell me why."

"I'm not quite comfortable with your lack of planning," he confessed. "I mean, by now you really should have more assets."

Staring at my computer screen, I felt a wave of nausea. Planning? Assets? Had he been auditioning for the financial advisor part all along—not the lover?

After my stint with the professor, I took a four-month sabbatical from my dating life and spent my weekends repainting my living room. Just recently I got up the courage to put myself out there again and agreed to have dinner with a forty-eight-year-old man who has never been married. "Tame my wild heart," his online ad began.

"I like this guy," I told a friend afterward. Then I mentioned his lifelong single status, and she turned suspicious.

"Career bachelor." She sniffed. "Red flag."

I don't know him well enough to judge. But I figure, if he's willing to take on my checkered past, I'm more than willing to consider his uncheckered one. I'm willing to see if store-bought actually is shinier than used.

Dump Day has come and gone, and I'm happy to report that everything but my *Cooking Light* collection was rescued by others. I picked up some flowerpots and a lovely old dictionary from a house over on Hudson. Slim pickings this year. Last year I struck gold with a set of voile kitchen curtains and a dresser that is still in need of refinishing—a job I have never found the time to do. Maybe next year I'll haul it back to the curb, and someone more ambitious will come along.

And so it goes for all of us: for me, Ron, the poet plumber, and the professor, who place ourselves within the confines of a personal ad hoping someone out there will connect with our fifty words and nervous voices on a recorded message. If we were really honest, our ads would read: "My heart has been shattered, and I'm scared. Will someone take a chance on me?"

Part Two

Finding

I THINK I LOVE YOU

Loved and Lost? It's Okay, Especially If You Win

Veronica Chambers

DATING FOR ME WAS ALWAYS LIKE THAT VIDEO GAME: YOU try to follow the dance moves, and the further you get in the game, the trickier the moves become, until you are just a flailing mess. I was clingy and desperate and wore my heart on my sleeve, falling madly in love repeatedly, only to meet with heartbreaking rejection at every turn.

Which is why it is nothing short of a miracle that two years ago I was swiftly and happily married.

Until then I was a case study in "He's Just Not That into You," or so I've been told. I haven't read

> *It's okay to fall deeply for one loser after another. It's okay to show up at a guy's house with a dozen roses and declare your undying affection.*

that book: friends warned me that it would trigger too many unpleasant memories. Apparently it is all about women like me: women who wear blinders about the men in their lives, who come on too strong and fall in love with the wrong people over and over.

I'm sure there are many of you out there. And if you're one of us, here's what I have to tell you, what I wish someone at some point had told me: It's okay.

It's okay to fall deeply for one loser after another. It's okay to show up at a guy's house with a dozen roses and declare your undying affection. It's okay to have too much to drink and call your ex twenty times and then to be mortally embarrassed when you realize your number must have shown up on his caller ID. It's okay to stand at a phone booth in Times Square on New Year's Eve, drenched like a sewer cat in the pouring rain, crying your eyes out because the man you are infatuated with has decided that he needs some space.

It's okay because I believe that all of these grand gestures and heroic attempts to follow E. M. Forster's simple advice to "only connect" are not really about this guy or that guy. Making a fool of yourself for love is ultimately about you, about how much you have to give and the distances you will travel to keep your heart wide open when everything around you makes you feel like slamming it shut and soldering it closed.

Not to digress into too much pop psychology, but I sometimes think that I never had a chance at being one of those girls who could play it cool. My parents' marriage was a soap opera saga of dramatic exits and mind games and affairs. When I was little, my father would force me to choose which parent I loved more. If I chose my mother, he would react with fury. If I chose him, he would smother me with hugs and kisses, luxuriating in his victory, then promise to come back for me soon.

Soon could mean two days or two weeks or two months. I learned early on that love meant never having to follow through on your promises.

My mother, bless her heart, tried to keep me from

becoming a desperate girl with a daddy complex. In seventh grade, I got my first boyfriend: one very handsome junior high school star athlete named Chuck Douglas. We went to different schools, so our relationship consisted of long, meandering phone calls, most of which were initiated by me.

One day, when my mother could not reach me after school for three hours straight, she came home early with the intention of beating some sense into me. When she found me sprawled underneath the dining table, the phone cord wrapped like a bracelet (or a handcuff) around my arm, she took pity. She led me into her bedroom and asked me how often I called Chuck.

"All the time."

"And how often does he call you?" she asked.

I shrugged.

"You can't chase boys," she said. "They don't like it."

I was thirteen. Chuck Douglas was dating me, a certified nerd, in a sea of buxom cheerleaders. My mother's words meant nothing. I was already lost to the cause.

In college, I discovered women's studies and somehow managed to wrap the words of Gloria Steinem and Angela Davis neatly around my now well-solidified boy craziness. "I'm a feminist," I declared. "I don't need to wait for a man to ask me out."

So I asked out guy after guy after guy: the very epitome of "he's just not that into you." I dated numerous gay men who hadn't yet come out. It became a kind of service after a while, coaching ex-boyfriends out of the closet. I went out with a techno DJ who invited me to go sailing with his parents. I hated his taste in music, and he was a terrible kisser, but I still cried a week later when he dumped me.

In my twenties I had two long-term relationships that nevertheless ended, and I found myself back out in the wilds of the dating world. At this time the hot self-help dating book was *The Rules*. There were many rules that were supposed to help you lasso a man, but the one I remember said that you should never accept a date for Saturday after Thursday.

The Rules reminded me of that conversation I had with my mother about the swoon-worthy Chuck Douglas. I understood that the rules were good for me, but so is tofu, and I just can't stand the stuff.

My friend Cassandra insisted that men are like lions; they want to chase their prey. She suggested that I smile at a guy I was interested in instead of barreling him over with conversation. "See what he does," she said. "If you're feeling playful, then maybe give him a little wink."

Soon after, I was invited by a friend to take a trip to South Africa. One enchanted morning my friend and I were having breakfast in the hotel restaurant. Across the room I spied a charming man with the kind of friendly face that you feel you have known forever. Leaving the restaurant, I stood up and saw that he was looking my way. I smiled. He smiled back. Feeling bold, I winked, then tripped on a step and fell on my face.

The next few minutes were dizzying as I was surrounded by hotel staff offering me ice and bandages. Then I heard a voice amid the cacophony; it was the man I had winked at. I turned away, mortified.

"You should see a doctor," he said.

I insisted that I was fine.

"Well, let me be the judge of that, because I happen to be a doctor."

He took me out to dinner that night and every night for the rest of my trip. We exchanged phone numbers, and even though I lived in New York and he lived in Sydney, Australia, I called and called him because I was so sure that what I felt for this man was, if not love, then certainly magic.

It wasn't. To give the guy a little credit, we lived continents apart. Even if he was that into me, it would've been a hard row to hoe.

It was about this time, when I was in my late twenties, that I read a nugget of advice, probably in a women's magazine, that I took to heart. This article suggested that if you knew you were going to meet the love of your life in one year, you would really enjoy this year. This seemed reasonable.

So while I still tended to wear my heart on my sleeve and to commit too quickly, I also had some really fun one-off dates with guys I knew were never going to call. I went to the theater and to hip-hop shows and tried to relax about the whole dating and mating thing.

About a year later I met the man who would become my husband. The friend who kept reintroducing us insisted that, unlike the vast majority of men I was meeting in New York, Jason was a guy who could hold his own. He was not a *Sex and the City* Mr. Big, a type I was well acquainted with: the übersuccessful guy who keeps you at arm's length. Nor was he a starving artist who was willing to fall in love while nursing commitment issues about things like holding down a job and paying bills.

Jason was a regular guy: he had a good job, owned a house, liked his parents. Eight months after our first date he proposed.

Suddenly the role I had been playing my entire dating life was reversed: I didn't want to get married. I'd never been angling for a ring. What I had wanted all through my twenties was a really great boyfriend: someone who called when he said he would, who would get up early and go running with me over the Brooklyn Bridge, and who would jump at the chance at weekend getaways in the Berkshires.

I wanted someone with whom I could read the Sunday paper in bed, who would sit next to me during foreign movies, who would bring me chicken soup when I felt ill, who would send me flowers on Valentine's Day, and sometimes for no reason at all.

Jason said he wanted all the same things, too. But to him the relationship I described was marriage, not dating.

So I said yes.

Which is probably why after two years of holy matrimony I still make the mistake of calling Jason my boyfriend. He is in every way the best boyfriend I've ever had. No one ever told me that a really great marriage can make up for two decades of horrible dating. No one ever said that all those guys who were just not that into you can be, for women, the psychological equivalent of notches on a bedpost.

I'm happy now that I dated the DJ, the doctor, the

candlestick maker. When I look back at those relationships, I can see that in the midst of all the drama I managed to have a goodly amount of fun.

What would have happened if any of those relationships had lasted, bumbling along in all their glaring wrongness? Instead of just being dumped and consoling myself with pints of Chunky Monkey and viewings of *Breakfast at Tiffany's,* I could have been facing any one of these men in divorce court, or being forced to see them every Saturday afternoon, when we met to swap custody of our children or our cocker spaniel.

Thankfully, all those men were just not that into me. They did me a bigger favor than I could ever have known.

Hear That Wedding March Often Enough, You Fall in Step

Larry Smith

YES, WE WERE ON AN IDYLLIC ROCK ON A POSTCARD-worthy cove on the New England coast. Okay, I did have a ring—seven actually, none with diamonds. Fine, there was fumbling and nervousness and the oh-so-slyly stashed champagne in the vegetable drawer in the refrigerator back in the cottage. But let's get one thing straight: I didn't say the words. I didn't need to ask. She didn't need to answer. It never mattered.

Will you marry me? Who wants to know? Who cares? Not me. Not her. Is there anyone else, really, whose opinion counts?

> *We'd been to twenty-seven weddings—twenty-seven!—in our seven years together. No one could accuse us of not supporting, with gusto, this hallowed tradition.*

We'd been together seven years. What with medical advancements, free-range chicken, and Pilates classes, I estimated we were good for fifty, maybe sixty more. We didn't need a piece of paper to make what we had more real. What we needed was to learn Spanish and surf in Costa Rica. We needed to buy an apartment together and discuss light fixtures.

Maybe we even needed to breed. We didn't need to get married.

This troubled the usual suspects (grandparents, mothers). But it also, to our surprise, concerned those we expected to embrace our "unconventional" lifestyle (the pierced, the gay, the younger siblings). At a coleslaw-wrestling contest in Daytona, Florida, a grizzled biker told her she was nuts ("What are you doing with this guy? He got money?") and called me an idiot for not sealing the deal ("You better hold on tight, boy, before someone takes her away").

What, exactly, was the problem? We didn't have one.

This wasn't a political statement. We'd been to twenty-seven weddings—twenty-seven!—in our seven years together. We'd made toasts, danced with stray cousins, coaxed extra bottles of booze from busboys. No one could accuse us of not supporting, with gusto, this hallowed tradition.

This wasn't the fallout of family trauma. My folks are high school sweethearts, married forty years, for better, for worse. Her parents divorced when she was in high school—not ideal, but not exactly unusual for someone born in 1969, nor, in her case, the cause of large therapy bills later.

This wasn't even a hipster, postmodern, too-cool-for-school stance. Despite a popular misconception, there was never a time when I thought getting married was a sellout to convention. In fact, I always assumed I would get married.

She'd tell you her dream as a young girl never involved

a man whooshing her off her feet, shoving a rock on her finger, and sending her down the aisle. She'd tell you she's always been tough-minded and independent—and never expected to be in a relationship this long. She'd tell you the whole thing has been a pleasant surprise, that she's shocked it's working out this well. I saw no reason to rock this boat.

Cut to the night before our wedding: let's call it May 2006. A cool breeze greets the guests at the rehearsal dinner in a funky café in Key West. The mixing and mingling subsides as a playful pastiche of our previous separate lives is projected at the front of the room. Roll video.

Mine comes on first. The *Dennis the Menace* youth. Inappropriate uses of the high school PA system that would make the Desperate Housewives blush. Kooky Atlantic City summers at my grandmother's house and staying out all hours with a series of playthings she and her best friend Bunny Bookbinder didn't approve of. A theme emerges: girls. He loves them. Short, tall, big, small. White, black, Asian. Older, younger. Laurence David Smith is girl crazy. What's more, he himself is no big deal to look at, so he's got to work harder. But he loves it. Look at him chase! Why give this up? Ever? Now we see him in his mid-thirties, living in New York—best place on earth for a decent-looking dude with a good job and no discernible drug or anger-management problems to become acquainted with a lot of women. He could go on like this for years—five! ten!—before settling down with a choice woman in his target demographic. Fun!

Her life story is the real crowd-pleaser, though. Here she is, being conceived by hippie parents, San Francisco,

1969. The brief but memorable child-modeling career. The slow, sure birth of a stubborn independent streak and indifference to boys during high school. The years at an all-women's college. Jobs at rollicking bars. Exploits in Indonesia. Dangerous love. Make no mistake, she's the one always being chased (and rarely caught) in this movie. Theme: don't fence me in. Marriage? Don't bet your lunch money on it.

The man who loves women and the woman who won't be corralled—makes for great video. You say: Tigers never change their stripes. We say: We're together, we're happy. Survey says: If it ain't broke, don't marry it.

What happened?

I'm not entirely sure. My path to carrying seven gold rings (one for each year we'd been together) in a hermetically sealed bag as I cautiously kayaked out to that rock was subtle, a combination of personal outlook, impossible-to-define emotional pull, and gut instinct that even now I am still piecing together.

There was never a tipping point, no eureka moment when I realized that doing the most traditional thing possible was a good idea. Some guys say they know immediately She's the One. Not me. Whether it's a sweater or software, it takes some time for me to know if I want to keep something, one reason I always save receipts. I can't say there was an instance when I looked into the pale blue eyes of the girl I met over corned beef hash at a café in San Francisco and thought, *This is it.*

Now, after eight years, I know. When did I know? Was it how she helped me deal with the death of my grandfather? The relief I felt when she finally answered her cell on September 11? That great hike in Point Reyes? Because she cried when the Sox finally won? The way my nephew greets her like a rock star when she walks into the room? Perhaps I should have known right from the start, that morning of our cross-country trip, when she required one last trip to Arthur Bryant's for a half slab of ribs for breakfast (and ten minutes into the meal saying to me, "Hey, baby, why don't you pop open a beer?"). Or did I not truly know until seven years later when we found ourselves forced apart for more than a year? Who can say? It's the big moments, maybe, but it's the little moments as much or even more.

I do know one thing: those twenty-seven weddings had a lot to do with it. They were joyous, righteous, nup-tastic affairs (as Woody Allen said about orgasms, "the worst one was right on the money"). The idea of putting our own personal stamp on a tradition we've now seen take so many shapes and forms—including but not limited to full Masses, lobster bakes, white doves, exploding chupahs, gigantic soap bubbles, freezing-cold skinny-dipping, and one quasi-orgy—has become more appealing, not less, with each one.

But that's the party, and there's never been any doubt that we'd know how to throw a grand one to celebrate our staying power. Getting married—with the blood tests and stamped reply cards and tax benefits—is much more than that.

Like I said, I always thought I'd get married, until I started realizing maybe I wouldn't, or at least didn't have to. I've had long-term relationships before and exactly zero pressure to pop the question. No one has cared less than my fiancée, which makes her Woman of the Year to my buddies who are feeling the heat from partners who want to see a tangible, sparkly finish line. And although I'm also crazy about her unflappable strength and independence, I see the self-doubting downside: Does this person really need me? Does she wear her steely self-sufficiency like a badge of honor that will be stripped away if some priest, judge, or ordained-for-a-day pal of ours starts yammering about the power of unions?

So I figured that one out (she needs me, duh; and anyone who has watched us interact knows how much I need her). And I figured the rest of it out by the way she pinches the skin of my elbow during the bride's father's *we-cannot-be-hearing-this* toast. I figured it out from the little squeeze of my hand during a beautiful ceremony, and her quiet tears landing on both our fingers. And I figured it out from the ever-so-slightly different look I saw in her eyes the last time a perfect stranger questioned my sanity for not locking this lady up. And slowly as ever, yet indeed as sure as it gets, it dawned on me—she *wants* to get married. And I want to get married. To her. There's nothing less original than marriage—this is perhaps the least original idea I've had in a long time—but I needed to get there myself, on my own terms. And after all these years (so many that people have long stopped asking), one thing I actually had going for me was the element of surprise.

So what the hell, let's do it. I still don't believe marriage is the only path to happiness or completeness as a person, but it's the right thing for us. So I asked her. Or, more accurately, what I said, sitting next to her on that silly island in a scene straight out of *Bride's* magazine, was something about love and commitment and not going anywhere and here are these rings I got you, and if you want to actually make it official, that's cool, and if you don't, that's cool, too. And if you want to have a wedding, I'm into it, and if you don't, who needs it. She's still unclear what it was I was asking, exactly, but when she got done laughing, she said yes. And then she threw off her clothes and jumped in the water.

My friends joke that I've been to twenty-seven weddings and now it's finally time for one funeral . . . for my singlehood. Which is sad like any funeral, sure, but this death is no tragic accident. I look at it more like euthanasia I'm performing on myself, a mercy killing.

I'm ready, babe. Pull the plug.

UPDATE: *Larry and Piper plan to marry on their tenth anniversary of dating, at the Point Reyes National Seashore, an hour north of San Francisco and just down the road from where they first kissed.*

Two Men, Baby on the Way, and Me

Rebecca Eckler

I WAS THREE MONTHS PREGNANT AND ENGAGED TO BE MAR-
ried when I met him. He and I were out for dinner with
mutual friends. He made me laugh. He was very cute.
And very single. He saw my ring and heard my announcement about the growing bump in my stomach.
Nevertheless, he paid for my dinner and walked me
home, and a couple of weeks later we made plans to go
see an early movie.

After the movie, I
invited him into my apartment and made him a
vodka and orange juice. I
drank water but felt first-
date tipsy anyway.

Of course, it wasn't a

> *It was easier to
> pretend that the Cute
> Single Man was the
> father than to explain
> that he was just a
> friend.*

date. How could it be, when I had a bump in my stomach and was engaged to the father of the bump? No, the
word *date* was never uttered. I was in bed, alone, by ten.
But before he left, this cute single man surveyed my
apartment and told me I should have more secure locks
on my sliding-glass doors. The next day, he dropped off
a broomstick handle with my doorman, which I was to
use to secure the sliding door in the back.

Where was my fiancé? He lived in a different city, thousands of miles away. We'd been together this way for years—apart, yes, but together. We saw each other once a month. Our arrangement was fine until I got pregnant, which had forced us to make decisions. We chose to get married (eventually) and live in his western city, but for me to remain for the duration of the pregnancy in my better-for-my-career eastern city, because it was, well, better for my career.

This confused many people. "Yes, I'm pregnant," I had to explain endlessly. "No, the fiancé is not here. Yes, I go to the obstetrician appointments by myself. Yes, he visits. Yes, I visit. Really, it's fine."

But now, inconveniently, I had met this new man who had brought me a broomstick for security. To friends, I started to refer to him as Broomstick. His other name was Cute Single Man.

Cute Single Man and I began to e-mail regularly. We played Scrabble. Soon we had a standing date on Thursday nights watching reality television. He would come to my apartment and bring me ice cream, sliced watermelon, and Big Macs, my craving foods.

When CSM and I went to Mr. Sub (another craving) late one Saturday night and the employee behind the counter asked us when we were due, it was easier to pretend he was the father than to explain that he was just a friend. After all, what kind of woman goes out with a cute single man at eleven on a Saturday night when she's pregnant with another man's child?

Also I didn't have a car, so CSM took me grocery shopping on Sunday afternoons. He carried the cases of bottled water. When we once shared an elevator with another pregnant couple, it was more natural for me to say, "We also can't wait for this thing to come out," than, "Well, I'm excited. I'm not sure he is. He's not the father."

When we went to the movies, people gazed at us with the warm approval generally bestowed upon pregnant couples. I suppose we looked wholesome and happy. And I couldn't help but think that he and I would have had a very good-looking baby.

At first, I thought CSM pitied me. Actually, I thought he was attracted to my big pregnant breasts. I was right in both instances.

After all, there I was, two cups larger than my pre-pregnant self, alone in a big city, pregnant, while the father was a four-hour plane ride away. But CSM shouldn't have pitied me. It was my choice.

CSM was becoming a version of the fill-in boyfriend, which many women in long-distance relationships have. The fill-in boyfriend takes you to the movies or to dinner, or sets up your DVD player. The only difference for us—besides the fact that I was pregnant and engaged—was that he was quickly becoming more than simply a version of the fill-in boyfriend.

"He's in love with you," my friend kept telling me. "Why is he attracted to an engaged pregnant woman? What's wrong with him? It's like you're the ultimate challenge."

Sometimes I did find his attraction odd, but like most women, I like to believe my personality is what attracts men. I didn't want to believe I was just a challenge or that he had commitment problems (though often I did think that). I also did not, or could not, believe that CSM was physically attracted to the pregnant me—in sweat pants, with cellulite on my arms and pimples on my chin.

Don't get me wrong. I wanted CSM to be attracted to me. I was pregnant, not dead. And I liked him, too. Very much, then too much, and then, yes, way too much. I would have said we were falling in love, but as it wasn't an appropriate time for me to be falling in love, I didn't say it. We certainly acted as if we were falling in love. I spoke to him first thing in the morning and at the end of every day. I missed him five minutes after he dropped me off. A night without seeing him felt like a month. He told me he had never cared for anyone like he cared for me.

And we fought like we were in a passionate relationship. One night I asked him to bring me chocolate ice cream. He brought me toffee-flavored instead. It was, I felt, the end of the world.

"Try it," he said. "You'll like it."

"I will not like it," I screamed. "I wanted chocolate ice cream. You never listen to me. It's always all about you!" I kicked him out of my house, like a madwoman. It was the pregnancy hormones.

I thought I had lost him forever that night, and I waited for hours by my perfectly functioning phone, wondering if it had been disconnected, hoping for him to call, and knowing it would be better if he didn't.

He did. I apologized. We made up.

Another time we went to a large party. I shouldn't have gone. I was six months pregnant by then, felt ugly and out of place, and needed a bathroom every five minutes. He refused to accompany me to the bathroom, asking why didn't I just find him afterward. He flirted with other women, or at least that's the way I saw it. And why shouldn't he have? We were at a party. It's not as if he were the father of my child.

I left the party without telling him, angry, jealous. He called me at 3:00 a.m., drunk and apologetic. I had to keep reminding myself he was not my fiancé, not the person I was going to marry and grow old with.

But when I had an obstetrician appointment, he would say, "Call me right after."

And I would. (Immediately after I called the fiancé.) I couldn't stop myself. My head was screaming, Stop! But my heart . . .

"It's a girl!" I told him. "I wanted a girl!"

"Fantastic!" he said.

Like the model expectant father, he loved placing his hand on my stomach when the baby kicked. "Wow," he'd say. "That's amazing."

He worried about me and about this baby that wasn't his. I worried what people would say about me if they knew about our relationship. He worried what people would say about him. I worried about my fiancé, whom I loved and didn't want to hurt and didn't want to lose. I worried about what the right thing was for my baby.

To the extent that we could, we kept "us" a secret. CSM did not tell his friends about me, and I told mine—those who knew—simply that I liked him and that he made me laugh.

But I knew we were crossing some line. If my fiancé were hanging out in his city with a cute single woman,

I would have killed him. CSM never spoke of the fiancé, and I never spoke of CSM to the fiancé. If the fiancé suspected, he turned a blind eye. The denial! We were all swept up in it.

When I was very pregnant and it was time to leave CSM to be with the fiancé, my heart cracked. I cried on the plane. I no longer had any idea what I wanted. But I was having a baby in a few weeks. My life was about to change completely, and I was mostly wrapped up with the facts: I had gained forty-seven pounds, I could barely walk, and I was going to have an actual human thing to look after.

My baby is now no longer a baby. She is seventeen months old. Around the time my daughter was learning to walk, the supermodel Heidi Klum became engaged to Seal, after she met and dated him while pregnant with another man's child. No one, it seems, was bothered by this. Likewise, in the movie *The Life Aquatic with Steve Zissou,* the very pregnant journalist character ends up in bed with another man, not the father of her baby. Yet we all want her to be happy, and we're happy she hooks up with another man.

But I'm not sure anyone is happy about me and CSM. It's been more than two years since that fateful dinner and a year and a half since I moved away, yet he and I are still in touch. I take frequent trips to my eastern city, and we see each other. We struggle to figure out what, if anything, we are. We talk, we fight, we don't talk. He misses me. I miss him. He hates me. I hate him. On and on it goes.

The fiancé and I have struggled, too. We have not married. We have not regained that clarity. We ask ourselves,

"Are we happy together?" "Are we meant to be?" Those are, and perhaps forever will be, our questions. Maybe they are everyone's questions.

And finally, of course, there are the "if onlys." If only I'd moved west to be with my fiancé at the start. If only I hadn't gone to that dinner. If only CSM and I hadn't met at such an inopportune time. If only we could plan falling in love like a scheduled C-section.

UPDATE: *Rebecca lives happily with her fiancé and her two-year-old daughter. She has not spoken to Cute Single Man in a very long time.*

The Third Half of a Couple

Howie Kahn

IT'S A BIG MORNING FOR ME: A BREAKFAST DATE AT MY place, and I'm cooking. I've scoured the markets and rounded up the best of everything: oranges for zesting, pears for roasting, balsamic for drizzling, goat cheese for crumbling and, to amp up my French toast, a vial of organic Mexican vanilla beans for eviscerating and flecking. I've even grated the cinnamon myself. That's just what you do when someone special is coming over.

> *It didn't take long for me to stop dating entirely.*
> *It seemed pointless, since I already had a part in a very solid marriage.*

After completing my knife work, I set the table (folding the napkins into caterer's shapes), float pink peony blossoms in a glass bowl, take a quick shower, and put on a well-worn black T-shirt and a good pair of ripped jeans. At 11:00 a.m.—right on time—the buzzer sounds.

I answer the door, and there they are, my "date": eager, radiant, and, most appealingly, married.

I know this setup sounds potentially kinky, but there's no sexual dynamic to report on here. No threesome will commence once the fruit is caramelized. My guests, Cory and Jake, are faithful to each other, and I'm not looking to mess that up. On the contrary, I depend on the stability of their marriage; I need them to stay together so I can go where they go and do what they do. Simply put, I'm their third wheel.

With them it's a role I was conscripted to from the start. When I moved to New York (for graduate school), Cory, my friend from college, already lived there and, luckily, had a spare bedroom. I promptly rented it and soon met Jake, her new boyfriend.

Since he was on hiatus from his work in finance, and I had class only twice a week, we spent a lot of time together, mostly tossing around balls of various dimensions.

About a month before Jake proposed to Cory, he came into my room—the one right next to Cory's—and held out a small lacquered box.

"Hey," he said casually, "can you hold onto this for me?"

I looked at his offering and gulped. My eyes misted over.

Proudly Jake gave me permission to open it, and carefully I did: the ring was glimmering, perfect, surprisingly tall.

"I don't want Cory to find it," he said. "So if you'll take it for now, I'm giving it to you."

"Yes," I whispered and deposited the diamond into my drawer on top of my graphing calculator.

Soon after, Jake took Cory to a farm in Pennsylvania to propose, and like me before her, she accepted. When they returned from their Dominican honeymoon, it became evident that married life fit us all handsomely.

Their needs were fulfilled by each other; my needs were fulfilled, in tandem, by them.

By then they had a home of their own but always had food and a seat for me at their table (this at a time when I owned no furniture and bought very few groceries). Cory invited me over to talk about books and movies. Jake brought me along to play pickup basketball with his friends. Cory and I attended theater and museums. Jake and I went to a Rangers game and watched the World Series. Cory counseled me on what I fondly referred to as the ever-widening gap between me and every woman on the planet. Jake weighed in on that one, too.

We had a good thing going, a completely heartening domestic routine. Our dinners and talks took up entire nights. Cory would often fall asleep in the middle of the conversation, and I'd exit quietly, feeling satisfied, loved.

It didn't take long for me to stop dating entirely. It seemed pointless, since I already had a part in a very solid marriage.

I'd always coveted this sort of steadiness, always aspired to have my own share of it. But it's never been easy. I'm no lothario, after all, and I've long felt cut off from any dating ritual that doesn't include leaving behind a calling card with an overweight and overcorseted aunt.

I'm anachronistic, more at ease pursuing one emotionally intimate moment than braiding bodies for hours on end with some smoky-haired stranger. That and the rigors of dating have simply pushed me to unhealthy extremes—even to the hospital.

A few summers back, I endured a bout of chronic

stomach pain. At the time the thing had its own seismic agenda: rumbling, simmering, gurgling, even spurting little smoldering bits of itself up into the back of my throat. This was my body's response to a brilliantly sassy but ultimately unreachable woman for whom, at the time, I lived and breathed.

In the examining room a doctor pressed his fingers into my midsection and probed my chest with his stethoscope. "Heart sounds fine," he said. "Very strong."

I wasn't surprised. Women don't begin to do damage to my heart until they've utterly ripped apart my stomach. I told him this. He nodded sympathetically, then sent me packing with a prescription for a bowel relaxer.

Post-hospitalization, I began seeing other women. But the result, sadly, was a brand-new set of pseudo-gastroenterological dilemmas, which made me late, loopy, or a little green when I arrived for a date. As I was getting ready, my stomach would churn until it felt as if it were on the verge of popping out a stick of butter. It would take at least twenty-five minutes for my discomfort to pass naturally. Or fifteen minutes and a Xanax. Or five minutes and a finger down the throat.

Cory and Jake proved to be my panacea, better than all the other remedies (Tums, psychotherapy, Julie Delpy in *Before Sunrise*) that made love seem to me, momentarily, like a thing without fangs. So I got close to them, clung to them fiercely. It felt almost as if I were following a biological directive, the one that permits little creatures to seek protection and nourishment by piggybacking on the hide of a much larger animal.

Some of what we did as a threesome, although my participation was de rigueur and always welcome, I probably should have let them do alone, as a couple. Like dimly lighted birthday dinners at which Cory looked like a bigamist sandwiched between Jake and me, or the trip to the Bronx Zoo, where we all shared ice cream cones and, at my urging, rode the Skyfari cable car four times.

At one point I noticed a few baboons cavorting on a grassy slope below: three of them tumbling down the hill. At the bottom, though, a pair of them, holding hands, started climbing back toward the top while the third strutted off alone.

Primates weren't the only ones sending me signals. Cory and Jake now had a message for me, too. I don't remember exactly how they said it. Did they announce over dinner that they were leaving me for another city? Or break the news under a streetlamp just as it started to rain? Or send carnations with a note? I have no idea.

Whatever the case, their explanation that they were moving from New York to Portland (Oregon! Not even Maine!) slid, as if lubricated by its absurdity, in one ear and out the other. Having been blissfully sheltered for so long by the elemental passivity of third-wheeldom, I didn't hear them, or couldn't, because I was no longer fluent in the language of breakups and relationship anxiety.

Leaving? Moving? Goodbye? The words all sounded tangled and distant, as if from an Urdu phrase book or a Kelly Clarkson song.

The night Cory and Jake left, I cried so hard that I hyperventilated for the first time in my life. Without a paper bag in sight, I stuffed an unlaundered hand towel into my mouth like a horse's bit and huffed out what felt like the holdings of my entire pulmonary cavity.

When I finally caught my breath and extracted the towel (it left gauzy strands of lint on my tongue and between several of my teeth), I was shivering on my bathroom floor, knees tucked up against my chest. Out loud I said, "What the hell is wrong with me? People leave all the time. Deal with it."

But I couldn't deal with it, so I called my dad. "What's wrong with me?" I asked him.

"It's hard," he said, "to have your safety net yanked out from under you. It hurts."

At this point—it was 2:30 a.m.—I slid a couple of melatonin discs under my tongue.

Dad paused. "Being on your own for a while—it's probably going to be good for you."

Next thing I knew the sun had come up, and my face was half frozen, striated from the air-conditioner I'd used as a pillow.

I always knew that going through a divorce would crush me, send me over the edge, induce beard growth and religious indoctrination and spectral dreaming. But I'd never said any vows of my own, so I couldn't let things get that far out of hand. Besides, I could still fight this, couldn't I? I could move to Portland, too.

I really thought about it: about leaving New York and incorporating granola into my diet. I'd learn to recycle, strap on the Gore-Tex and spend weekends tromping around sub-alpine berry patches. In Oregon I could preserve my date-free, risk-free reality.

But that would be pathetic, cowardly. Even the baboon at the zoo was able to walk away, and he's supposed to be my evolutionary inferior.

I started focusing on my convalescence. Rilke and Grey Goose and Häagen-Dazs mango ice cream each played pivotal roles. But the real defibrillatory jolt came from what I now consider to be an alternative source of healing: online dating (Cory's idea).

I didn't go on any dates right away, but the shock of getting so much attention from strangers based solely on my posted photograph lifted my spirits considerably. I even started believing that some special girl out there just might have something more sublime to offer me than the usual ulcer. This sudden surge of faith wasn't exactly matrimonial bliss, but it felt like progress, an opportunity to get back in the game.

I *would* rebound, I realized, and that deserved a reward. So I decided to take a little trip. To Portland, of course.

UPDATE: *Howie still visits Cory and Jake in Oregon. Meanwhile, he has latched on to another couple, Dana and B.J., who live across the street and provide him with frequent meals and weekend trips.*

Elvis and My Husband Have Left the Building

Liza Monroy

MY EX-HUSBAND IS GAY, AND I KNEW IT WHEN I married him. We were only twenty-three, at the start of our promising careers, but he, alas, was at the end of his student visa. So I married Rickie to keep him from being sent back to his gay-intolerant Muslim homeland, where he'd have to live a life of lies, secrecy, and fear.

I acted out of love, no compensation requested or received. We simply got in the car, drove northeast out of Los Angeles, and five hours later Elvis was singing, "I'm in love, I'm all shook up," as we danced down the aisle of the Little White Wedding Chapel, me in a hot pink slip dress and my groom in his brown leather jacket, ribbed cream turtleneck, and khakis.

> *Our wedding was over in five minutes, but nobody could say our love wasn't genuine. It might have been more genuine, of course, if Rickie had been standing next to the preferred love of his life, a man.*

When we reached the altar, the Elvis impersonator stopped his hip-swinging jig. "Do you promise to polish each others' blue suede shoes?"

I beamed at my almost-husband. "I do."

"Do you promise to walk each other's hound dogs?"

"Of course," Rickie said.

"I'm more of a cat person," I replied, "but sure."

It was over in five minutes, but nobody could say our love wasn't genuine. It might have been more genuine, of course, if Rickie had been standing next to the preferred love of his life, a man. But a man wouldn't have been able to help him the way his best girlfriend could.

I had first noticed Rickie four years earlier, in college, when he walked into our advanced film production workshop. He was hard not to notice, with his wild black hair and coffee-colored cashmere turtleneck that matched his eyes. Our friendship was born over doughnuts and coffee at 5:00 a.m., freezing on a Boston street corner as we prepared to shoot our first exterior.

After graduation we moved to Los Angeles and rented a place together in West Hollywood, the land of shirtless men. Rickie got an internship on a studio lot while I freelanced in the art department of a company doing hip-hop videos.

We were constantly lost in the San Fernando Valley during our trips to Ikea or to sign up for Central Casting, but domestic life was sweet. Rickie cooked his famous spaghetti sauce for me whenever I'd had a rough day. I helped him shop for ties for his job interviews and drove him around when his Nissan wouldn't start.

But once Rickie's internship ended and he could no longer claim student status for his visa, he discovered that no entertainment company would sponsor him for a work visa.

I'd told him many times I would marry him if he ever had any visa trouble, and he'd never taken me seriously. I'm not sure I took myself seriously, either. But now, as he explained his grim situation over drinks at our favorite bar, it suddenly became a reality.

True to my word, I gulped my cocktail, got down on my knees, and proposed.

He hopped off his barstool, knelt beside me, and took my hands. "I'd be honored to be the envy of straight men everywhere."

"Straight men?" I said, looking around. "Where?"

Over the following weeks, like the engaged couple we were, we mapped out our finances and strategized about whom to tell and how much. Rickie called his father in the Middle East and told him we were marrying for the green card, and his father, who of course didn't know that Rickie was gay, actually hoped we'd fall in love during the process. I decided not to tell my mother, who lived in Europe and wasn't likely to find out, or so I thought.

I was nervous but happy. I was marrying Rickie not only so he could pursue his American dream but also because I needed him. And my love for him, though not sexual, made our marriage feel authentic to me.

What's strange is that even though our arrangement was unconventional, I started to have rather conventional expectations of Rickie. I expected him to pay the bills, to be there for me, and to come home at a decent hour. At times it seemed the only difference between our marriage and a "real" one was that we weren't having sex. Then again, maybe that didn't set us apart from a lot of straight couples. But still I wondered: Does love without sex count as marriage in the eyes of the law? On occasion we even talked about what a perfect child we could have if we were to go the artificial insemination route.

Newly armed with his work permit, Rickie edited movies as a freelancer and worked part time at a restaurant while I landed a job in the mailroom at a talent and literary agency. Occasionally I'd forget I was actually married, but reality hit every time I filled out employee forms and had to check the "Married" box. I felt like I was playing some kind of bizarre joke.

Word got out at my office that I was married, and I couldn't deny it. While some of my colleagues knew the truth, others thought I had a "real" husband and had just married young. Scandal ensued when I fell for a coworker and we began dating.

"You shouldn't date him," Rickie said. "We have to maintain appearances."

He was right. Unfortunately he didn't do such a great job of this himself. He went out nearly every night, partying with different guys. And six months into our marriage, he still didn't have a full-time job, which finally led to a stereotypical "married" argument one evening when I came home to find him watching *The Simpsons* instead of looking online for jobs, as he'd promised.

"I did this for you," I lectured, sounding just like my mother. "What are you doing for yourself? With freedom comes responsibility."

After our fight Rickie managed to get hired full time at the film editing company. "You're my wife," he told me. "I need to make you happy."

And things were better, until one weekend when I was color-coordinating my wardrobe and Rickie knocked lightly on my door.

"Which should go first after the whites?" I asked him.

"Sweetie, I have to tell you something, and I don't know how you're going to react."

"When have you ever not known how I'll react? You know me better than I do."

"This is different. The other day I went to get tested. Just a routine thing."

I went numb. "Tested?"

He came over and hugged me. "I was in that examination room for forty-five minutes. And when I came out, my friend Jeffrey was already crying. He knew they don't keep you in there unless something's wrong." He held my shoulders and looked at me. "You're not going to ask for a divorce?"

"I can't believe you'd think that." But I wondered: What would this mean for us? And what would it mean for his chances at the green card he still awaited?

Before we could sort it all out, Rickie got a stunning e-mail message: he'd won the green card lottery, a government visa program with fewer requirements. I couldn't believe the paradox. After all we'd done—our marriage, our secrecy, our sacrifices—his green card, in the end, had more to do with luck. It had nothing to do with me.

We were free to divorce immediately, but we didn't. Instead we moved to Manhattan. We were used to our situation, and we dreaded starting up with another round of paperwork, lawyers, and bureaucrats. Besides, being married had its advantages, especially when it came to getting an apartment in New York. The broker treated us like serious candidates instead of the low-income people in our twenties we were, and we snagged a charming two-bedroom in a great neighborhood.

In our new life Rickie and I went every morning before work to a nearby café for Mexican coffee and fresh fruit. The one time I went for coffee without him, the cashier asked me where my boyfriend was.

"He's not my boyfriend," I said. "He's gay."

"Oh thank God you know!" she exclaimed. "Here I was thinking, that poor girl, her boyfriend's gay and she doesn't even know it."

I knew it all right. I also knew things were changing between Rickie and me. I'd run into an old boyfriend and we'd started seeing each other; Rickie had also started dating someone new. Still, we didn't divorce.

A new boyfriend was one thing. A Manhattan co-op board was quite another. My mother and I had decided to buy an apartment together. She was still in Europe but wanted a place of her own when she visited New York, and I was ready to live on my own. We found a place and got all the way to the interview with the board members before it occurred to me that Rickie's name was all over my tax returns. If my mother found out about the marriage during the conference call with the board and threw a fit, we'd lose the apartment.

I had to tell her. But first, I called Rickie.

"The co-op board will need to know you don't have any rights to the property. We need to file for divorce." I paused. "I'm sorry it has to end this way."

"It's okay," he said. "It had to happen sometime."

The very next day Rickie took care of the paperwork. He said he was the only one in line at divorce court happily humming along to his iPod. The reason I filed, according to the report he completed on our behalf, was "neglect," legalese for his lack of performance in bed.

The conversation with my mother was not as cheery. "You got married?" she yelled. "To Rickie?"

"Don't worry," I said. "We're divorced now."

"You'd better be divorced."

I swallowed. "Just so you know, it was my idea to get married."

"For his green card?"

I thought for a moment, then told her the truth. "Mom, I married him because I wanted to."

Now, almost two years later, Rickie has good doctors and is healthy and thriving. I'm married again, to the old boyfriend I ran into. He isn't an American, either, but he's straight, and he's already established in his career. It is the most conventional of marriages, complete with actual sex and plans for babies down the line. The only unconventional thing I do anymore is go out with my ex-husband for shopping and pedicures. How many divorcées can say that?

UPDATE: *When Liza and her husband took their vows on a Mexican beach, it was Rickie who walked her to the altar. Rickie now has a steady job he enjoys, is writing a new screenplay, and is in a serious relationship.*

Our Bodies, Our Imaginations

Jean Braithwaite

MY HUSBAND HAD GIVEN UP ON SEX. FOR A WHILE HE kept saying he was just in a slump—it was dissertation stress—but by now that obviously was not the whole story.

Was it because I'd gotten fat again? Paul had met me only a few years after my anorexic period ended, and I didn't refatten all the way until after we were married. Now I was rapidly approaching my pre-anorexic maximum, and people who hadn't seen me in a while would look startled before glancing tactfully away.

> Raven, she called herself. I'd never meant for it to go further than some racy letters.

"It's nothing to do with you," Paul said. "It's just me."

But that wasn't necessarily true. The fact that Paul was fat himself—quite a bit fatter than I was at the time—didn't mean he couldn't find my body repulsive; it only meant he wouldn't be able to admit it if he did. Maybe Paul's libido problem was medical. Maybe it was a combination of things. Whatever; he didn't intend to do anything about it.

Meanwhile, my own libido was plenty high. I looked at both men and women. I'd been corresponding with a woman who had placed an ad in the Women Seeking

Women section of the *Tucson Weekly.* Raven, she called herself. I'd never meant for it to go further than some racy letters. I had envisioned a steady supply of personalized pornography delivered to the post office box I'd rented just for this purpose. Somehow I hadn't grasped at the outset that the source of that supply was going to be a real person. After a few months of writing each other, I fell for her. Just on the basis of words. We had never exchanged pictures. I was sure that what she looked like wouldn't make any difference to me.

I was working in a used book store at the time, and as a game I'd look at each female customer I waited on and say to myself, "This could be Raven." Then I'd practice taking my sexual feelings and centering them on that specific body. I never had any trouble accomplishing this, except when the woman was very young because I already knew Raven was older than me.

"Do you have physical preferences?" I wrote. "Body types that you prefer or don't prefer?"

"Not really," she replied. "Well, okay, if I'm honest, there is one thing that puts me off."

She didn't say what the one thing was, and I didn't ask. But I knew it had to be fat. What else was there? She probably suspected, too. We kept writing anyway, stirring each other up.

My Raven correspondence was not a secret from Paul. He even encouraged it, asking about her, offering to bring the mail from my post office box when I was sick. It took the pressure off him, I guess. He agreed that I could have a fling with Raven if he could also have a fling with another woman some day. I said all right, partly because I didn't think it would ever happen. He had to say that to save his pride. It's a deal, I said, if I actually bag Raven. Deal, he said, and we shook hands. "Raven probably won't ever want to anyway," I thought.

I kept on playing my game at the bookstore. If a woman came in who was dark-haired and in her late thirties, my breath would speed up. "This really could be Raven, for real." If the woman was pretty, my lust mixed with despair and a kind of anger. "Raven would never want me—she is so shallow!" I was capable of desiring her regardless of her body's shape. If the woman was black, no problem—a black Raven would suit me fine. If the woman limped, I'd think, "Yes, let Raven have something physically wrong with her, something serious enough to offset my fat."

By now, Raven and I were cautiously negotiating— by mail—a first meeting in person. I sent her my phone number and asked her to call me on Friday after midnight. I was aflame. If Raven found my body objectionable, perhaps I could simply offer to blindfold her. Then there would be no problem, right? Then I would be whoever and whatever she wanted. I was that desperate.

It was on Wednesday, late in the afternoon, that the man with no nose walked into the bookstore. My friend Mariely and I were working alone. Mariely was paleskinned, dark-haired, prettier than average without being a great beauty, a serious student with a thoughtful face. At around twenty years old, she was too young to attract me, but a Raven who was Mariely plus another fifteen years would have suited me very well indeed.

Mariely took one look at the man with no nose and fled to the back room. I shared her feelings. He was pretty hard to look at. When I say he had no nose, I don't mean that the end of it was missing, or that there was a discreet bandage over a flat place, or even that there was some kind of malformed lump instead of a regular nose. I mean he had a gaping red and black hole in the middle of his face.

"How are you this afternoon?" I said. I made myself look at him and smile. I saw, or perhaps I only imagined I could see, a dangling pair of bones inside the cavern where his nose ought to have been. I wasn't usually that outgoing with customers, but I made a special effort to chat with the man with no nose because I was ashamed at how much he repelled me. I made myself touch his hand as I gave him his change.

The man with no nose remained at the register, talking cheerfully, for several minutes. My jumpiness subsided slightly. It became easier to maintain eye contact and smile. If I knew him for a friend, I thought, I'd get used to him. "What if he were Raven?" I thought. "What if Raven were actually a man, this man?" I could do it. I could get over that hurdle. Given time, I could come to love and desire this person, I was sure. Bitterly, I thought again of Raven's likely rejection of me, and I felt myself, in this moment, morally superior—not that it was any big comfort.

The man with no nose finally left the store, and Mariely came out from the back room.

"Oh, I'm so ashamed!" she said.

"Don't be," I said. "It's only natural; I felt the same way." But I was complacent just the same. I hadn't run; I had conquered my feelings.

On Friday night, when Raven called, I was not so composed. In fact, I could hardly breathe. Her voice so disoriented me at first that I thought she had a speech defect. After a few minutes I realized it was simply a Southern accent, all sunshine and slow honey.

"You don't sound like I expected," I said. I don't know why I'd failed to imagine any particular voice for her. I'd imagined countless bodies and faces over the months we'd been corresponding, but never a voice.

"We're certain to have a few surprises," she said.

"Yes," I said. "Listen, you remember we wrote one time about body types?" Suddenly I felt sick. I wondered if the noseless man ever had blind dates, and what his thought process was in the anxious moments before—"Oh, by the way, there's something I'd better mention before we meet, just so, you know, it's not a shock when you first see me . . ."

"I'm fat," I said, just like that.

"Oh." Her voice was so laced with disappointment I almost felt sorry for her. After a long pause she said, "I'm sorry. I guess I'm not as open-minded sometimes as I'd like to think I am."

"Raven," I said. "Don't worry." And I meant it. But in the back of my mind, I started planning a longer campaign. If I could get over my initial repulsion by the man with no nose, maybe Raven eventually could get over her repulsion by me as well? "Do you still want to meet?" I asked.

"Yes," she said. "We can be friends, at least. When would you like to get together?"

"Tomorrow?"

"Tomorrow's fine," she said.

We met in a twenty-four-hour coffee shop, where I was shocked to find myself exchanging nervous hellos with a rail-thin, short-haired, boyish-faced blonde. She looked like Opie of Mayberry, or Dennis the Menace. Why on earth, I wondered, would a blond woman ever choose Raven for a pen name? All at once my desire, that great burden of desire that had sat on me for months, the desire I breathed and walked around inside of, the desire so desperately strong that it was absolutely indifferent to the bodily details of its object—my desire vanished.

Temporarily.

After a few weeks, my scattered fantasies, ever resilient, managed to regroup and realign themselves around the actual body of Raven. I hoped Raven would be able to accomplish the same feat with me, and for a while it seemed she had. She even started introducing me as her girlfriend. But ultimately, despite our best combined efforts, we were never able to get past the obstacle of my body. And one day, over the telephone, she called it quits. To soften the blow, she said she hoped we could still be friends, exactly as she had during our very first conversation.

When Paul came home I told him what had happened. I was trying to be stoic, but he could tell I was upset.

"Friends?" he said. "Tell her to go to hell. She never deserved you. She wasn't good enough for you, honey."

But of course, at that point in our marriage Paul and I had gone from being lovers to friends as well. So while I appreciated his outrage on my behalf, I also understood its subtleties. And I understood that desire, the great driving force of desire, is sometimes merely a trick of the mind not everyone can master. "I don't know," I said to Paul. "I'm not sure that's the right way of looking at it."

Three Men and a Woman

Stephen Elliott

ANGELINA AND I ARE IN AN ART GALLERY THAT DOUBLES as a dance club. A DJ stands on a sheet of plywood over milk crates playing house music with a heavy bass line. It's still afternoon but already there are a few office workers here loosening their ties, putting their earrings back in.

With us is Tristan. He and Angelina have known each other fifteen years, since high school. He has flushed cheeks, feminine features, wears black jeans and a leather jacket. He helps Angelina clean, shop, run chores, carries her things. Angelina refers to Tristan as her pockets. Tristan refers to Angelina as his girlfriend. Girlfriend, he feels, comes closest to summing up their relationship.

> When I tell Angelina I am worried that between Tristan, her husband, and her job, she won't have enough time for me, she says, "Tell me what you need to make this work."

I tell him I think he should use a paragraph. That a word isn't going to explain it. But what is bothering me more is that *girlfriend* is the term I've been using. She told me she doesn't like it, but I use it anyway, for the same reason Tristan does.

My paragraph would have to include that Angelina is married. That there is a child at the house four days a week. That not only is she married but she also has Tristan, meaning there are three men in her life, minimum. That what we have is not nonmonogamy, it is polyamory. That I love her and that sometimes I think this could maybe work, and then other times I see nothing but a bunch of potholes, a couple of landmines, and a train wreck.

The after-work crowd is trickling in. Button-ups have been replaced with undershirts. I talk with Tristan and watch Angelina dance. She kicks her legs, spins. She looks like a fighter, dark hair pulled back, swinging fists, elbows bent.

"I have to dance with her," I say, "before she dances with someone else."

"It's not a zero-sum game," Tristan says.

I don't even know what he means. He's trying to help me. I'm trying to understand him. Already there are three men dancing near her, all of them turned to show their availability.

The day I met Angelina's husband, I was crossing the bridge and called to say I would be there shortly. The bay was filled with tankers nosing into port and sailboats like pieces of paper. I was just rolling onto the span over Treasure Island, could already see the landfill, the abandoned military site. Angelina said, "Okay, come over."

"You don't want to wait on the corner?" I asked.

"You have to meet him eventually," she replied.

They live back from the street in a two-bedroom mud-colored bungalow. I was standing in the doorway when he stepped out of the kitchen. The meeting was awkward but not awful. "Oh," he said as we shook hands. He was better-looking than I expected and three inches taller than me. He wore light jeans and a striped shirt. I was wearing a necklace, leather pants, and a sleeveless top. We looked our roles: the suburban father and the other man.

I could hear Angelina speaking with their son in the other room. Her husband and I made some small talk about his job, and then Angelina and I were gone.

I try not to question Angelina's marriage or her situation with Tristan. It's not my place to second-guess other people's desires. One evening I confessed that I didn't understand her relationship with her husband.

She laughed. "You don't even understand our relationship."

Angelina and I make each other CDs, see movies together, go shopping. We sit late into the night telling stories about our families. Angelina's father kicked her out when she was fifteen. I left home when I was thirteen and never went back. The truth is this is the healthiest relationship I've ever had. When I tell her I am worried that between Tristan, her husband, and her job, she won't have enough time for me, she says, "Tell me what you need to make this work."

I see Angelina about four days a week, and on days when I don't see her we talk on the phone. She's negotiating with her husband to spend a night each week at my apartment. She'd like to see a situation where I come over for big family events, like Thanksgiving and New Year's. But none of us is ready for that.

The music is louder, the room hotter, the crowd thickening, all of us with hearts stamped on the insides of our wrists.

She and I have moved so quickly and had so many opportunities to fail. Angelina says that my lack of relationship experience is usually a red flag for her. I say being married is usually a red flag for me. Her husband is upset because having multiple sexual partners is one thing and falling in love is something else. She says this is the first time she's fallen in love since meeting her husband nine years ago.

"I almost didn't show up one day," Angelina says, resting her wrists on my shoulders. "I panicked."

"If you hadn't shown up I would have been so disappointed," I say.

"I would have called," she says.

"That wouldn't have helped."

Tristan sits while we dance. I wonder if he is not some mirror for me; if he weren't real, I would create him. I like Tristan. I have a magazine in my bag and want to offer it to him, but it's too dark to read. I wonder how much of his life he spends watching Angelina dance, her jacket next to him, her cigarettes in his pocket. I ask myself if I could do what he's doing, if I could sit for hours and watch Angelina dance with other people. The first answer that comes to mind is no. But the second answer is yes. Yes, if she weren't going home to her husband. If she were going home with me. If we were going to sleep together, to lie next to each other in my bed. If she were going home with me I could wait all night. But she isn't.

In fact, most of my problems have nothing to do with Angelina's marriage. They spring instead from the insecurities of new love. Not long ago Angelina came to my apartment. She was late, and I looked from my window and saw a black car pause and then continue down the street. I thought it was hers and went downstairs thinking she couldn't find parking and would come back around and I would get in and we would drive together. But the car never returned, and I began to crack. It was unbearably hot, and bright enough to see all the broken glass, dirt, and old paint stains on the curb. By the time an hour had passed my face was burning.

And then she arrived, wearing a patterned summer skirt and a spaghetti-strap top, carrying a heavy bag. I laughed, taking the bag from her. "I thought I saw your car," I kept saying. But she'd just been stuck in traffic. She kept stroking my head saying, "You poor baby." I was inches away from crying. I pushed my face into her collar, gripped her tightly.

Inside the club we sit apart from Tristan. He doesn't know where we are, but we're only ten feet away. The club is full, and people climb around us, hiding their jackets below our bench and their sweaters on the ledge above. We're cushioned and surrounded by their clothing.

Angelina and I are exhausted from dancing. Our shirts are soaked. One time she said to me, "I haven't placed any limits on you. You place limits on yourself." And to help, I've been reading a book about polyamory. The book recommends that you own your decisions. No one can make you do anything. The important thing is not to get in a cycle of blame, the book says, but rather to inform your partner of your feelings. Most relationships are doomed anyway; it's their nature.

I squeeze Angelina's arms as she turns, throwing her legs over mine. When I first met her I was shocked by her raw physical beauty. I didn't think the fact that she was in an open marriage would affect me one way or the other. I wasn't thinking long term. I had no idea of Angelina's capacity for affection. Some think that love is a finite resource, like food. That love given to one person is love taken from someone else. Others believe that the more you love, the more love you're capable of. It's what enables families to have more than one child.

Outside it has gotten cold. I peel off my wet shirt and replace it with three layers I brought for the bike ride home. Recently a woman I've always liked, who lives in New York, confessed that she would like to tie me up the next time I was in town. I asked Angelina if it was okay, and she told me she was jealous. It was my first time suggesting another woman.

"I know it's hypocritical," Angelina said. After five days she decided it was fine, that it was probably even good for us. She said people who claim not to be jealous are fooling themselves, it's just what you do with it.

I walk Tristan and Angelina to her car. They're going back across the bay, where the giant grocery stores are. I'm staying here in the city, where it's crowded. I've always lived in cities, and I've wondered if this city is even big enough, if there are enough people for me. I like crowds, diversity, opportunity.

I kiss Angelina at the overlighted parking garage. The theatergoers insert bills and punch buttons on the bright yellow parking machines. Tristan lingers near the corner, one elbow on a newspaper box.

"I love you," I tell her.

"I love you, too," she replies.

I'm seeing her tomorrow, in the evening. Tomorrow is Thursday, and Tristan will be there again. And then I won't see her until Tuesday.

Angelina will be home soon, and I'll sleep alone tonight. I think about the long weekend looming as I bicycle past neon signs south of Market, too dark to see the potholes now.

UPDATE: *Five months after this essay appeared, Stephen and Angelina broke up. Then they got back together. Then they broke up again. Then they got back together before finally breaking up for good.*

A Go-Between Gets Going

Kirsten Allen Major

I MET KRISTA AFTER AN ABRUPT BREAKUP WITH A LIVE-IN boyfriend. I needed a new place to live, and responding to an ad, I found refuge in what felt like the Brooklyn Annex for Aging Spinsters, an apartment of three women between thirty-three and forty, nursing various sorrows and set in our various, irritating ways. Krista was one of my new roommates.

At first I was nervous around her; she was a serious Christian to my skittish heathen, with a mother who expressed hopes that she would find "a nice Christian boy." But she wasn't the roommate who insisted on establishing a sign-up sheet for the shower, and soon I found myself liking her: she was intelligent, vulnerable, and kind. I spilled my stories of dejection. And she told me about Marcus.

> *She wouldn't tell him she still loved him in spite of everything. Did I dare disturb the universe?*

She and Marcus, a brilliant and tormented graduate student studying medieval theology, had twice decided to get married; he'd pulled back and ended their relationship both times.

This is the kind of deep betrayal that generates the rage of the ages, and I waited to hear about his horrid behavior and fatal character flaws—but no. Krista had only sweet memories of Marcus. I eventually saw that it was not his treatment of her that was making her miserable; it was that she loved him and he was gone. It also seemed clear to me that Marcus had balked out of fear, not lack of affection.

Not that telling her any of this helped. I told her what I thought she should do, and though she thought I was crazy, she would mention it every now and then. "Why would I contact him and tell him that, after everything, I still love him?" she'd ask. "That's idiotic." He'd left her, after all. She'd told him that, this time, the breakup was final. He was to leave her alone.

Listening to this made took me back to the night when, ten years before, I'd dug in my heels and told someone, "Well, if you're going to be so busy, let's just stop seeing each other."

He was the great love of my life, and I never told him that. Instead I'd struck back, eager to punish him for hurting my feelings. I was young and thought he would be easily replaced.

But I had learned through some very miserable years that there is something worse than rejection, and that is not risking rejection, even certain rejection, to tell the truth. I had lived with a bluff and my supposed pride and more regret than I can express. And now my past was being replayed before me.

Three months into my tenure at the Annex, we all got the boot. I rented an apartment in the East Village. Krista stayed with me while she looked for a new place, and after that our friendship became one of lunches. We remained closer than two ex-roommates might, but not so close, I hoped, that I would continue to dwell on her broken relationship with Marcus. Still, the sense that I was watching needless tragedy only mounted in me.

In the spring, after a year's silence, Marcus sent Krista a long e-mail message, telling her that he was going to Berlin for the summer and confessing that he had never met anyone who measured up to her; and just in case the plane crashed, he wanted her to know that he loved her.

"What should I do?" she asked me.

"Tell him that you want him back."

"But he didn't ask."

"You told him never to ask you again."

"But he was the one who left."

I was sure he was testing the waters. In any case, she sent him a cold splash back: "Have a good summer. I will always love you, too."

"He didn't reply," she sniffled after a couple of weeks.

"You wrote him two lines after he wrote you an essay."

"But I said I loved him."

"People say, 'Have a nice summer, love you,' in school yearbooks."

Months later she said, "I was trying to convince myself that Marcus's faults meant we'd be miserable, but you know what? I was having a good time. I liked the way he was."

"Tell him you want him back."

"But he didn't ask."

"But you told him never to ask you again." And we had the same conversation.

At the same time, I knew I was being overly romantic, that the better advice would probably be to move on. I encouraged her to try online dating, which produced for her a summer of e-mail administrivia: she filled out forms, stared at electronic suitors, corresponded with them. But her thoughts always drifted to Marcus and stayed there firmly, and she told me so.

"Tell him you want him back."

"But he didn't ask."

"You told him not to." And again we had the same conversation.

I encouraged her to go on a blind date with a friend's friend.

She did, twice; it came to nothing. Then, in September, she told me that on a Saturday night she had lighted candles and played music in an attempt to cheer up but instead felt horribly depressed. She fell silent. Then she spoke with weight on each syllable: "I. Just don't think. I am. Ever. Going to get over Marcus."

Times before, when I've made fatal romantic efforts on my own behalf, I first would think, *Do I dare disturb the universe?* Some would call doing the same thing over and over and expecting different results psychosis: I decided to call it a leap of faith. That in this case I would be leaping uninvited into other people's lives was no longer enough to stop me.

I'd never met Marcus, never spoken to him, and it took me a month to work up the nerve to dial his number. "You don't know me," I stammered when he answered. "I'm a friend of Krista's, and she's fine, there's nothing to worry about. But I need to talk to you about her, in person. So if you're ever in the city——"

Three weeks later there he was, sitting in an empty conference room at work, looking every bit as intense as I'd imagined. After minutes of circumlocution I squeezed my eyes shut and said, "Krista still loves you. She saved a message you left on her cell phone two years ago so she'd always have the sound of your voice. She told you never to come back, but that's because she was devastated that you left. She misses you terribly."

His shoulders relaxed, but his response otherwise ranged from inconclusive to unpromising. At one point he said, "There's no sense in dating other people. They aren't Krista." But then he enumerated his problems with making a serious commitment to her.

I tried to stay neutral: my goal was not to talk anyone into anything. After fifteen minutes I thanked him for listening and saw him out. Then I plunged into a period of guilty deception in my friendship with Krista.

After all, what could I tell her? That I had divulged her feelings to her love and that he might or might not contact her? No. I knew I'd done a terrible thing, but I began to cast it in a different light. I told myself that what I had done was hopeful, that all those romantic movie plots and Jane Austen endings had to have some basis in reality, right? I began to feel better about my interference, musing about faith, destiny, the Fates.

And in fact the universe did seem to be coming through. The day after I met Marcus, Krista sent a group e-mail message with her new cell phone number and included him.

He wrote her back at once: "I look for your face in crowds."

"What should I do?" she asked me.

"Tell him the truth."

"I don't know."

A week went by, then two.

Krista phoned me one Sunday morning. "Marcus called."

"That's fantastic! Did you tell him?"

"He said, 'You have a meddling friend.'"

I was silent.

"Kirsten, how could you do this to me?"

The lunacy of what I'd done suddenly descended upon me. I had not liberated love; I'd created a new opportunity for her to suffer. Who does something like this? I wasn't a saint; I was insane.

"What are you going to do?" I whispered.

"I'm not going to do anything."

Marcus had not asked her to come back, but he said he had a few things he wanted to tell her in person. She agreed to see him the next Sunday. It was possible, I realized, that he wanted to hold her hand while he told her as nicely as possible to please get over him.

It was October, and that Sunday was cold and overcast. I was having problems with my cell phone, which also serves as my home phone, and spoke to Krista for only a few minutes that morning. I paced around with my stomach boiling. When I thought Marcus had left, I called her repeatedly and got no answer. Afternoon turned into evening. I imagined the worst. Finally, at ten o'clock at night, my phone rang.

"Are you all right?" I asked.

"Yes."

"Is he still there?"

"No."

"What happened?"

"Well—" And then my phone went dead.

I was in my pajamas. I threw on a coat in which I found three quarters and ran to a pay phone on the corner of Fifth Street and Avenue A. There was a lot of noise on the street, and as I tried to dial, someone started asking me for my other two quarters and explaining the situation that caused him to need my two quarters.

It was on that corner, fending off the guy in need of quarters while trembling in my pajamas, that I learned how my hideous project had played out.

It took Marcus *seven hours* to get to his point. But in the end he said that all the things he'd previously wanted out of life had changed. He no longer wanted to live like a monk. What he really wanted was to be married to Krista, and he knew this with utter clarity. They had known each other for six years, and it was time. It could be in any way and at any time she chose, but please, would she marry him?

She said the oddest thing was that as he spoke, she felt perfectly calm.

Several months later, I stood at their wedding and wept through the entire ceremony.

UPDATE: *Krista and Marcus live in Brooklyn, where they recently celebrated their first anniversary.*

Part Three

Breeding

WHAT TO EXPECT
THAT YOU'RE
LEAST EXPECTING

DJ's Homeless Mommy

Dan Savage

THERE WAS NO GUARANTEE THAT DOING AN OPEN ADOP-
tion would get us a baby any faster than doing a closed
or foreign adoption. In fact, our agency warned us
that, as a gay male couple, we might be in for a long wait.
This point was driven
home when both birth
mothers who spoke at the
two-day open adoption
seminar we were required
to attend said that finding
"good, Christian homes"
for their babies was their
first concern. But we
decided to go ahead and
try to do an open adop-
tion anyway. If we became parents, we wanted our
child's biological parents to be a part of his life.

> She'd chosen us
> because we didn't look
> old enough to be her
> parents, and she didn't
> want us to start acting
> like her parents now.
> She'd get off the
> streets when she was
> ready.

As it turns out, we didn't have to wait long. A few
weeks after our paperwork was done, we got a call from
the agency. A nineteen-year-old homeless street kid—
homeless by choice and seven months pregnant by
accident—had selected us from the agency's pool of pre-
screened parent wannabes. The day we met her, the

agency suggested that all three of us go out for lunch—
well, four of us if you count Wish, her German shepherd;
five if you count the baby she was carrying. We were
bursting with touchy-feely questions, but she was wary,
only interested in the facts: She didn't want to have an
abortion and couldn't bring up her baby on the streets.
That left adoption. And she was willing to jump through
the agency's hoops—which included weekly counseling
sessions and a few meetings with us—because she wanted
to do an open adoption, too.

We were with her when DJ was born. And we were in
her hospital room two days later when it was time for her
to give him up. Before we could take DJ home, we literally had to take him from his mother's arms as she sat
sobbing in her bed.

I was thirty-three years old when we adopted DJ, and
I thought I knew what a broken heart looked like, how it
felt, but I didn't know anything. You know what a broken heart looks like? Like a sobbing teenager handing
over a two-day-old infant she can't take care of to a
couple who she hopes can.

Ask a couple hoping to adopt what they want most in
the world and they'll tell you there's only one thing on
earth they want: a healthy baby. But many couples want
something more: They want their child's biological
parents to disappear permanently so there will never be
any question about who their child's "real" parents are.
The biological parents showing up on their doorstep,
lawyers in tow, demanding their kid back is the collec-
tive nightmare of all adoptive parents, endlessly discussed
in adoption chat rooms and during adoption seminars.

But it seemed to us that all adopted kids eventually want to know why they were adopted, and sooner or later they start asking questions. "Didn't they love me?" "Why did they throw me away?" In cases of closed adoptions there's not a lot the adoptive parents can say. Fact is, they don't know the answers. We would.

Like most homeless street kids, our son's birthmother works a national circuit. Portland or Seattle in the summer; Denver, Minneapolis, Chicago, and New York in the late summer and early fall; Phoenix, Las Vegas, or Los Angeles in the winter and spring. Then she hitchhikes or rides the rails back up to Portland, where she's from, and starts all over again. For the first few years after we adopted DJ, his mother made a point of coming up to Seattle during the summer so we could get together. When she wasn't in Seattle she kept in touch by phone. Her calls were usually short. She would ask how we were, we'd ask her the same, then we'd put DJ on the phone. She didn't gush; he didn't know what to say. But it was important to DJ that his mother called.

When DJ was three, his mother stopped calling regularly and visiting. When she did call, it was usually with disturbing news. One time her boyfriend had died of alcohol poisoning. They were sleeping on a sidewalk in New Orleans, and when she woke up, he was dead. Another time she called after her next boyfriend started using heroin again. Soon the calls stopped, and we began to worry about whether she was alive or dead. After six months with no contact, I started calling hospitals. Then morgues.

When DJ's fourth birthday came and went without a call, I was convinced that something had happened to her on the road or in a train yard somewhere. She had to be dead.

I was tearing down the wallpaper in an extra bedroom one night shortly after DJ turned four. His best friend, a little boy named Haven, had spent the night, and after Haven's mother picked him up, DJ dragged a chair into the room and watched as I pulled wallpaper down in strips.

"Haven has a mommy," he suddenly said, "and I have a mommy."

"That's right," I responded.

He went on. "I came out of my mommy's tummy. I play with my mommy in the park." Then he looked at me and asked, "When will I see my mommy again?"

"This summer," I said, hoping it wasn't a lie. It was April, and we hadn't heard from DJ's mother since September of the previous year. "We'll see her in the park, just like last summer."

We didn't see her in the summer. Or in the fall or spring. I wasn't sure what to tell DJ. We knew that she hadn't thrown him away and that she loved him. We also knew, though, that she wasn't calling and could be dead. In fact, I was convinced she was dead. But dead or alive, we weren't sure how to handle the issue with DJ. Which two-by-four to hit him with? That his mother was in all likelihood dead? Or that she was out there somewhere but didn't care enough to come by or call? And soon he would be asking more complicated questions. What if he wanted to know why his mother didn't love him enough to take care of herself? So she could live long enough to be there for him? So she could tell him herself how much she loved him when he was old enough to remember her and to know what love means?

My partner and I discussed these issues late at night, when DJ was in bed, thankful for each day that passed without the issue of his missing mother coming up. We knew we wouldn't be able to avoid or finesse the issue after summer arrived in Seattle. As the weeks ticked away, we admitted to each other that those closed adoptions we'd frowned upon were starting to look pretty good. Instead of being a mystery, his mother was a mass of very distressing specifics. And instead of dealing with his birth parent's specifics at, say, eighteen or twenty-one, like many adopted children, he would have to deal with them at four or five.

He was already beginning to deal with them: The last time his mother visited, when DJ was three, he wanted to know why she smelled so terrible. We were taken aback and answered without thinking it through. We explained that, since she doesn't have a home, she isn't able to bathe often or wash her clothes.

We realized we'd screwed up even before DJ started to freak. What, after all, could be more terrifying to a child than the idea of not having a home? Telling him that his mother chooses to live on the streets, that for her the streets were home, didn't cut it. For months DJ insisted that his mother was just going to have to come and live with us. We had a bathroom, a washing machine. She could sleep in the guest bedroom. When grandma came to visit, she could sleep in his bed and he would sleep on the floor.

We did hear from DJ's mother again, fourteen months later, when she called from Portland, Oregon. She wasn't dead, only thoughtless. She'd lost track of time and didn't make it up to Seattle before it got too cold and wet; and whenever she thought about calling it was either too late or she was too drunk. When she told me she'd reached the point where she got sick when she didn't drink, I gently suggested that maybe it was time to get off the streets, stop drinking and using drugs, and think about her future. I could hear her rolling her eyes.

The reason she'd chosen us over all the straight couples was because we didn't look old enough to be her parents. She didn't want us to start acting like her parents now, she said. She would get off the streets when she was ready. She wasn't angry and didn't raise her voice. She just wanted to make sure we understood one another.

DJ was happy to hear from his mother, and the fourteen months without a call or a visit were forgotten. We went down to Portland to see her, she apologized to DJ in person, we took some pictures, and she promised not to disappear again.

We didn't hear from her for a year. This time she wasn't drunk. She was in prison, charged with assault. She'd been in prison before, for short stretches, picked up on vagrancy and trespassing charges. But this time was different—she needed our help. Or her dog did.

Her boyfriends and traveling companions were always vanishing, but her dog, Wish, was the one constant presence in her life. Having a large dog complicates hitchhiking and hopping trains, of course, but DJ's mother is a petite woman, and her dog offers her some protection. And love.

Late one night in New Orleans, she told us from a noisy common room in the jail, she'd gotten into an argument with another homeless person. He lunged at her, and Wish bit him. She was calling, she said, because it didn't look she would get out of prison before the pound put Wish down. She was distraught. We had to help her save Wish, she begged. She was crying, the first time I'd heard her cry since that day in the hospital six years before.

Five weeks and $1,600 later, we had managed not only to save Wish but also to get DJ's mother out and the charges dropped. When we talked on the phone, I urged her to move on to someplace else. I found out three months later that she'd taken my advice—she was calling from a jail in Virginia, where she'd been arrested for trespassing at a train yard. Wish was okay—he was with friends; she was only calling to say hello to DJ.

I've heard people say that choosing to live on the streets is a kind of slow-motion suicide. Having known DJ's mother for six years now I'd say that's accurate. Everything she does seems to court danger. I've lost track of the number of her friends and boyfriends who have died of an overdose, alcohol poisoning, or hypothermia.

As he gets older, DJ is getting a more accurate picture of his mother, but so far it doesn't seem to be an issue for him. He loves her. A photo of a family reunion we attended isn't complete, he insists, because his mother isn't in it. He wants to see her this summer, "even if she smells," he says. We're looking forward to seeing her, too. But I'm tired.

Now for the may-God-rip-off-my-fingers-before-I-type-this part of the essay: I'm starting to get anxious for this slo-mo suicide to end, whatever that end looks like. I'd prefer that it end with DJ's mother off the streets, in an apartment somewhere, pulling her life together. But as she gets older that resolution is getting harder to picture.

A lot of people who self-destruct don't think twice about destroying their children in the process. Maybe DJ's mother knew she was going to self-destruct and loved DJ so much that she wanted to make sure he wouldn't get hurt. She left him somewhere safe, with parents she chose for him, even though it broke her heart to give him away, because she knew that if he were close she would hurt him, too. Sometimes I wonder if this answer will be good enough for DJ when he asks us why his mother couldn't hold it together just enough to stay in the world for him. I kind of doubt it.

UPDATE: *After more than a year and a half without contact, DJ's mother suddenly called two days after his eighth birthday. At the time of the call, she had a short-term job and a place to stay. She asked Dan to send pictures of DJ to her current address. She had plans to be back on the road by summer.*

His Genes Hold Gifts. Mine Carry Risk.

Bonnie J. Rough

I CARRY A GENE FOR A SERIOUS DISORDER, BUT MY HUS-
band, who hopes for children, married me anyway.

I remember the black Seattle rain as we drove at night three years ago. Having dated since college, we were in the middle of our increasingly common debate about whether we should get engaged.

"I know I'll never find anyone better than you," Dan said. "But you have to understand that I'll always wonder what it would have been like to be a single twentysome-thing."

> *In the twenty-first century, "God's will" is not a force Dan and I have to accept. "What is our will?" we ask ourselves.*

This is how our marriage talks always went. What would we miss out on if we married, two best friends who had been side by side since college?

Water spun over the tires as we sloshed through the city. Dan had gone quiet. I watched his face as he drove. I often watched his face as he drove—still do. He must have felt my eyes, but he is a professional concentrator, a former college basketball star who, among other feats, set a division record for making the most free throws in a row—sixty, over his sophomore and junior seasons.

Now, at twenty-nine, he still hits the bull's-eye, slips the football between telephone wires, lands a soil-footed weed in the yard bin like a precisely struck shuttlecock.

He drove on. As light and rain patterns bloomed over his face, his expression softened. "So," he said, "tell me more about this genetic thing in your family."

I sat up straight. I felt that I was about to deliver the most important speech of my life. "It's called ectodermal dysplasia," I said. And then I told him everything I knew. I explained that my grandfather and my younger brother had both been born with sparse hair, missing tooth buds (which required them to wear dentures, even as children), and no sweat glands, making hot weather unbearable and even dangerous.

I explained that women carry the gene, and risk passing it along to their sons. So if he and I were to have a boy—the son, yes, of an extraordinarily gifted athlete—there would be a good chance he'd be burdened with it. It goes without saying that it's pretty hard to play basketball, or any sport at all, if you can't sweat.

Dan took all this in without a word. Finally he said, "Is there anything they can do about it?"

"My mom told me scientists recently found the gene with the ED mutation, which half of my eggs have. I think that means doctors can pick out healthy eggs to fertilize."

Dan didn't ask for more. But a few months later, he did ask me to marry him.

My grandparents, and then my mother and father, made their babies on faith. They knew the ED was there, and there was nothing to do about it but pray.

When my brother Luke was born, his skin was so dry

and flaky that the doctor said, "We should take him down for an X-ray just to rule out ED."

Later, Luke's pediatrician poked his head into my parents' hospital room and said simply, "There are no tooth buds."

A friend had brought a bottle of champagne, and my parents opened it. A nurse then wheeled their pink-faced son, with a head of dandelion fluff, into the room. My parents looked at my brother, who was very quiet and moved his lips with the concentration of an old man, and poured the champagne. Toasting, they said together, "God's will be done." And they cried long into the night.

But now, in the twenty-first century, "God's will" is not a force Dan and I have to accept. "What is *our* will?" we ask ourselves. We could save up fifteen thousand dollars to have my eggs harvested and combined with his sperm. Doctors would then implant a few fertilized embryos without the ED mutation, and we'd have to accept the possibility of twins, even triplets. We're students again, so fifteen thousand dollars for anything—even a healthy baby—sounds staggering. And having triplets sounds equally unfathomable. But my real worry is more complicated.

If we went this route, doctors would freeze our remaining healthy embryos until we were ready for another child. I know this method is a miracle for couples who can't have children otherwise. But I can't help wondering whether there's meaning attached to a natural conception—one that occurs by fate, inside a mother— as opposed to an embryo being chosen, frozen, thawed, and implanted. I know that plenty of happy, healthy people have been conceived this way, but I confess: I hope that my children can begin their lives within the warmth of my body.

Why don't we just adopt? This is an unsettling question because it points to what must be our selfishness. But the idea of creating a life from our two bodies seems to us a consummation of sorts. Maybe this means we need to work on our relationship—that we already, dangerously, see having children as a way of fulfilling something missing between us. But then, something is missing: our echo through time.

When Dan and I visited the grave site of his great-great-grandparents, I remember thinking with awe, *These are the ancestors of my future children.* History is the only purchase I have on my life—knowing the stories that meld to make my story—and it seems like a fulfillment of some kind, a continuation of a narrative, for a child to know the real, biological melding of Dan and me.

For Dan, it may be simpler. He has uncommon athleticism, shining health, beautiful teeth, sharp concentration, perfect aim. He wants children sooner rather than later so he can have the knees to play basketball with them—hard, sweating, laughing basketball—when they are in high school. Dan has genetic gifts he wants to give.

I have a lesbian friend who has struggled to become pregnant. It takes time and negotiation to secure a suitable sperm donor, and potentially a lot of money if acquaintances don't work out. "Heterosexual couples don't realize how good they have it," she said to me one day. "All they have to do is hop in the sack a few times."

Dan and I could do that. Creating human life is so free, and so common, that it becomes plausible to create and then destroy. At twelve weeks of pregnancy, we could have our fetus tested. A few weeks later, results would arrive, and we could choose to keep our baby or not.

This, my pro-choice heart realized one night at dinner, is not an option for me. "I couldn't do it, Dan. I couldn't carry a baby with a doubt in my soul. What would that do to him? He should know from the start that I love him and want him. I want him to feel acceptance, not worry. As late as sixteen weeks? That's way, way too far along."

"I think so, too," he said, filling me with a relief I hadn't known I wanted.

Later, I asked Dan if he'd rather adopt a healthy child or have one of our own with ED. "Have our own with ED," he said.

In some ways, we're lucky. ED is no Down syndrome, no cerebral palsy or cystic fibrosis. It doesn't affect mental capacity or motor skills. It doesn't cap life span. The more we talk about ED, the littler it tends to sound. My brother, after all, is healthy and strong, getting good grades in his first year of college. He seems to know the name of every kid he sees on his way to class. In poker, he beats the pants off every guy in his hall and spends his winnings on books and food and, this month, his first suit; he's taking a smart girl with curly blond hair to the Charity Ball.

But Luke grew up in Seattle, where the weather is kind to him nearly all year, where top prosthodontists are plentiful, and where our father has a job with decent dental benefits. Growing up, I came to see ED as a mere inconvenience. Sometimes it brought heavy expenses for our parents, sometimes it caused physical embarrassments for my brother. But it never seemed cataclysmic.

So I fumbled for words recently when I found myself explaining to my brother that Dan and I hoped to dodge ED. I wondered if he was thinking, *What's so bad that they'd try so hard to avoid it?* As I stammered, Luke interrupted me with a "duh" look. "I wouldn't want your kids to have it," he said.

And neither, of course, would we. Dan was with me on a summer trip last year as I peered into my grandfather's story for a writing project. His family and schoolmates told us about his childhood in western Nebraska—part of the Great Desert, with cactus paddles crowding the wheat. The heat often prevented him from helping on the farm, or doing anything at all. He'd sit in the ice barn alone, melting into the white blocks. If the playground sizzled at recess, it didn't matter who was watching; he'd creep like a dog beneath the snowberry bushes. People considered Earl feeble, and tended to him like a baby. He grew into a reckless man, desperate to prove he had no limits—financial, physical, or emotional. At forty-nine, he died penniless, addicted to prescription drugs, and alone.

On our drive home to Iowa from Nebraska, I asked Dan what he thought of what we'd learned.

"When you think about Earl's life," he said as we whipped through the sweltering summer cornfields, "it seems like we should do whatever we can to avoid passing it on."

Still, I sometimes dream of a baby boy who reminds me of my brother. He has the same clever humor, sharp eye, and wise ears.

Despite his ED, the boy seems perfect to me. He is astoundingly bright. Before he's old enough to talk, he sits on my lap with a good-natured smile, making amused remarks about humankind. Then he turns and clings to me like a gentle koala, loving me deeply. I have begun to wonder if he is saying in his patient way, "Don't rule me out."

UPDATE: *Bonnie and Dan Rough hope to start a family in the next few years. They haven't decided for certain which method they'll use in hopes of achieving their first pregnancy, though Bonnie reports, "We've grown less anxious about the means and more eager for the end result."*

Online Images Open a Heart, Then a Home

Debora Spar

For about a year, for the first time in my life, I was addicted to a Web site. Well, two Web sites, actually, both of which did the same thing. They listed beautiful children, tragic children, children whose photographs were displayed in colorful rows or banner headlines, looking out from the desktop and pleading with someone to take them home. There were some babies in the mix, and some older kids. Most were toddlers, clasping toys or sporting huge bows in their hair. Technically, all of these children were available; "waiting" in the parlance of adoption, for their "forever families."

> One of those children, I giddily felt, was mine. My kid, misplaced somehow, and determined to find her way home.

Each morning, I would scroll through these hundreds of kids, sorting them by age or country or gender. The toughest category, and my most frequent pick, was "Date added." There, you could see the spectrum of options: the newest kids—just in! just born!—and those who had been waiting for a long, long time. I knew I couldn't actually adopt any of these kids online, but the sites were so seamless that it often felt as if I could. You find a kid, click on his photo, and get whisked off to an adoption agency, where you're presented with more information designed to rip your heart out: "Rashid is a cutie pie who is waiting for a Mommy and Daddy to bring him home." "Yamile likes to write and draw, and dreams of being a doctor when she grows up."

There was no good reason for me to be messing around on these sites. I had two school-age sons already, plus a job that devoured both time and energy. My husband and I both came from small, tight-knit families, and neither of us had any connection to adoption. And yet there I was every morning, pushing my work aside and logging on to check on "my" kids.

Initially, it was all too painful: I wanted Yamile and Rashid and whomever else I discovered in my morning haunts. I wanted the beautiful little girls from Cambodia, and the hungry toddlers from Haiti, and the older Russian siblings who probably had no chance of ever being adopted.

Over time, though, I got faster and pickier. I raced through the listings with a harder heart and waited for the inevitable blow: for the kid whose picture jumped off the screen and made me start to cry. I never found a pattern to my preferences. Sometimes it was the little girls who bowled me over, sometimes the older boys. Sometimes it was kids whom I couldn't possibly adopt, like a family of three teenagers from Guatemala, and sometimes it was those who seemed easier, like a chubby-faced toddler from Ukraine. It didn't matter. I'd see their pictures, and in some strange way I'd start to fall in love.

Eventually, I took the next step. I told my husband what I was up to, and showed him the pictures I had piled on my desk. He was surprised at first, of course, but the pictures tore his heart as well, and slowly he realized how committed I had become. So we agreed—tentatively, hesitantly—just to find out more.

On a brilliantly sunny June day, I went to a local adoption agency, confessed my obsession with the photo listings, and received the first pile of what would soon be mountains of paperwork. And while I was there, I was attacked by photos again: by the serious older children that this agency placed, all with the same sad smile, posed in front of the same orphanage wall. One of those children, I giddily felt, was mine. My kid, misplaced somehow, and determined to find her way home.

For the next several months, my husband and I grappled with this sudden odd calculus. I couldn't explain what was driving me to those pictures. He couldn't understand what was missing, or wrong. Everything about adoption seemed scary and unnecessary. We worried about the health of an unknown child. We worried about our boys, about our jobs, about how our families would deal with an unconventional addition.

Mostly, though, we worried about our choices. Because when we had decided to have babies the old-fashioned way, the decision had been simple: yes or no, now or later. Now it was infinitely more complex, involving all those horrible variables that hit me each morning from the online sites.

How do you pick a child who already exists? What do you choose? If there are pictures, you are inevitably choosing on looks— brunette versus blonde, short versus tall. For girls, this process seems particularly cruel: a beauty pageant that plucks one little creature from the orphanage and leaves the others behind.

And so as we wound our way toward an eventual decision, my husband issued his only ultimatum: we weren't going to pick this child ourselves. We weren't going to plow through any more photos, or through the glossy newsletters that now arrived regularly in the mail. Instead, we would pick an agency and let them—or God, or someone—choose for us.

It was tough, this vow of blindness, and occasionally I cheated. When no one was watching, I would trawl again through the photo listings, half hoping, half dreading that my child would somehow find me. Then, an ironic nine months after we started, the agency finally called: they had our daughter; her file was on its way.

The next day, my normally reticent son—the son who had stayed aloof from this whole process—called me breathless in the middle of a meeting. He had ripped open the brown envelope and seen the girl who was soon to be his sister. "Mom," he screamed. "She's the most beautiful girl in the world. And she looks just like me."

That night, we watched the video, a polished presentation that was clearly designed to market a small child. We saw the pouffy pink dress and the shoes that were way too big. We saw a little girl who couldn't stop talking, who loved to build with blocks, and who sang very loudly and distinctly off-key. My son was right: she was the most beautiful girl in the world. This time, for the first time, my husband fell hard. "That's her," he said. "Let's go get her."

Six weeks later, we flew to Ekaterinburg, an industrial city on the western edge of Siberia. Boris, our driver, sped us past blocks of neglected apartment buildings and streets crammed with vendors. Soon we pulled up to the orphanage, a whitewashed cluster of buildings tucked behind a convenience store.

The first meeting was exquisitely hard. Because what do you say when you meet your daughter for the first time and she's already six? We followed the instructions closely: to give her a doll, some stickers, and to repeat the few comforting phrases we knew in Russian. The thing that captured her attention, though, was exactly what had captured our attention in the first place: photos. Pictures of us at home, with the boys, with the cat. Clearly, the photos were more intriguing to her than we were; it seemed that the image of a home, rather than the presence of two grasping strangers, was what gradually reduced her terror and allowed her to trust.

When we left four days later, as Russian law demands, to await our court hearing, the photo album remained. All of the other trinkets—the stickers, clothes, toys— quickly disappeared into the communal nooks of the orphanage. But the album stayed. When we returned six weeks later, she was clutching it still, imagining her new life from a handful of photos.

That was three years ago. After a frenetic few months, our daughter blended almost seamlessly into our lives, convincing us—in the way of all parents—that no other child could possibly have been ours. She builds like her father, sings like her brother, and talks, as we all do, too much. Although she clearly doesn't bear a genetic relationship to our family, we constantly find a resemblance: the same blue eyes as her brother, the same craving for pickles. It's not really a physical resemblance, but it works just as well.

Her room is cluttered with the usual jetsam of nine-year-old girls, but her three most treasured possessions never budge from her bedside. The little album we brought to her in Russia; another—compiled later—of the friends she left behind; and two snapshots, thankfully saved by the orphanage, of her as a toddler, posing in a crowded kitchen with grandparents whom we never knew.

These days, the photos move in the opposite direction. Once a year, under Russian law, we mail an update to the local authorities in Ekaterinburg. I've never understood precisely who sees the update—the judge, perhaps, or maybe the orphanage director—but I find myself selecting the pictures with ritualistic concern. I want them to represent the best of both her worlds. I want whoever looks at this record to see the trappings of her new life, the soccer games and ballet lessons and birthday parties. I want them to see her happy, with the family that's now hers. But I also want them to know that this child they've sent us is still who she always was: fiercely independent, full of joy and grace and pride.

My daughter, meanwhile, uses the annual photos to send what she sees as missives back to her friends. She wants them to see a new dress, or a picture of her skating. She wants them, lately, to see her at the beach, so that they can catch a glimpse of the warm waves that will never reach Siberia.

I don't return to the online photo listings very often anymore. I suppose I shouldn't go at all, but every once in a while something pulls me back. Several weeks ago, a boy leaped out at me. He made me look at his shy face, at the self-conscious way he stood before the camera. He made me read the few brief sentences that described his life. And he made me, in an instant, want to go get him.

So I did what I shouldn't have done, and heard what I didn't want to hear. I called the agency and spoke with a friendly, enthusiastic woman who informed me that, yes, he was still available and, no, no one else had ever expressed an interest in him.

I can't adopt this boy. This time around, I know that. But I can't help hoping that someone else will see this child and recognize him as their own—a distant child, a stranger, who becomes the most beautiful boy in the world.

UPDATE: *Debora and her husband's daughter has been with them for nearly four years now and continues to thrive.*

Sending a Lost Boy to the Wilderness to Find Himself

Richard Reiss

IT'S DARK. I LIE IN BED WITH MY EYES OPEN. THE WIN-
dows are closed, but I can still hear the gentle midnight
roar of the New Jersey Turnpike, a mere quarter mile
from the front door of my safe suburban home.

Safe, that's a joke.
Walk through my house,
see what my fourteen-
year-old son has done—
a pile of broken picture
frames, a hole in the wall,
a closet without a door, a
few shards of glass still
beneath a recently repaired
window.

> *His mother and I grew
> convinced that our love
> was not enough to help
> him, so we looked into
> having him taken
> away to people
> who could.*

At two I go to my son's room to check on him, and he
asks me to rub his back. His skin is cool to the touch as my
hand slides across the suppleness of his young developing
muscles. His thick hair is the color of henna. His eyes are
dark and sophisticated. He is lean and muscular, with
long, elegant hands. He is a striking young man just as he
was a striking young boy.

What he doesn't know is that these will be the last

hours in his bed, in our house, for a long, long time. Yet he must sense something's up; he can't sleep.

I can't either. I haven't even tried.

It's been a relatively good week: no major fights, not much cursing. Our "R-rated house," as his younger brother describes it, recently has been closer to PG, which makes this even harder. But the irresolvable problem, the breaking point for us, is that he has stopped going to school; he simply refuses. Instead, he stays up late and then sleeps in and hangs around until his friends come home from school, when he leaves to join them.

Our son's birth mother is a woman he has never known, a woman who answered our ad in the newspaper. My wife and I had endured the trials of infertility—three years of shots and tears and bloody toilets, and absolutely not one second of joy. Like so many others, we were desperate, young, and naïve.

Then we got him, our boy, and he was a star, a chatterbox, a wiz, the delight of all who were lucky enough to cross his path. A few years later, my wife gave birth to a boy, and then another. And soon after, our first son was adored not only by his parents but by his younger brothers, too. We felt blessed—certainly, we were blessed.

So it's hard for us to imagine how this child, surrounded by so much love, could turn out to be so lost. Perhaps it was the ADHD? Or the plethora of medications that never worked for more than a few weeks? Perhaps it was the loss of someone he never knew—his biological parent?

At age three he began to show a temper. At six he developed an attitude. At ten he struck a classmate. At fourteen he was spiraling out of control. His mother and I grew convinced that our love was not enough to help him, so we looked into having him taken away to people who could—we researched it, examined the costs, talked to everyone we could find. And we've put up all of our assets to pay for it: mortgaged our house, spent his college fund. It's all gone to this. A financial hardship, yes, but how could we not?

Back in our bedroom, my wife says to me, "What's going to happen?"

"I don't know. I just hope he doesn't wake up his brothers."

At 4:00 a.m. they arrive, right on time. I open the door and hear, much louder now, the sound of cars rushing by on the New Jersey Turnpike. But their car, its engine cooling in my driveway, is quiet.

Two young men step out. One is big but not huge. The other is average-size.

"So how do you do this?" I ask. "What if he resists?"

"It's rare that anyone resists," says the average-size one. He goes on to explain a process called de-escalation. They are experienced, bright, articulate; they make a living coming into strangers' homes and taking away their unsuspecting children to youth boot camps, private boarding schools, or, in our case, a therapeutic wilderness program. They are paid a lot of money by parents like us who hope that somehow, some way, our beautiful babies can be fixed.

We enter our son's room. I press against his shoulder to wake him.

He looks up and sees the escorts. "What did I do now?"

I tell him to get up and get dressed. "You shouldn't be surprised," I explain. "You knew this is what would happen if you didn't go back to school."

He curses and punches the wall.

"We love you," my wife and I say, and then, per the escorts' instructions, we leave the room.

From our bedroom we hear the muffled sounds of conversation but can't make out the words. There is no shouting. I think I hear him crying but maybe that's wishful thinking. I hope he cares enough to cry.

I hug my wife. We are not crying. We are too nervous to cry. How much time has gone by? Five minutes? Ten? And then footsteps, the door closing, and we look out our bedroom window to see the car making its way back to the turnpike.

In the morning I go to work and wait for the call to let me know he has arrived safely. I can't stay home and think about it. I need to be distracted. I need to call my parents, to explain it all to them, and in doing so accept my failure as a parent. It's not easy. My mother cries.

And then I get the call; he's there.

In the wilderness of North Carolina he will not see or speak to his friends. He will not sneak out in the middle of the night. He will not be brought home by the police. He will not come within ten miles of a cigarette. He will not curse at us or break anything of ours. He will not see a movie, have sex, or go on the Internet. He will not receive phone calls from strangers. He will not get in trouble for missing school; his school is the wilderness now.

In the wilderness I will not come into his room when he is sleeping and kiss him on the head. Instead, a counselor will check on him. At bedtime the counselor will take away my son's shoes to make it more difficult for him to run away.

Every night that he's gone I silently call out his name as I lie in bed, hoping to reach him telepathically, hoping he's thinking of me. He is, of course, thinking of me. He's thinking of his mother, too. He writes us horrific letters, rife with the contempt and venom that often filled our home. They are idle threats from a frightened child. His counselors assure us that he is doing well and in time his attitude will change. Living in a sleeping bag and under a tarp, they say, does that to a person.

Our son's wilderness experience will last seven weeks before we are reunited. When we do see him that first time, he is cold and nasty to us, having recently learned that he is not coming home but instead going straight from camp to boarding school. Yet that evening, before we leave for the boarding school, we spend an emotional night together in a ten-by-twelve cabin with no heat, no water, no electricity. We speak about life and family and honesty in a way we never have, and it feels like a breakthrough.

After this visit it will be another seven months before he finally sets foot in the house he grew up in. His younger brothers miss him. We miss him. But now he goes to school . . . imagine! It's amazing what a person can do when there are no distractions.

A full nine months after he was taken away on that awful night he is home again, and for two whole days, before he returns to boarding school, he is loved by us and by his brothers. Yet I worry that the boy we had whisked away all that time ago is still lurking under the façade of his smile.

Later I hear him above me in his room. It's midnight and he can't sleep. I hear his footsteps, then the sound of his door opening and closing. It's hard not to think what this meant before.

A few days earlier I visited him at his therapeutic boarding school, where he introduced me to his teachers and friends. He was confident and poised. We hugged and laughed. "How's school?" I asked. "It sucks," he said. But he smiled and we both knew that's what all the kids say.

He's not the same boy, but we don't tell him that. He has changed, but he doesn't completely see it, and it's wonderful that he can't. In another year he'll see it even less.

Part of me is confident that we have done the right thing. As painful and difficult and expensive as this process has been, it's clearly been worthwhile; maybe it even has saved his life. But now, during the few days he's home, I sense the reemergence of frightening patterns: the mess in his room, the piles of dishes in the basement where he hangs out, the pounding music. Are these signs of trouble or normal teenage behavior?

"Can you bring in the garbage cans?" I ask tentatively, probing him.

He shoots me an unpleasant look and mutters an under-the-breath remark. Still, he brings in the cans and places them against the wall in front of a gaping hole he made one day with the angry swing of a golf club.

I am quietly terrified again, but what scares me, I realize, is not his behavior but my inability to know how to read it. I have no idea what typical teenage angst and opposition looks like when it comes to him, and I worry I'll never know.

My wife doesn't understand why I'm so upset. "He's been nothing short of great," she says.

And she is right. I have to believe that.

Now it's late and he's asleep; his room is quiet, dark. I walk down the stairs toward the kitchen. On the wall of the stairway is his baby portrait. I lean toward it, kiss his beautiful one-year-old face, and pray that the worst is over.

UPDATE: *After several visits home from his current program, Richard's son has decided that he is ready to be home permanently, though while home he also has returned to some of his old behaviors. Consequently, Richard and his wife find themselves again facing a heart-wrenching choice: allow their son to come home against the advice of every professional who has worked with him over the last year and hope he can function well in the home environment, or send him to a more restrictive school with more therapy, more attention, and more rules, which would push him, temporarily, even farther away from his family.*

Looking for Love at the Sperm Bank

Linda Dackman

PULLED UP IN FRONT OF A RED BRICK BUILDING WITH TUR-
rets. The place looked like a run-down miniaturized
Elizabethan castle. I had to laugh. What an odd place for
a sperm bank.

The mission at hand was terrifying: I'd come here to
choose a partner, a father for my yet-to-be-conceived
child. To do so I had to
select anonymous sperm
from among the bank's
verified swimmers.

> *So now it was my turn
> to come here, to this
> unlikely sperm castle,
> seeking an anonymous
> donor. I just had to
> find him.*

Choosing in gen-
eral—or rather, making
practical choices—is not
exactly my forte, which
may explain why I've had plenty of boyfriends but have
never been able to figure out whom I could settle down
with. So at forty-two I was still like a teenager, single,
stupid, spinning from steady to steady. But unlike a
teenager I was running out of time to find the perfect
man and create the perfect family. Still, I wanted to have
a baby, even if it meant doing the whole thing on my
own.

Now, at the castle, I entered a dark wood-paneled hall,
the floorboards creaking with my steps along the tatty red

carpets, until I came to a frosted glass door with TSBC inscribed in black letters, like a detective's office in an old film noir. The initials stood for The Sperm Bank of California. I buzzed, heard a buzz back, and walked in.

"Hi, I'm Shellie," a young woman said. She wore flowing cotton pants, a turquoise tank top, Birkenstocks, and a tight band of beads around her neck. Her long hair was light brown and frizzy.

After greeting her I asked, "What was this building before?"

"A funeral parlor," she said, matter-of-factly.

A funeral parlor? And now it was a sperm bank? She had to be kidding. This was taking the idea of full circle too far.

"Everything, our comings and goings, are carefully timed here," Shellie said, beginning my tour. "That's to protect the identity of the donors and the recipients. We have separate rooms, arrival times, and hallways, so never the twain shall meet."

I looked at the closed doors along the hall and wondered who might be lurking inside and what they might be doing.

She pointed through a doorway. "These are our tanks, where the frozen sperm are stored."

The tanks were large, round silver containers, not much different from beer kegs. But instead of a spigot at the top there was a wheel, the sort used to batten down submarine hatches. It wasn't an antiseptic room. Just a room. To judge from the flocked wallpaper, it might have been a vigil room for the funerals that were once held here.

Now that I was touring the place, I marveled that my friend Tom had actually gone to the trouble of coming here months before, entering one of these rooms and, with the aid of his imagination or maybe a magazine, producing, all on my behalf. "A designated donor," Shellie called him.

I marveled, too, that my friend Michael had been so kind as to stop by on his way to work to pick up nitrogen-frosted thermoses with Tom's cold, drowsy sperm inside and take them across the bridge to me at the doctor's office in San Francisco.

But after months of trying to conceive this way I gave up. Tom is a wonderful friend, an ex-boyfriend and a talented professor, and I very much liked the idea that he would be the father of my child. But apparently his sperm weren't going to work for me.

So now it was my turn to come here, to this unlikely sperm castle, seeking an anonymous donor. I just had to find him.

Shellie explained how the system worked. "You pay by the hour and go through the files of available donors privately," she said. "You select three, and we see whose sperm is available at the time you are ovulating."

So it wasn't even a single donor I had to choose but a collection, a triumvirate.

The initial roster was short and concise, providing only ethnicity, height, weight, hair, and eye color, career, and availability. I picked ten to consider more thoroughly. Shellie then took those files and escorted me into what looked like a student dorm room, complete with a futon covered in an Indian cloth that resembled Shellie's pants. There was a table, a lamp, a desk, and a chair. There were no windows, but several cheerful posters of puppies and kittens adorned the walls, a hint of new life without being so overt as to promise a new baby.

Shellie left me alone, and I sat down to read through the files. A door opened and shut in the hallway, and a moment later I heard a man's voice.

I wanted to run and look, but I knew it was against the rules. I felt I was playing *Let's Make a Deal,* trying to guess who or what was behind Door Number One and Door Number Two.

One young prospect excited me, a tall man of Japanese and Jewish descent. Jewish, like me, and Japanese as a nice twist. I'd had a half-Japanese boyfriend once, a medical student, and had liked him a lot. But would a mixed-race child be a mistake, an even greater disadvantage for this poor imaginary kid than being raised by a single mother? My heart raced, my Pergonal-enhanced ovaries ached, and my stomach took flight. This process was so preposterous. I knew love was supposed to be blind, but come on.

There was anguish when I opened the next file. This donor's family's medical history seemed as bad as mine— cancer all over the place, as well as poor vision, headaches, and allergies. Ah, this was going to be a problem, this eugenics, where there ought to be emotion. The information in these files was so abstract, so sterile, so tinged with the depressing reality of paternal grandmothers with diabetes and fathers with heart disease.

What about personality, love, intellect, passion? All I had to go on was the hieroglyphics of handwriting. I couldn't visualize any of them. From what I understood they were mostly kids, college students in need of tuition money, with mothers who were probably younger than I. I'd probably be better off grading their college English papers and picking a father for my child on that basis. What was I doing here?

Unfortunately I was looking for love, still trying to make an intuitive selection, not a rational one. I tried to fall for something on each page, some soaring words in their short essays, but there was barely the flair of a crossed *T* to swoon over.

How, I asked myself, did I end up amid these worn blue files with numbers on them? How did this become my love life? Why hadn't I stuck with that medical student I liked in grad school? How was it that in my late twenties I spent four years with Allan, and upon my departure, when he offered commitment and a child, I knew I wasn't interested? Why all those years lost on that tall, fair-haired, but dark, damaged, and brooding German? And of course the artists. Don't get me started on the artists.

It's a good thing Shellie knocked on the door. She seemed used to exactly this type of crisis. She scanned the files I was considering and began giving me hints. "This one here is very cute," she said. "He's a popular choice."

I wondered if her hints were within regulation, what the rules were.

"This one looks the most like you," she said about another.

He was interested in the arts, just as I am. He probably can't get a job, I mused, suddenly screening for psychological characteristics and their economic impact. "He seems *too* sensitive," I explained, rejecting him. I was on the brink of a nervous breakdown.

"What about him?" I asked Shellie. He said he had freckly skin—not my favorite—but I saw gorgeous handwriting, broad interests in the sciences and arts, and, best of all, a high sperm count.

"Not available until April," Shellie told me. "But number five-thirty-seven over here is a professor of philosophy and has good coloring. And he's good-looking, at least in my opinion."

Her opinion? An awful lot was hinging on her opinion, this woman in Birkenstocks, a brand of shoe I was never once tempted to buy. But she was all I had. And more important still, she'd at least laid eyes on these men.

"He doesn't seem to have much in the way of artistic leanings," I lamented.

Shellie nodded like a patient therapist, not bothering to mention that I was contradicting myself. She was no doubt mindful that another client needed the room.

"He's smart and academic," she said. "He ought to naturally appreciate the finer things."

But the freckly donor's lack of availability had caught in my mind and lingered there. I sensed, in a perfect metaphor for the rest of my romantic life, that it was precisely his unavailability that appealed to me. "I still kind of like the freckly kid with the high sperm count," I said, trying to relieve the tension and the paralyzing uncertainty I felt. After all, I knew it was this paralyzing uncertainty that had landed me in a sperm bank in the first place.

Shellie just looked at me.

"Okay, I'll take the philosopher this time," I said, relenting. "But I would like to reserve the unavailable freckly kid for next time. And maybe the Japanese Jewish kid as the final backup?"

Shellie nodded and smiled.

I had made my choice. As inelegant as this process had been, as limp and emotionally exhausted as I was, the matter was done.

What's more, I understood that whatever the outcome—success or failure, whichever father, baby or none—by going forward I had at least ensured some of what I sought in an actual baby, a commitment to life. And what more fitting place to come to such an understanding than in this funeral parlor turned sperm bank?

UPDATE: *While undergoing her six months of insemination, Linda faced a battle with her insurance company, which denied her claims for infertility treatment (as she was undergoing them) because of her status as a single woman. In the end, she finally got her benefits. But that's all.*

Now I Need a Place to Hide Away

Ann Hood

IT IS DIFFICULT TO HIDE FROM THE BEATLES. AFTER ALL these years they are still regularly in the news. Their songs play on oldies stations, countdowns, and best-ofs. There is always some Beatles anniversary: the first Number One song, the first time in the United States, a birthday, an anniversary, a milestone, a Broadway show.

But hide from the Beatles I must. Or, in some cases, escape. One day in the grocery store, when "Eight Days a Week" came on, I had to leave my cartful of food and run out. Stepping into an elevator that's blasting a peppy Muzak version of "Hey Jude" is enough to send me home to bed.

> *As parents do, I had shared my passions with my children. But now that passion was turned upside down, and rather than bring joy, the Beatles haunted me.*

Of course it wasn't always this way. I used to love everything about the Beatles. As a child I memorized their birthdays, their tragic life stories, the words to all of their songs. I collected Beatles trading cards in bubble gum packs and wore a charm bracelet of dangling Beatles' heads and guitars.

For days my cousin Debbie and I argued over whether "Penny Lane" and its flip side, "Strawberry Fields Forever," had been worth waiting for. I struggled to understand *Sgt. Pepper*. I marveled over the brilliance of the *White Album*.

My cousins and I used to play Beatles wives. We all wanted to be married to Paul, but John was okay, too. None of us wanted Ringo. Or even worse, George.

It was too easy to love Paul. Those bedroom eyes. That mop of hair. Classically cute. When I was eight, I asked my mother if she thought I might someday marry Paul McCartney.

"Well, honey," she said, taking a long drag on her Pall Mall. "Somebody will. Maybe it'll be you."

In fifth grade, in a diary in which I mostly wrote, *It is so boring here,* or simply, *Bored,* only one entry stands out: *I just heard on the radio that Paul got married. Oh, please, God, don't let it be true.*

It was true, and I mourned for far too long.

Of course by the time I was in high school, I understood my folly. John was the best Beatle: sarcastic, funny, interesting looking. That long thin nose. Those round wire-rimmed glasses. By then I didn't want to be anybody's wife. But I did want a boy like John, someone who spoke his mind, got into trouble, swore a lot, and wrote poetry.

When I did get married and then had children, it was Beatles songs I sang to them at night. As one of the youngest of twenty-four cousins, I had never held an infant or baby-sat. I didn't know any lullabies, so I sang Sam and Grace to sleep with "I Will" and "P.S. I Love

You." Eventually Sam fell in love with Broadway musicals and abandoned the Beatles.

But not Grace. She embraced them with all the fervor that I had. Her taste was quirky, mature.

"What's the song where the man is standing, holding his head?" she asked, frowning, and before long I had unearthed my old *Help!* album, and the two of us were singing, "Here I stand, head in hand."

For Grace's fourth Christmas, Santa brought her all of the Beatles' movies on video, a photo book of their career, and *The Beatles 1* tape. Before long, playing "Eight Days a Week" as loud as possible became our anthem. Even Sam sang along and admitted that it was arguably the best song ever written.

Best of all about my daughter the Beatles fan was that by the time she was five, she already had fallen for John. Paul's traditional good looks did not win her over. Instead she liked John's nasally voice, his dark side. After watching the biopic *Backbeat,* she said Stu was her favorite. But soon she returned to John. Once I overheard her arguing with a first-grade boy who didn't believe that there had been another Beatle.

"There were two other Beatles," Grace told him, disgusted. "Stu and Pete Best." She rolled her eyes and stomped off in her glittery shoes.

Sometimes, before she fell asleep, she would make me tell her stories about John's mother dying, how the band met in Liverpool, and how when Paul wrote the tune for "Yesterday," he sang the words "scrambled eggs" to it.

After I would drop Sam off at school and continue with Grace to her kindergarten, she'd have me play one of her Beatles tapes. She would sing along the whole way there: "Scrambled eggs, all my troubles seemed so far away."

On the day George Harrison died, Grace acted as if she had lost a friend, walking sad and teary-eyed around the house, shaking her head in disbelief. She asked if we could play just Beatles music all day, and we did. That night we watched a retrospective on George. Feeling guilty, I confessed that he was the one none of us wanted to marry.

"George?" Grace said, stunned. "But he's great."

Five months later, on a beautiful April morning, Grace and I took Sam to school, then got in the car and sang along with "I Want to Hold Your Hand" while we drove. Before she left, she asked me to cue the tape so that as soon as she got back in the car that afternoon, she could hear "You've Got to Hide Your Love Away" right from the beginning. That was the last time we listened to our Beatles together.

The next day Grace spiked a fever and died from a virulent form of strep. Briefly, as she lay in the ICU, the nurses told us to bring in some of her favorite music. My husband ran out to his car and grabbed 1 from the tape deck. Then he put it in the hospital's tape deck, and we climbed on the bed with our daughter and sang her "Love Me Do." Despite the tubes and machines struggling to keep her alive, Grace smiled at us as we sang to her.

At her memorial service, eight-year-old Sam, wearing a bright red bow tie, stood in front of the hundreds of people there and sang "Eight Days a Week" loud enough for his sister, wherever she had gone, to hear him.

That evening I gathered all of my Beatles music—the dusty albums, the tapes that littered the floor of my car, the CDs that filled our stereo—and put them in a box with Grace's copies of the Beatles movies. I could not pause over any of them.

Instead I threw them in carelessly and fast, knowing that the sight of those black-and-white faces on *Revolver,* or the dizzying colors of *Sgt. Pepper* or even the cartoon drawings from *Yellow Submarine,* the very things that had made me so happy a week earlier, were now too painful even to glimpse. As parents do, I had shared my passions with my children. And when it came to the Beatles, Grace had seized my passion and made it her own. But with her death, that passion was turned upside down, and rather than bring joy, the Beatles haunted me.

I couldn't bear to hear even the opening chords of "Yesterday" or a cover of "Michelle." In the car I started listening only to talk radio to avoid a Beatles song catching me by surprise and touching off another round of sobbing.

I tried to shield myself from the Beatles altogether—their music, images, conversations about them—but it's hard, if not impossible. How, for example, am I supposed to ask Sam not to pick out their music slowly during his guitar lessons?

Back in the sixties, in my aunt's family room, with the knotty-pine walls and Zenith TV, with my female cousins all around me, our hair straight and long, our bangs in our eyes, the air thick with our parents' cigarette smoke and the harmonies of the Beatles, I believed there was no love greater than mine for Paul McCartney.

Sometimes now, alone, I find myself singing softly. "And when at last I find you, your song will fill the air," I sing to Grace, imagining her blue eyes shining behind her own little wire-rimmed glasses, her feet tapping in time. "Love you whenever we're together, love you when we're apart." It was once my favorite love song, silent now in its *White Album* cover in my basement.

How foolish I was to have fallen so easily for Paul while overlooking John and George, to have believed that everything I could ever want was right there in that family room of my childhood: cousins, TV, my favorite music. But mostly I feel foolish for believing that my time with my daughter would never end.

Or perhaps that is love: a leap of faith, a belief in the impossible, the ability to believe that a little girl in a small town in Rhode Island would grow up to marry Paul McCartney. Or for a grieving woman to believe that a mother's love is so strong that the child she lost can still hear her singing a lullaby.

UPDATE: *A year after Grace died, Ann, her husband, and their eleven-year-old son traveled to China to adopt a baby girl, whom they named Annabelle. Annabelle is now two, and Ann reports that the girl's spirit and presence has brought hope and joy back into their household.*

The New Nanny Diaries Are Online

Helaine Olen

OUR FORMER NANNY, A TWENTY-SIX-YEAR-OLD FORMER teacher with excellent references, liked to touch her breasts while reading *The New Yorker* and often woke her lovers in the night by biting them. She took sleeping pills, joked about offbeat erotic fantasies involving Tucker Carlson, and determined she'd had more female sexual partners than her boyfriend.

How do I know these things? I read her blog.

She hadn't been with us long when we found out about her online diary. All she'd revealed previously about her private life were the bare-bones details of the occasional date or argument with her landlord and her hopes of attending graduate school in the fall.

In part I felt empathy and sadness for this younger version of myself.
But I also feared she would judge my life and find it wanting.

Yet within two months of my starting to read her entries, our entire relationship unraveled. Not only were there things I didn't want to know about the person who was watching my children, it turned out her online revelations brought feelings of mine to the surface I'd just as soon not have had to face as well.

I hadn't exactly been a stranger to the sexual she-nanigans of our previous babysitters. One got pregnant accidentally by her longtime boyfriend and asked me for advice. Another was involved in a mostly off-again relationship with a fidelity-challenged college football player. Yet those were problems I could feel superior to and that made me grateful for the steady routine of marriage and children.

This was something else entirely.

It all began one day late last fall when we were tending to my toddler and she murmured to me, "I've started a blog. I'll give you the link."

I wrote the address in my appointment book but didn't rush off to my computer to look up her site. It wasn't until a month later, after she told me she'd post the Sharon Olds poem "Life With Sick Kids," on a day when both of the boys were ill, that I decided to be polite and take a look.

I read the poem, then scrolled down to the next entry. And the next. Amid the musings on poetry and fanatical analysis of the *Gilmore Girls* was a sweet scene of sex with a new boyfriend, accounts of semi-promiscuous couplings, and tales of too much drinking for my comfort.

My husband thought her writing precociously talented but wanted to fire her nonetheless. "This is inappropriate," he said. "We don't need to know that Jennifer Ehle makes her hot."

I defended her—at first. Didn't she have a right to free expression? It wasn't as though she were quaffing Scotch or bedding guys, or the occasional girl, while on the job. Besides, weren't all recent college graduates keeping Web logs?

But there was more to my advocacy. Suddenly, with her in my employ, I felt I was young and hip by proxy. I might be a boring mother of two, but my nanny, why, she dined in the hippest Williamsburg restaurants and rated the sexual energy of the men and women she met. I was amused—and more than a bit envious.

I was about to turn forty. I'd been married almost fifteen years. My ability to attend literary readings and art gallery openings was hampered by two children, and my party life was relegated to the toddler birthday circuit. I imagined the snoozefest that would ensue if I were to post:

SPENT THE MORNING AT THE GARFIELD TEMPLE
PLAYROOM. TRIED TO READ PAUL KRUGMAN
WHILE OTHER PARENTS GAVE ME DIRTY LOOKS
AS MY YOUNGER SON ATTEMPTED TO FILCH
THEIR KIDS' DUMP TRUCKS.

I told my friends about the blog, and even my childless acquaintances were riveted. They called, begging for more details. "Did she wear the rose negligee, the pink see-through slip, or the purple Empire-waisted gown?" demanded one after perusing a post on the proper outfit for first-time sex. "She didn't say."

But I was not as comfortable with the situation as I pretended. The blog had brought odd similarities to the fore. I don't want to overstate the case: I was not bisexual, and I did not come from a strictly religious background, as my nanny did.

Yet we had enough in common—if I took her statements at face value—to make me uneasy. In my twenties I, too, felt passionately about nineteenth-century English literature but had long since let it go, barely able to concentrate on the *New York Times,* let alone Henry James. I, too, had had an abortion back then. And trouble with depression? Check. Self-righteousness and inflated self-regard? Affirmative.

When our nanny asked permission to bring her laptop to work so she could work on her graduate school applications while the baby napped, I said yes. Then I wondered if she was whiling away time with flirtatious e-mail messages—something that she revealed on her blog she sometimes did. And when she came down with a stomach virus twice during a period when the rest of us were sick only once, I wondered about her confessions of boozy nights out followed by coming to work hungover. Paranoia, perhaps, but reading the blog seemed to encourage such thoughts.

Yet I did not confront her. In part I felt empathy and sadness for this younger version of myself. But I also feared she would judge my life and find it wanting.

As I read her words I was transported back to my own youth and those feelings of awkwardness, fear, false bravado, and self-importance. I could have told her that I understood her life more than she realized, that I had not always been the boring hausfrau she must see. I could say that I, too, once stayed out late, drank too much, and slept with the wrong people. I, too, once found my work obligations a tedious distraction from creative pursuits and thought myself superior to my surroundings, just as she appeared to.

Yet my awareness of this prior life and my knowledge that I'd outgrown it didn't spare me from feelings of intense doubt about my current life, times when I was convinced I'd made the wrong choices, days when my husband and I would spend hours tearing into each other over who should clean the tub after a child mistook it for the potty. On the other hand I also got to revel in days when I loved my life and children so much that it hurt.

But there was another element of her posts that unnerved me. Most parents don't like to think that the person watching their children is there for a salary. We often build up a mythology of friendship with our nannies, pretending the nanny admires us and loves our children so much that she would continue to visit even without pay.

When our nanny referred to our house on her blog as work, in a seemingly sarcastic fashion, she broke the covenant. The more she posted, the more life in our household deteriorated. It almost seemed that as she created the persona of a do-me feminist with an academic bent, it began to affect her performance. The woman who was loving if a bit strict toward the children became in our view short and impatient, slamming doors and bashing pans when my toddler wouldn't sleep and sighing heavily if asked to run an errand.

Instead of opening a dialogue, I monitored her online life almost obsessively. I would log on upstairs to see if she was simultaneously posting entries below me on her laptop while the baby was napping. Too often she was.

Looking at archived entries one afternoon, I read her

reactions to an argument my husband and I had had when she was in the house. "I heard a couple fighting within the confines of couples therapy-speak," she wrote. "I wanted to say, smack him, bite her."

It went on like that for three ghastly pages.

"I seethed," she added.

Well, so did I. But mostly I felt hurt. My issues, my problems, my compromises, my entire being seemed to be viewed by her as so much waste.

Mortified into silence, I didn't tell my husband about the post. Nor could I tell her how disturbing the situation was becoming. I was beginning to realize either her employment or the blog would have to come to an end.

A few days later her anger boiled over. "I am having the type of workweek that makes me think being an evil corporate lawyer would be okay," she wrote. "Seriously. Contemplated sterilizing myself yesterday."

Whatever her reasons, whatever her frustrations, this was unacceptable. She had finally crossed my threshold of tolerance.

My husband let her go the following Monday, while my younger son and I were attending a Music for Aard-varks class. Even though she had posted entries about how discontented she was with our house and children and must have known there was a pretty good chance I'd read them, she appeared shocked. My husband didn't bring up the blog with her and instead cited other factors for her dismissal. He did not, he told me, care to find himself a character online.

She did not write that we had fired her. Instead she posted an entry about her "day of bad news," including a graduate school rejection, adding that her worst fears about other people were confirmed.

As for why she ever told me about her blog in the first place, I suppose I'll never know. Sometimes I suspect she was unhappy in my house and hoped our seemingly bourgeois souls would be so shocked we'd let her go, exactly as we did. Other times I believe she wanted me to assume a more maternal role, and I failed her. But perhaps that is self-aggrandizement.

I still read her blog, though not as frequently. Her life has settled down. She writes of domestic nights with her significant other and posts less often about coitus. (Well, okay, they did have sex on the floor of his new abode, a Williamsburg loft.) She'll soon be leaving New York to attend graduate school. It's a life of passion and uncertainty, in which chance meetings can lead to the as-yet-unimagined.

In many ways it used to be my life. I miss it still. And I don't.

Something Like Motherhood

Carolyn Megan

I'M DRIVING MY NIECE AND NEPHEW TO THE MUSEUM OF Science. At the end of our outing, when I take them home, their father—my brother John—will tell them that their mother's latest cancer treatment has failed and that she will die. But for now, my niece, who's nine, rifles through my glove compartment and discovers a tampon. She tears open the wrapper, ejects the tampon, and begins swinging it by the string.

"What's this?"

"It's a tampon," I say.

"What's it for?"

> My niece and nephew are alive and here and need taking care of now.
> And I have stepped in without hesitation. Yet the very concern that informed my decision not to have children has come true.

It seems like a loaded question. To understand tampons means first understanding menstruation, which means understanding the whole life cycle. I have no idea what John and my sister-in-law, Sarah, have told her up to this point. "Well, you know how babies are made, right?"

"No," she says.

My nephew, thirteen, who is playing with his Game-Boy in the backseat, says: "Oh, boy. Here we go."

"What?" she says, sitting upright.

How should I respond? I don't want my niece to feel awkward about her sexuality, and anyway I want John to have the opportunity to discuss this with her himself. I begin to talk around the edges but pause as I approach a toll booth, at which point my niece drops the tampon and reaches for the radio dial. I'm off the hook.

Later, when I tell John about the conversation, he replies, "I can't tell her what it is to be a woman. You'll probably be the one who helps her with all of this."

I realize he's probably right. Over the past eighteen months, as Sarah's condition has worsened, I've assumed more than a few parental duties. I've driven to my niece and nephew's soccer games, attended school events, gone to pediatric appointments. I've lain awake at night rubbing their backs, tried to relearn algebra, studied the Civil War, bought McDonald's, nixed Chuck E. Cheese's, doled out medicines, done loads of laundry, said no more times than I've felt comfortable, said yes more times than I've felt comfortable.

During this time I've found myself moving into situations with a calm parentlike demeanor while admitting on the inside that I have no idea what I'm doing.

After delivering the children to John and Sarah at their house, I wait outside the room where they meet. The plan is that John and Sarah will tell the kids together and that I will then enter to be with them as they process the news. When John opens the door, he whispers, "They're devastated. They want you to come in, but they don't want to talk."

I walk into a tableau of shock and grief. Sarah sits on

the couch, half asleep under the influence of pain killers, resting her hand on my niece, who is sobbing. My nephew cries and walks around the room with his arms crossed in front of his body, so much the body language of a teenager now.

I walk over and hug him; he leans up against me, letting out stifled sobs, his arms still crossed. In that moment some part of my heart opens and a new love pours out, not a recalibration or reconfiguring of the love I have, but a new well tapped. No separation of myself with him. And in that moment I think: *I will do anything for you.*

But will I?

Early in Sarah's illness, when John was already imagining a world without her, he asked whether my partner, Michael, and I would consider moving in with them. "You won't have to do anything. It would be just to have you there as a presence in the house."

I never answered him. I said things like "We'll see how this unfolds" or "Don't go there yet." Stall tactics. Each time he asked, I felt trapped, an impending sense of desperation and doom. It's the same feeling I had years ago that led to my decision not to have children.

The decision came from my desire to be fully in my life as a writer rather than to raise a child. Having a child was not how I wanted to make meaning of my life, not how I wanted to give back to the world. And the reason for this was my sense that I would love too fiercely, too desperately at the cost of my *self*.

I knew my children would always come first and my art second, and I sensed the resentment I would feel about that. So I made a choice and said no to the idea of a child. But my niece and nephew are alive and here and need taking care of now. And I have stepped in without hesitation, something I could never regret.

Yet the very concern that informed my decision not to have children has come true: all my energy, love, and passion are focused on my niece and nephew, and I mourn the loss of a part of myself that has been pushed aside. In essence John's question of whether I might move in leaves me once again choosing whether or not I want to have children.

When I'm out with my niece and nephew, strangers already assume I'm their mother. I ask the sales clerk at a clothing store where the kids' T-shirts are, and she asks, "How old is your daughter?"

"Nine," I say. She points me to the girls' section, where there are a number of shirts trimmed with flowers.

"I might have better luck in the boys' section," I tell her. "She's a tomboy and would much prefer a soccer shirt."

The clerk laughs. "Oh, one of those."

It's so easy to slip into this role, so comfortable. Easier than explaining my not having kids to people who inquire. Easier than having to assure others that I love kids and that my decision isn't a reflection of a troubled childhood, not an act of selfishness. It is simply a choice. But in that moment with the sales clerk, I experience the ease of being in the mainstream, and it is a relief. This scene repeats itself: hugging my niece and nephew when they come off the soccer field, waiting for them at the bus stop, hearing my niece yell as she runs in from playing outside, "Mom! We need a drink!" When she finds me in the kitchen, she laughs and says, "I mean, Aunt Carolyn."

Anyone observing us would assume I am their mother. But I'm not and don't want to be. Yet given all that has happened, how can I not be?

People have always had their own ideas about why I don't have children: "Was it the divorce?" "Never found the right person at the right time?" "Biological clock?"

Now the story has a more positive spin: "Isn't it amazing how things work out?" "You didn't have kids, and now you can be there for your niece and nephew." "It's like it was meant to be."

Literature is rife with spinster aunts who move in with families when a sibling or in-law dies. They care for the ill parent and stand vigil until death. They step in and become surrogate mothers, platonic "wives" who efficiently take over the ministrations of the household and children.

There is an expectation of sacrifice: your life, your story, for the sake of the new story unfolding.

I'd like to believe that I don't need to be present all the time in order to be a mother figure to my niece and nephew. I'd like to believe that knowing they are loved and nurtured, whether I am there every day or not, will shore them up and give them the grounding they need to move healthfully into their adult lives.

But the day-to-day concerns pull at me. My nephew has athlete's foot. Under his littlest toe there is a large crack that he insists is from scraping the toe on a pool.

A small matter, really, except that my brother hasn't had the chance to buy foot ointment.

Other worries: clean clothes, the lice outbreak at school. Why is my niece's friend teasing her? Has anyone talked to my nephew about wet dreams? Is it okay that he shuts his bedroom door to be alone? Is there any vegetable that they'll eat? Are they having too much sugar? Of course John worries about these things, but he is exhausted. And the toilet is broken, the dryer has a squeaking sound, the dog is limping, there's no milk for tomorrow morning's cereal.

And then there is the meeting for parents whose children are in the school production of *The Hobbit*. My nephew is one of the dwarfs, and this meeting is to discuss the logistics and who will have the coveted roles of stage manager, prop master, and costume designer. There are only women present.

They talk about last year's production, laugh, and claim intimacy with one another and the process of putting on a show.

"We need to discuss how to get the working parents involved," one of the organizers says. The others nod in agreement. "This needs to be a community event."

I am there because I don't want my nephew to feel as though he doesn't have someone supporting him. I'm there because a friend of mine, whose mother died when she was young, once told me that she always felt like an orphan being fobbed off onto various caretakers. I don't want my nephew to feel like an orphan.

Yet I feel like an imposter, an outsider. I couldn't care

less about the power struggle for who will be the stage manager. I am bored. I'd rather be home and am anxious to get back to my writing.

But I find being away from the kids a continual ache and worry.

I wonder how they are and miss being near them, touching them. I'm interested in their stories, in the young people they are becoming.

And although I am not a mother and never will be, this pull feels like it must be a kind of motherhood: as difficult as I expected, yes, but also full of wonder.

Adolescence, Without a Roadmap

Claire Scovell LaZebnik

A T LEAST HE'S GOOD-LOOKING," I SAY TO MY HUSBAND whenever the subject of our oldest son's dating future comes up. And he is good-looking, our son, with his blue eyes, wavy hair, broad shoulders, and warm smile. He's also got a deep voice (he works at it) and a gentle manner. It's hard to believe girls won't fall in love with him. And maybe they will.

But he also has autism. When he's tired or sick, he forgets words or uses them incorrectly; often it requires enormous effort just for him to maintain a conversation. It's as if he has no native tongue and essentially has had to memorize our language word by word.

> For a long time our son was a little boy with autism, which was a certain kind of challenge. Now that he's a teenager with autism—and a teenager who notices girls—we're faced with something else altogether.

Now he's working on our customs. You see him eagerly watching other kids, looking for clues and lessons, signs he can follow into the world of the average teenager. It's a world he's desperate to be part of. He dresses like them, adopts their gestures, mimics their rudeness, and even douses himself, as they do, with Axe deodorant body spray.

He'll be in the middle of a group of kids and they'll laugh. Then he'll laugh, a second too late and too loud. He knows he needs to laugh to fit in; that much he's learned from observation. What he can't seem to learn is what made the joke funny and why everyone gets it but he.

For a long time our son was a little boy with autism, which was a certain kind of challenge. Now that he's a teenager with autism—and a teenager who notices girls—we're faced with something else altogether.

"Hey, Mom?" he says as we're walking out of a store. "That girl was hot." He thinks he's talking in a whisper but he isn't, really, because he has voice modulation problems and has trouble hearing what his own voice sounds like. The lifeguard in the bikini at the beach is also "hot." So is Jessica Alba, whose picture he printed and carefully glued on to his binder, next to a photo of Keira Knightley.

The term *hot* may be an affectation he picked up from his friends, but his appreciation of skinny girls with big breasts seems to be genuine, as we realized when we discovered he'd started using the Internet the way other teenage boys are likely to only when they think no one is watching.

We put content filters on our browser software, and his father sat down with him to go over some basic rules: Wait until you're in love to have sex. Always wear a condom. Hide your pornography where your mother won't find it. He'll remember all this because they're rules, and he's very good at remembering rules.

It's the other stuff—the emotional, he
stuff—that's going to be hard.

I know he wants to find a girl and fall in love. Sometimes people say that kids with autism aren't capable of
love. That's ridiculous. My son loves deeply. He just doesn't
communicate well. The instincts we rely on when we're
first falling in love (being able to sense what someone else is
thinking, becoming aware of a sudden connection, anticipating another person's desire) don't come naturally to him.

I want the girls he meets to know that just because he
speaks a little oddly and sometimes struggles to understand what they're saying doesn't mean he wouldn't make
a great boyfriend. I want them to see what a good heart
he has, how he would never manipulate or hurt them,
how he would be grateful, obliging, and loyal. But how
many girls will be able to get past the frustrations of his
disabilities to appreciate that part of him?

Would I have been able to?

And these things can't be forced anyway, no matter
how good-hearted someone may be.

Last year he got friendly with a girl he met in a social
skills class. She was what those of us in the world of special needs describe as "lower-functioning." She attended
a special-needs school, but even there she felt she was the
object of ridicule and abuse. I never knew if her account
of insults and cruelties was accurate, but I'd hear my son
talking to her on the phone, offering his unwavering
support. "That's terrible!" he'd cry out after listening for
a while. "They shouldn't do that."

I'd listen to him and think, "What woman wouldn't
want a man who comforted her like that, who was

willing to listen and believe and always be on her side?"
It gave me hope.

In the end, though, he broke up with her, if "breaking up" is even the right term for ending what they had.
Her litany of complaints bored him. And in all honesty
she wasn't the slightest bit "hot." Although he never
mentioned it, I suspect this also may have been a factor in
his decision.

Since then, the only girls he's asked out have been at the
other end of the spectrum, and they've all rejected him—
for the most part (and as far as I know)—quite kindly.

Still, he aims high. Recently he asked out a girl who
was already dating the star athlete of the entire middle
school, an eighth-grader who was captain of the baseball
and basketball teams. When I suggested that maybe a girl
like her was out of his reach, my son just looked confused. The social intricacies of popularity that separate
students into cliques and loners mean nothing to him
because they're unstated, unquantified. Most of us just
sense them instinctively. He can't.

Obviously I could let myself be crushed by these
rejections, especially if he were. But so far he doesn't
seem to mind; there's an advantage to his emotional
obliviousness. He's still young, though, and none of his
friends is really dating, so he probably doesn't feel so left
out yet. Still, I worry about whether girls will keep
rejecting him throughout high school and into college,
while the other kids start successfully pairing off. What
if he starts to wonder if anyone will ever love him?

You can, I've discovered, teach your child to make
polite conversation (ask questions, listen attentively, then

ask more questions), to be a good host (offer refreshments, suggest activities, and choose the one your guest says he'll enjoy), to please his teachers (show up on time, behave well in class). But how do you teach him to fall in love with someone who will love him back? What rules can you lay down for making someone's heart leap when she sees him?

When our son's autism was diagnosed at the age of two and a half, there was no clear prognosis. We didn't even know if he'd ever learn to talk. But we found talented people to work with him, and he improved, slowly at first and then more rapidly. By the time he graduated from elementary school, he had no discernible behavioral or academic problems.

People congratulated us. Our son had emerged. Someone met our kids at a party and a friend mentioned that one of them had autism. "Which one?" the person said, genuinely bewildered, and then guessed the wrong child.

But that was from a distance. Up close it's clearer that our son is marked and challenged, fundamentally and permanently. And up close is where relationships live. Up close is what love is all about. And sex? Well, that goes without saying.

This leads to what is perhaps the scarier question: What happens when a girl finally says yes? A year or two ago, going out meant nothing more than a kind of glorified playdate. But I overhear the kids in his class flirting, and there's a strong edge of sexuality to it. My son's body has matured, and physically, if not developmentally, he's not a little boy anymore.

Just as he's learned our language and our customs with a lot of hard work and memorization, he'll soon have to learn how to navigate the world of sex. But how? Through imitation and observation? Through rules we teach him? No. The same kids he has studied and imitated to gain other social skills are going to be fumbling in the dark themselves, behind closed doors. And in this particular game I don't foresee his father and me doing much coaching from the sidelines. He'll truly have to find his own way.

Then again, I've seen him rise to similar challenges in ways I never anticipated. I was told, for example, that kids with autism can't be empathetic because they're incapable of being able to perceive and relate to someone else's suffering. He can learn that he's supposed to say, "That's terrible!" when someone complains to him about an injustice. But the ability to notice and respond to the nuances of another person's emotions and moods isn't supposed to be in his repertory. And it's true that when he was younger I could sob in front of him (something I did all too often back then, I'm afraid), and he would simply continue his play, oblivious to my emotions.

Not long ago, however, when I was fixing a snack in the kitchen for all my kids while they sat around the table doing their homework, something about the situation reminded me of my mother, who'd died recently, and I quietly began to cry.

My three younger children didn't notice. But my son looked up and said, "What's wrong, Mom? Are you okay?" and came over to give me a hug. I literally smiled through my tears.

Somehow he had learned something they said couldn't be taught. I'll take that as a good sign.

UPDATE: *A few months after this essay appeared, Claire's son was "fixed up" by a friend, who gave him the e-mail address of his own girlfriend's best friend. The two corresponded online for a day or two before he announced he had "a girlfriend." Eventually they met, double-dating with his friend and hers. After, they spoke on the phone daily, he escorted her to her school semiformal and made her a CD for Valentine's Day. They kissed. He said romantic things to her. In short, he was just like other boys his age. And then (perhaps a little too much like other boys his age) he lost interest in the relationship and broke up with her.*

Part Four

Staying

THE TIES THAT BIND

A Body Scarred, a Marriage Healed

Autumn Stephens

I GOT THE CALL ON A SUNNY JULY MORNING IN 2001, WHILE my husband was at work and my children were in day care, and big, blowsy roses bloomed like crazy all over my backyard. According to the biopsy, the milk ducts of my right breast were riddled with cancer cells. Latent cells, at the moment, but if they ever took it into their pointy little heads to detonate, the oncologist said, all hell could break loose.

He suggested we go for the preemptive strike and fight it. And who was I to argue? One of my late-life babies was still in diapers, the other

> *There are easier ways to heal a marriage than by getting cancer. But that is how it was for us.*

barely able to write his name. We would try a lumpectomy, we decided. If that didn't work, we would just cut the breast off.

My husband took the news of my illness stoically, almost as if it were something he already knew. Not so much as an arched eyebrow revealed surprise or dismay. Like many men, he prefers take-charge calm to histrionics. So, for that matter, do I. But that night, there was no sleep for me: I lay in the dark, trembling and alone with my fears. My husband could live without me, I knew. He had done so before—by choice. Despite his bouts of ambivalence about our marriage—and consequently, mine—I have been with (and without, and then with again) this man for more than a quarter of a century. Not all scars are visible to the naked eye.

Incomprehensible, it sometimes seems, that the Volvo-driving, tax-paying, insomniac mortgage holder whose ring I wear on my fourth finger was once a gangly nine-teen-year-old who so stirred my soul, the blue-eyed boyfriend I met in the college co-op we both lived in, a haven for latter-day hippies and student activists. We became lovers one early spring night when the lights went out at a party fueled by alcohol and LSD. All win-ter, we had been circling each other: He was afraid, I real-ize now, of my sharp tongue; I suspected (not altogether incorrectly) that he was a much nicer person than I.

We had never been on a date, never engaged in any of the formal rituals of courtship that previous generations took for granted. But that night, in the dark, we found each other, and in the months and years that followed, while other couples merged and broke apart and merged again in new configurations, we stayed together. Eventu-ally we married, then promptly betrayed each other in ways both explicit and ephemeral. For us there was to be no giddy, go-for-broke flush of newlywed euphoria; no honeymoon babies and no grand real estate purchase demonstrating our faith in a shared future. When the going got tough, there was nothing concrete to tie us down.

Two years to the date from our barefoot beachside wedding, my husband said he wanted a divorce. For weeks afterward, I felt so shattered that I was sometimes afraid to move, lest I fall apart; so susceptible to rejection that I scarcely dared show my wounded face, my loser's face, to the winner-loving world.

You can get used to anything, though. Here is what my new single life was like: lonely, liberating, productive. Quiet, in contrast to the silent, screaming despair that had characterized my marriage. And safe. Alone, I could not be stabbed in the back, my serenity hijacked by someone else's demons. Over time I settled deeply into myself. Sometimes, writing on deadline, I didn't leave my apartment for two or three days; I barely slept or changed my clothes. This I perceived not as pathology but pleasure, the full expression of a certain driven, antisocial aspect of myself that I tend to experience, or perhaps merely to romanticize, as the "real" me.

So when, five years later, my husband and I suddenly and unexpectedly reconciled (a chance meeting, an explosive kiss, déjà vu all over again) I thought hard before consenting to give up my bachelor-girl studio. With some misgiving, I co-signed the loan application for the big gray Victorian in Berkeley that we planned to fill, as soon as possible, with a family.

And then the aforementioned rose garden, and dinner parties, and the great relief of our parents that there would be grandchildren after all. Snapshot of a Happy Couple, at long last. Although a more penetrating portrait, a marital biopsy, would have revealed how mistrust still constricted the woman's heart; how the husband bloodied his inner cheek with his teeth, biting back his frustration. History repeats itself, doesn't it? For many years I waited, harboring my bitterness, for the other shoe to drop.

And so, finally, it did—although not quite in the fashion I had expected but with a diagnosis of cancer. The easy trade I thought I'd brokered—my saggy, forty-three-year-old breast in return for a shot at a nice, long, quotidian life—didn't go off as smoothly as I had anticipated. Neither my doctors nor my husband and I were shocked when the lesser surgical evil, lumpectomy, failed to rout the cancer. No one had promised it would. What came as a bolt from the blue was the raging postsurgical infection that blindsided me two days later and from which I did, in fact, almost die.

The summer of 2001 slipped away as I lay in bed, hooked up to IV meds, too preoccupied with my own condition to notice time passing. It took weeks of those IVs, first at the hospital, then at home, before I was healthy enough to have my breast—what remained of it, anyway—removed.

When the plastic surgeon talked about repairing my mutilated chest, reconstruction was the term he used. The word always makes me think of the Civil War: the blood-soaked battlefields, the doomed effort to heal and move on while the smell of death still hangs in the air.

I rejected his proposition out of hand. To be fair, there were medical reasons. But there were other reasons, too. Back when my husband and I were young, the feminist party line was that man-woman differences should not be emphasized. Perhaps because of that, I have seldom been able to summon—much less sustain—a viable sense of femininity. In fact, I've never even really understood what people mean by the word, but whatever it is, I am certain that a matched set of mammaries doesn't define it.

And yet, as my appetite vanished and my weight dropped to what it was in sixth grade, sometimes, thinking of how fragile I looked and how wounded and delicate I felt, the word *feminine* did indeed float into my mind. A bud on a severed branch. Even now, noticing a newly patched portion of a city street, the dark asphalt scar, I am acutely aware of my upper chest. That flat, empty surface where I sometimes feel tingling and sometimes feel pain, but where most of the time I feel nothing.

But my husband: let's not forget about my husband. For of course this is not my history alone. During that time, it could not escape my captive attention how much my husband, my once ambivalent husband, cared for me. The man cared—specifically and pragmatically. With his own two hands, he bandaged the nothingness that I did not want to see. Uncomplainingly drained the plastic tubing that drew pus and blood from my chest; matter-of-factly measured that foul fluid in a cup and recorded its quantity, as the surgeon had blithely, sadistically ordered us to do. And over and over, the ritual of scrubbing skin, smoothing the latex gloves over his familiar, competent hands, inserting the IV into my tense but upturned arm, until finally my apprehension subsided and I looked up with unadulterated trust into his tired but still-blue eyes.

There are easier ways to heal a marriage than by getting cancer. But that is how it was for us. Do not, however, imagine us with our gazes forever entwined, our lips locked in a grand finale kiss. Life goes on. And like many women in their forties, I lament that my libido is not what it once was. I'm preoccupied with the children or work, or I'm simply weary, thinking of nothing except how much I would like to be asleep. The last thing I want to do is to move, or be moved. Nor do missing body parts tend to have an aphrodisiac effect on the flickering spark of midlife sex drive. I'm speaking strictly for myself here; my husband doesn't seem to mind. Make no mistake: if we were to divorce again, it would be from lack of sex, not lack of breasts.

But you're not thinking, are you, that I should be grateful that my husband still finds me alluring, that he cleaves to my disfigured side? I concede it's not the ideal denouement, to forsake all others for someone who turns out, in the end, to be so nakedly flawed. Yet haven't we all done precisely that, every one of us who has ever vowed fidelity to another imperfect human being?

Believe me, if I could, I'd spread myself out on the sheets like a lush landscape of sensual delights, the full complement, everything a lover could desire. But I do what I can; I make a sporadic effort, and it is true that we are close to each other afterward. He wraps his arm around my shoulder, and I attempt to amuse him, or at least to speak of topics other than our boys' behavior and tasks that remain to be done.

One afternoon last summer, my then three-year-old and I were strolling down the sidewalk, pausing, as we do, to examine the many objects of interest—pebbles, ants, cigarette butts. That day we were in luck: a gorgeous trumpet flower, orange and mauve and, indeed, somewhat resembling a miniature musical instrument, had fallen from the vine. But when my happy boy held up the blossom for me to admire, he saw that the underside was mottled and brown. Consternation wrestled with determination on his young face. "Mommy," he said, his voice quavering, "can we pretend it's perfect?"

In pretending, we sometimes forget. But in pretending, we also remember. Naked before the mirror, I marvel at the sight of my ribs, now so cleanly articulated. Mine—mine in part, anyway—is the bony, unembellished torso of a teenage boy, not unlike that of my husband at nineteen, when sex was the sticky glue that bonded us, blurring boundaries so that it was impossible to tell where one of our bodies stopped, where the other began. But now, of course, it's obvious which is mine. Mine is the one with the thin pink scar running northeast to southwest, pointing toward my heart.

UPDATE: *Autumn remains married and in good health.*

Truly, Madly, Guiltily

Ayelet Waldman

I HAVE BEEN IN MANY MOTHERS' GROUPS—MOMMY AND ME, Gymboree, Second-Time Moms—and each time, within three minutes, the conversation invariably comes around to the topic of how often mommy feels compelled to put out. Everyone wants to be reassured that no one else is having sex, either. These are women who, for the most part, are comfortable with their bodies, consider themselves sexual beings. These are women who love their husbands or partners. Still, almost none of them is having any sex.

*I love my children.
But I am not in love
with them.
I am in love with
their father.*

There are agreed-upon reasons for this bed death. They are exhausted. It still hurts. They are so physically available to their babies—nursing, carrying, stroking—how could they bear to be physically available to anyone else?

But the real reason for this lack of sex, or at least the most profound, is that the wife's passion has been refocused. Instead of concentrating her ardor on her husband, she concentrates it on her babies. Where once her husband was the center of her passionate universe, there is now a new sun in whose orbit she revolves. Libido, as she once knew it, is gone, and in its place is all-consuming maternal desire. There is absolute unanimity on this topic, and instant reassurance.

Except, that is, from me.

I am the only woman in Mommy and Me who seems to be, well, getting any. This could fill me with smug well-being. I could sit in the room and gloat over my wonderful marriage. I could think about how our sex life—always vital, even torrid—is more exciting and imaginative now than it was when we first met. I could check my watch to see if I have time to stop at Good Vibrations to see if they have any exciting new toys. I could even gaze pityingly at the other mothers in the group, wishing that they, too, could experience a love as deep as my own.

But I don't. I am far too busy worrying about what's wrong with me. Why, of all the women in the room, am I the only one who has not made the erotic transition a good mother is supposed to make? Why am I the only one incapable of placing her children at the center of her passionate universe?

When my first daughter was born, my husband held her in his hands and said, "My God, she's so beautiful."

I unwrapped the baby from her blankets. She was average size, with long, thin fingers and a random assortment of toes. Her eyes were close set, and she had her father's hooked nose. It looked better on him.

She looked like a newborn baby, red and scrawny, blotchy-faced and mewling. I don't remember what I said to my husband. Actually I remember very little of my Percocet- and Vicodin-fogged first few days of motherhood except for a friend calling and squealing, "Aren't you just completely in love?" And of course I was. Just not with my baby.

I do love her. But I'm not in love with her. Nor with her two brothers or sister. Yes, I have four children. Four children with whom I spend a good part of every day: bathing them, combing their hair, sitting with them while they do their homework, holding them while they weep their tragic tears. But I'm not in love with any of them. I am in love with my husband.

It is his face that inspires in me paroxysms of infatuated devotion. If a good mother is one who loves her child more than anyone else in the world, I am not a good mother. I am in fact a bad mother. I love my husband more than I love my children.

An example: I often engage in the parental pastime known as God Forbid. What if, God forbid, someone were to snatch one of my children? God forbid. I imagine what it would feel like to lose one or even all of them. I imagine myself consumed, destroyed by the pain. And yet, in these imaginings, there is always a future beyond the child's death. Because if I were to lose one of my children, God forbid, even if I lost all my children, God forbid, I would still have him, my husband.

But my imagination simply fails me when I try to picture a future beyond my husband's death. Of course I would have to live. I have four children, a mortgage, work to do. But I can imagine no joy without my husband.

I don't think the other mothers at Mommy and Me feel this way. I know they would be absolutely devastated if they found themselves widowed. But any one of them would sacrifice anything, including their husbands, for their children.

Can my bad motherhood be my husband's fault? Perhaps he just inspires more complete adoration than other husbands. He cooks, cleans, cares for the children at least 50 percent of the time.

If the most erotic form of foreplay to a mother of a small child is, as I've heard some women claim, loading the dishwasher or sweeping the floor, then he's a master of titillation.

He's handsome, brilliant, and successful. But he can also be scatterbrained, antisocial, and arrogant. He is a bad dancer, and he knows far too much about Klingon politics and the lyrics to Yes songs. All in all, he's not that much better than other men. The fault must be my own.

I am trying to remember those first days and weeks after giving birth. I know that my sexual longing for my husband took a while to return. I recall not wanting to make love. I did not even want to cuddle. At times I felt that if my husband's hand were to accidentally brush against my breast while reaching for the saltshaker, I would saw it off with the butter knife.

Even now I am not always in the mood. By the time the children go to bed, I am as drained as any mother who has spent her day working, carpooling, building Lego castles, and shopping for the precisely correct soccer cleat. I am also a compulsive reader. Put together fatigue and bookwormishness, and you could have a situation in which nobody ever gets any. Except that when I catch a glimpse of my husband from the corner of my eye—his smooth, round shoulders, his bright blue eyes through the magnification of his reading glasses—I fold over the page of my novel.

Sometimes I think I am alone in this obsession with my spouse. Sometimes I think my husband does not feel as I do. He loves the children the way a mother is supposed to. He has put them at the center of his world. But he is a man and thus possesses a strong libido. Having found something to usurp me as the sun of his universe does not mean he wants to make love to me any less.

And yet, he says I am wrong. He says he loves me as I love him. Every so often we escape from the children for a few days. We talk about our love, about how much we love each other's bodies and brains, about the things that make us happy in our marriage.

During the course of these meandering and exhilarating conversations, we touch each other, we start to make love, we stop.

And afterward my husband will say that we, he and I, are the core of what he cherishes, that the children are satellites, beloved but tangential. He seems entirely unperturbed by loving me like this. Loving me more than his children does not bother him. It does not make him feel like a bad father. He does not feel that loving me more than he loves them is a kind of infidelity.

And neither, I suppose, should I. I should not use that wretched phrase "bad mother." At the very least, I should allow that, if nothing else, I am good enough. I do know this: when I look around the room at the other mothers in the group, I know that I would not change places with any of them.

I wish some learned sociologist would publish a definitive study of marriages where the parents are desperately, ardently in love, where the parents love each other even more than they love the children. It would be wonderful if it could be established, once and for all, that the children of these marriages are more successful, happier, live longer, and have healthier lives than children whose mothers focus their desires and passions on them.

But even in the likely event that this study is not forthcoming, even in the event that I face a day of reckoning in which my children, God forbid, become heroin addicts or, God forbid, are unable to form decent attachments and wander from one miserable and unsatisfying relationship to another, or, God forbid, other things too awful even to imagine befall them, I cannot regret that when I look at my husband I still feel the same quickening of desire that I felt twelve years ago when I saw him for the first time, standing in the lobby of my apartment building, a bouquet of purple irises in his hands.

And if my children resent having been moons rather than the sun? If they berate me for not having loved them enough? If they call me a bad mother?

I will tell them that I wish for them a love like I have for their father. I will tell them that they are my children, and they deserve both to love and be loved like that. I will tell them to settle for nothing less than what they saw when they looked at me, looking at him.

Back from the Front, with Honor, a Warrior's Truth

Helen Gerhardt

J OHN WAS A LOVE CHILD, CONCEIVED ON THE DRIVER'S seat of my rusty old Volvo as I sped toward my National Guard headquarters in March of 2002. I was aglow with unexpected discovery, my body flush from hours of cuddling skin to skin with my newly beloved.

But I had lingered too long and now was pushing the speedometer toward ninety in a seventy-mile-an-hour zone, trying desperately to get to the armory in time for morning formation. I was speeding toward what I knew would be a very slow day: probably an apathetic rehash of gas mask maintenance, maybe a quick check under the hoods of our seldom-used trucks, and most certainly a cud-chewing on the latest rumors of our possible deployment to the war on terror.

> **When I joined the army I had never anticipated any future need to censor my life, had never imagined the flesh-and-blood form in which my true love would one day appear.**

When I rushed into formation, a minute late and shining with happiness, Sergeant Bryan twisted around, looked me up and down, and winked. "Guy wouldn't let you go, huh?"

I smiled back. Why disabuse him of that notion?

But as soon as formation broke, a small clump of my fellow soldiers gathered to tease me and pursue details of the scoop. I hadn't dated anyone since I joined the company two years before, soon after the end of my twelve-year marriage to a man I still cared for, if I couldn't live with him. A couple of guys in the unit had manfully tried to rectify my lack of companionship, flirting with me, asking me out, and my ham-handed response to their attempts had raised a few eyebrows and fueled speculation about my sexual orientation that was not spoken to me but that I could read clearly on several faces. Of course they were wrong, I'd thought. They just weren't taking into account the complexities of a bruised heart.

Sergeant Durk grinned up at me from his pink pug face. "Is it lust, girl, or is it love?"

"Come on," Sergeant Bryan demanded. "Details, details—who is he?"

I looked back at Sergeant Bryan with affection. He had so innocently asked, but I could not tell. And it was killing me, the fact that I had to keep all those glorious, life-changing details of my new love hemmed in and humming between my ears. I wanted to tell the world about it. I certainly didn't see how it was possible to spend eight long hours pretending it was just another drill day.

"I see," Sergeant Bryan said. "Gonna hold out on your redneck army buddies?"

The alias I'd thought of on the way to the armory trembled at the edge of my lips. And then it tumbled out. "Well," I began.

And so John was born, breaking records for growth as he sprang from my head with all the reflective glow of a newly polished shield and armed with all the sharp edges of my fresh memory. "He's a little tubby, just turned forty, salt-and-pepper hair cut mighty short. He's finishing his doctorate. He's going to be applying for teaching jobs next year. Yes, he's in English, too. We met in class."

The story poured out with such confidence—it was the truth, after all, except for one small, inconvenient fact. But how great it felt to besottedly report the relevant details of my unexpected love, to regale my fellow soldiers with tales of my man, who was only a slight twist of the helix and the tongue away from the whole truth.

John at first seemed to be a low-maintenance guy. Put away with my uniform, and quickly brushed to a shine along with my black boots once a month, he always sprang to duty with military efficiency.

But as the year wore on, my act began to take its toll. Early on I had excused John's absences at Guard socials by proudly declaring how devoted he was to his studies. But that line wore thin as my fellow soldiers' spouses, boyfriends, and girlfriends continued to show up by their sides while I, yet again, attended solo.

"Yeah, well, John's definitely a workaholic," I complained with an anger that felt disturbingly authentic. When my real love and I began to plot a discreet cohabitation, I tried to allay any suspicion that my lover's voice might raise if Guard members were to call my home by explaining that John wanted to save money by moving in with my "roommate" and me. But finally, when we got the news of our deployment to Iraq, I felt as if my wall of deception was about to collapse.

My true love began to campaign for John's elimination with editorial ruthlessness: "Kill him off now! This is the perfect time."

"But I've been talking about our engagement. We were looking at rings last month."

"Everybody knows deployments change things. With such a long separation coming up, maybe he thought it would be wiser to wait rather than act hastily."

As usual, my lover's practicality was inarguable, and over the next few months I laid down a back story for the coming virtual breakup. As other guardsmen swore the undying love of their own lovers and spouses, I indicated that, no, John certainly wasn't thrilled by the prospect of my yearlong deployment in Iraq. "And he's been offered a job in Texas," I added. "We don't see how he can turn it down with the job market like this."

I had friends and family who wondered very loudly why I didn't just come out and tell the truth rather than so carefully script John's exit. After all, why not take the opportunity to let the truth get me off what could be a truly deadly hook?

But I couldn't do that. When I joined the army in 2000, I had never anticipated any future need to censor my life, had never imagined the flesh-and-blood form in which my true love would one day appear. I had raised my hand and sworn the military oath to redeem a decade of debt, to escape the years of assembly lines, waitress aprons, and janitor buckets that had kept me afloat. Thanks to the army, I had just received a degree in English, and for this I was grateful.

Like my country, teetering on the edge of a war with unknowable costs, I had decided to borrow now and pay later. As I saw it, I owed for what I had received, and it would be a sniveling, wimpy misuse of my love to back out just when the bill was due to my country and the men and women I served with. I did not really buy the bill of goods they'd sold everyone to star-and-spangle our reasons for preemptive invasion, but I had sworn to obey my commander in chief.

So while I told my worried friends and family that I would not bear the fictional burden of John to Iraq for my fellow soldiers to innocently pry at, I would have to remain silent about who I was for the duration of my overseas service.

In February 2003, as my unit gathered in the freezing gray dawn to get on the bus to the predeployment processing camp, I broke my carefully planned news to the sergeant I respected the most.

"So, will John be there to see you off next month?" Sergeant Collum asked.

"No," I said. "He went ahead and took the job in Texas. We decided we had to see what happens when all this is over."

He did not look surprised. Unlike others in my unit, he'd never asked why John didn't show up for our group celebrations. I knew he was a savvy man, but I could not know what he guessed of my real situation—if his restraint had served as willed ignorance or respectful tact.

Suddenly it occurred to me that my deception had worked two ways. The falsehoods I'd spread to keep my fellow soldiers from knowing the real me were at the same time preventing me from knowing the real them. I could now see that during the time I'd been covering for myself, I'd stood increasingly apart from my unit and my superior officers—friendly, but not a friend.

And in a few months we all would be in a war zone together. Over the coming year I would convoy thousands of miles with Sergeant Collum and the other members of our transportation unit, past deteriorating mosques, begging Iraqi children, and roadside explosives. I could never have guessed that the loneliness of maintaining my silence with him and others I cared about would be harder to bear than being shot at or bombed.

Now Sergeant Collum looked at me. "It won't work out for a lot of these guys," he said quietly. "They think it will, but it won't."

A month later, as new recruits marched by our predeployment barracks singing songs of home and lost loves, I sat down and wrote to my man for the first time. We'd been told that for security reasons, all of our correspondence would be subject to inspection, and I sort of hoped that would be the case here, that my letter could serve as a final flourish to end the illusion.

"Dear John," I wrote, "I'm afraid we can't go on like this." And just like that it was over. Or so I thought.

Now it is 2005, and I have done my time in the wilderness. For twelve months I hauled your ammunition and guns, your concrete barriers, and your charred Humvees that no thickness of back story could armor for the flesh within. I served honorably, remained faithful to my true love and to my country, and I came back in one piece, with even my silence intact.

But in the wake of all these deceptions, small and large, innocent and deadly, my ongoing silence eventually became its own burdensome lie—one that I simply could no longer bear.

So that is my truth, or at least the best I could do under the circumstances. I know you didn't ask. I had to tell anyway. The fact is, I would very much like to continue to serve as my true self. I hope you'll understand.

UPDATE: *Although Helen's active drilling obligation with the National Guard ended, she still has two more years to serve as part of the Individual Ready Reserve. She does not plan to reenlist as long as the Don't Ask, Don't Tell policy remains in effect.*

Sleeping with the Guitar Player

Jean Hanff Korelitz

IN THE AGES OF MAN, THERE ARE THE CLASSICS—INFANCY, childhood, adulthood. We have the midlife crisis, of course, so dear to therapists and second wives everywhere. There is adolescence, which in some men seems to last . . . oh, well, when does it end? But in the last few years I've experienced, via my husband, another masculine stage, one I'd been blissfully unaware of. This is the time of a man's life that I must now and forever think of as the guitar-in-the-basement phase.

> Gradually I began to understand this wasn't just about my husband. There were hordes of men out there, roughly his age, frolicking in guitar wonderlands and shoring up amp arsenals in their own basements.

Six years ago, when my husband, Paul Muldoon, a poet who teaches at Princeton, brought home an electric guitar, carried it down to the basement of our house in New Jersey, and plugged it in, I was laughing too hard to absorb the enormousness of what was happening. I knew he loved music. Growing up in Ireland during the 1960s, he was present at the birth of British rock, and he knew far more about American blues and its influence on both sides of the Atlantic than I had ever cared to learn. He leaped into action when U2 tickets went on sale and had dragged me, over the years, to many, many concerts I despised. (I once fell asleep listening to Bob Dylan at the Beacon Theatre.)

Still, I failed to realize that the very loud sounds coming from beneath the living room floor portended great changes for our family. I was pregnant with our second child at the time, and to be honest, I wasn't focusing very well. When Paul played his guitar in the basement, the whole building vibrated, and I would sit there, one story up, swaying with nausea. When I couldn't stand it any longer, I went to the top of the basement stairs and flicked the light to get his attention. "Please. Stop." He stopped. But not for long.

This was not, I would soon discover, a mere matter of purchasing a single musical instrument. We were on an acquisition conveyor belt of more guitars and related equipment, the charms of each soon negated by the undulations of the next. After that first guitar, a Cort, and its sidekick amplifier, Paul ordered up a Fender Stratocaster, a Gibson Les Paul, a Marshall amp, a reissue of a 1952 Telecaster ("like the guitar Keith plays"), an Ibanez acoustic/electric, and a Fender Acoustasonic amp.

It was a new and unwelcome side of a man I thought I'd known pretty well, a man who never shopped, who wore a watch with a cracked plastic band, and who drove an old unlovely car, knocked askew by a deer a decade ago. Now he was making special trips to Sam Ash in New York City (I imagined the salesmen nudging one another, "Here comes another guitar-in-the-basement dude, dude."). It was getting crowded down there under the floorboards.

Gradually, I began to understand that it wasn't just about my husband. There were hordes of men out there, roughly his age, frolicking in guitar wonderlands and shoring up amp arsenals in their own basements. In the weeks after September 11, when I began each sad day with the Portraits of Grief in the *New York Times,* I read again and again of men commuting home from their working lives, descending their basement stairs, and rocking their Jersey or Westchester or Long Island houses to the rafters.

Once, at a friend's dinner party, Paul was seated next to a terribly dull financial manager I'd been shackled with during cocktails. To my surprise, they quickly began an avid conversation, which lasted all through the meal. I kept my eye on them, at a loss to imagine what they might possibly have found to talk about, let alone with such animation. "He has a Stratocaster in his basement," Paul said happily as we drove home. "He just got a wah-wah pedal."

Inevitably, Paul started to play with some of these men. There was a lawyer who possessed an entire recording studio in his apartment, then a professor of Renaissance poetry with a vast collection of guitars. Initially, heading out after dinner with a guitar packed into the backseat was a grand occasion, a thrilling adventure for him, if not for me, but soon it became a more routine outing. "You don't mind if I rehearse tonight, do you?" he'd ask. Rehearse? I'd think, baffled. He was still learning basic chords on the instrument. Rehearse?

It took a long time for me to figure out what I was dealing with. But I'm a woman, which means that, in my heart of hearts, I have long understood that certain things are never going to happen in my life. I won't, by way of example, be modeling swimsuits for *Sports Illustrated,* representing my country as an Olympic gymnast, or dancing Coppélia for the New York City Ballet.

I have dealt with these disappointments and, in the idiom of our age, moved on. But my husband—my wonderful, endearing husband, who is extremely successful at writing and teaching poetry—believed, at the age of fifty-three, that it was utterly possible for him to become a rock guitarist. On a stage. In front of an audience.

Our twelve-year-old daughter dubbed the new band Freaks with Guitars, but the actual name encompassed more subtle humor. They were called Rackett, and by now the three older men had been joined by three cute young guys, just out of college. They started writing songs: the Renaissance poetry professor on music, my husband on lyrics.

A couple of those cute young guys could really sing. The Renaissance poetry professor was a superb guitar player, actually. Within months, the recordings made in the lawyer's studio were sounding not all that different from the music my twelve-year-old was blasting in her room. The keyboardist, who runs his own breath-mint company, began to talk about producing the eventual CDs.

I no longer bothered to try to talk some sense into my husband. What sense, after all? My notion of reality had departed the day I came home to find Paul playing, over and over, a recorded phone message from one of the few rock stars we both revered, Warren Zevon. Mr. Zevon had read some of his poetry. When Paul hit Play on the answering machine, I heard the author of "Werewolves of London" and "Excitable Boy" pronounce my husband "The best damn poet on the planet."

In due course they would meet, become friends, and write two songs together, including "My Ride's Here," the title track of Mr. Zevon's penultimate album. Books about the music business began to accumulate in our bathroom. Paul formed a publishing company to register his lyrics, and became a member of ASCAP. Copies of *Spin* and *Guitar World* began to arrive monthly, along with an inexhaustible supply of Sam Ash catalogs. Rackett was offered its first gig, in a Greenwich Village club. The band's catalog of original songs stretched to thirty, then fifty. Bruce Springsteen produced a live recording of "My Ride's Here" for Warren Zevon's posthumous tribute album.

I refuse to conclude from all this that I have been unknowingly married to a rock star for nigh on eighteen years. I simply could not have been that unobservant, failing to notice the spandex in the closet, the tour bus in the garage, the groupies at the mailbox. Nor is this a story about years of hard work, prodigious innate musical talent, and patient honing of "craft" reaching their inevitable, just conclusion.

It occurs to me that much of his success in this odd endeavor derives from the fact that he just didn't know the whole thing was impossible, that his dearth of musicality, advanced age, and lack of rock star lips meant that it was flatly impossible for him to become the thing he had decided he wanted to become. Then again, some of that obtuseness might have derived from being male in the first place.

Unlike women, for whom menopause serves as an unignorable transition, a line dividing one part of life from another, men have no midlife marker to brake before, or even to steer around, in the hinterland from their youth to their age; there is only a great, elastic middle. Is it any wonder they lose track of where they are, and think they can do anything? And evidence being what it is, I'm forced to concur. Should Paul waltz in tomorrow and announce that he has decided to become an engineer, a painter, or a matinee idol, I'm afraid I will be forced to give him the benefit of the doubt.

Onstage, he looks like a middle-aged Irish poet, bespectacled, dressed in the same rumpled suit he teaches in. He is not a great musician and still can play only seven chords (which is four more than you need, he points out). But to succeed at anything is just so unlikely in the first place. Why should the fact that he's fifty-three and a musical neophyte make watching his band rock out onstage any more bizarre for me? Why should I be so surprised by the possibility of being surprised?

Then again, one of the great pleasures of being shocked by some amazing thing a loved one does is being aftershocked by something in ourselves. I'll admit that I have now done things I never thought I'd do, like bounce up and down in the dark basement of a rock club with a host of twentysomethings, an activity that might have recalled my lost youth had I ever done it when I myself was a twentysomething. I have seen things I never thought I'd see, like a group of college students raising a sign with Paul's name on it in the audience at a Rackett performance.

And I have said something I never thought I'd say, at the stage door of a New York club, as I attempted to carry his guitar—one of his guitars!—downstairs to the dressing room. The bouncer, after giving me a very dubious look, wondering, perhaps, if I hadn't just wandered in off a New Jersey soccer field (which was precisely where I'd been a few hours earlier), asked if he could help me.

"That's all right," I told him, hoisting the guitar. "I'm with the band."

UPDATE: *Rackett's first CD,* Don't Try This at Home, *was recently released.*

Out from Under the Influence

Kevin Cahillane

MY FIRST DATE WITH JULIE DID NOT BEGIN WELL AND ended even worse. For starters, I didn't show. It was Saturday evening of Presidents' Day weekend, and I was drinking gin and tonics and watching hoops in the Telephone Bar and Grill on Second Avenue, whiling away the time before I was supposed to meet her at John's Pizzeria, just down the block. The next thing I knew it was hours later and the phone was waking me from my slumber in my apartment on East Twelfth Street.

> *I made her a promise that I would stay sober. Two months later, though, I was back with old friends and to my old self.*

I stumbled out of the building and ran to John's, where Julie ended up crying defiantly on the sidewalk, her words lost to me but their meaning clear: never again.

After she left in a cab for the Upper West Side, it could have been just one of those first dates from hell that eventually becomes funny in the retelling. But it wasn't that simple. We worked together at an advertising agency, she as a human resources coordinator and I as one of the human resources she coordinated. She was the first person I'd met at work. I'd only passed the typing test because she had added an extra five minutes to the egg timer.

With that and a smile she'd hooked me, and I started spending my nights constructing elaborate and clever e-mail messages to her that I would pass off as spontaneous the next day. She began to drop by my desk with a frequency that I attributed more to her need for my ragged charm than my need for the memos she was distributing.

Now all that groundwork appeared lost. And on Tuesday I'd have to face her again.

I continued to drink all weekend, wallowing in regret, and on Sunday I sent her a hundred dollars' worth of roses, bought with money I didn't have, along with a note of apology. Unfortunately I also left her a voice mail message that consisted of Hootie and the Blowfish's "Hold My Hand" in its entirety.

When Tuesday rolled around, I stayed home. Wednesday, the same.

I knew this kind of denial was not a practical long-term strategy, so on Thursday I got dressed and tried to return to work. But my nerves were shattered, my head cloudy. I had crossed the line, as I sometimes did, from functional alcoholic to clearly not.

Finally I called Julie. "Did you get the roses?" I asked.

Yes, she had, and they were lovely, but she felt it was a rather grotesque gesture all the same. "You're an alcoholic," she said, not unkindly. "You need help."

I had already reached this conclusion myself at age sixteen, but no one had ever said it directly to me. Julie suggested I make an appointment for the next morning with a doctor associated with the agency's employee-assistance program. I did. I was love-struck and free-falling, and if she'd asked me to jump off a bridge, I might have done that, too. But again I stumbled out of bed disoriented and arrived at the doctor's half an hour late, rain-soaked.

His West Fifty-seventh Street office was lush and quiet; somewhere a fountain trickled tranquilly. He was bearded and kindly but he got right to the point.

"Now, what brings you here?" he asked.

"I drink."

"How often?"

"Daily."

"Have you been drinking this morning?"

"Affirmative."

"What about your arm?"

"I have a cat."

"Must be some cat."

"I don't really have a cat."

"I think you like to see the physical manifestation of your psychic pain."

"Who doesn't?"

He diagnosed me with acute alcoholism, which wasn't exactly breaking news, and recommended that I seek treatment pronto at an inpatient rehabilitation clinic.

"If it's okay with Blue Cross," I told him, "it's okay with me."

I was twenty-four years old.

I returned to my apartment, where I hadn't paid rent in some time, and waited for a call from the benefits people at work. I had been with the agency for only six months, and only as a favor to my aunt, who had worked there for several years. From my shaggy wardrobe to my computer illiteracy, it was pretty clear I was not Madison Avenue material, but she had snagged me an interview anyway.

Julie, my unlikely advocate, called and told me that my benefits were shipshape and that I was good to go. So I went, but not before draining several forties to steel myself for the phone calls I had to make to family and friends to ensure that I wasn't reported AWOL.

When the van arrived to pick me up, the grizzled driver told me that most people were drunker than I was. Somehow this made me feel worse, as if I couldn't even self-destruct correctly. As the van sailed north on the FDR Drive, I thought the bright lights of the big city never looked quite so intoxicating as when you were leaving.

Nearly three weeks later I appeared at Julie's cubicle in my only suit. She hugged me and told me I looked great. I told her she did, too. She found some envelopes for me to stuff and papers to photocopy, tasks I completed with unprecedented zeal. She looked amused each time I reported on my progress and requested more work.

At the end of the day I took off my jacket, sat in her cubicle, and told her about rehab.

"Nobody thought you'd come back," she said.

As I got up to go, I briefly touched her knee as if I were some repressed character in a Merchant-Ivory movie, and then I walked home through the streets of Manhattan.

We met that weekend in Central Park and talked as we walked. Julie was from Canton, Ohio, a daughter of a schoolteacher and a football coach. She was a Phi Beta something or other, and her best friend was her sister, a graphic designer in Chicago. She had chosen the ad agency over Merrill Lynch because it felt more humane. Me, I was just a guy from New Jersey whose path of least resistance had led through the Lincoln Tunnel.

The recovery literature warned of the dangers of starting a romance days (or even weeks, sometimes years) after coming out of the drink, but I wanted company on my lifeboat, and Julie seemed ready to grab an oar, if warily.

At our next date in the park, she climbed a rock and declared me too raw to date. "I think we should just be friends," she said.

I didn't begrudge her this decision. If you were to take Julie's suitors from over the years and place them in a police lineup, I clearly was the one who most likely belonged. We walked through the Ramble, across the Sheep Meadow, and to a clearing where the skyscraping hotels of Central Park South looked luminous in the gloaming. As the light disappeared behind the Palisades and a full moon shone, she turned to me and said, "If we weren't just friends, this would be kind of romantic."

During our hermetically sealed days and nights that followed, I made her a promise that I would stay sober.

Two months later, though, I was back with old friends and to my old self. Julie and I attended a wedding at the Jersey Shore, where, unbeknownst to her, I knocked back drink after drink. I simply could not see anything past the clinking ice cubes and undulating limes in seemingly every person's glass. I danced with the groom's sister, who whispered in my ear to give her a call if I ever decided to "lose the blonde." One old acquaintance looked at me quizzically as I poured a few back during our conversation and said, "You a little thirsty?"

On the return to the city, we became ensnarled in traffic awaiting a DWI checkpoint. Terrified, I kept up the ruse by telling Julie it was a good thing I'd quit drinking when I had. Such is the bottomless cup of duplicity that we drunks drink from. When the officer simply waved me through, I felt such joy and relief that I vowed I'd had my last drink. And except for a few minor lapses in the next month or so, it was.

Two years later, we were married on a steamy June day in a tiny church in an industrial corner of Canton as guests fanned themselves with their programs. The night before the wedding, a group of the hopeful and faithless had gathered for the rehearsal dinner in a restaurant in old downtown Canton. There was the requisite mix of drinks and well wishes, and I still had the sense that my mouth and arm could conspire against my brain to raise a little hell, but they didn't.

When it came my turn to toast, I recited the speech I had outlined on a cocktail napkin at the Indians game the night before. I forget every word of it now except for the last line, which I borrowed from a Bruce Springsteen song. I promised Julie that for better or worse, for richer or more likely poorer, I would love her with all the madness in my soul. It was one part vow, one part pose, and one part roll of the dice.

Then I lifted my glass in the air and put it back down.

It's been ten years since my last drink, and it's not like rolling a boulder up a mountain every day. In fact it's no effort at all. I don't attend meetings, speak in jargon, or mouth the Serenity Prayer when flummoxed. The accumulation of thousands of days without alcohol has simply made it a reflexive nonhabit.

Julie and I have ordinary jobs, a home in the suburbs, and a minivan for our 2.5 children (two now and one due in December), who, genetically speaking, could have hoped for better. Soon enough they will surely tell me so.

But I don't know. The thing is, would their mother and I ever have gotten together if I hadn't been a drowning alcoholic in need of her outstretched hand? Sometimes I can't help but wonder if the burdens we carry don't end up carrying us.

Jill and Jill Live on the Hill, but One Must Boil the Water

Tzivia Gover

MY STRAIGHT MALE FRIENDS DON'T BELIEVE IT WHEN I tell them, but it happens. I'll be lunching with some women who are grousing about their husbands: perfectly nice guys who will never just listen to their problems but always have to solve them, who won't write a thank-you note—even to their own mothers—and who give their child one bath and think they deserve a medal. At some point these women look wistfully in my direction and say, "I'd be a lesbian, too, if I could!"

I wallow in their lesbian envy for as long as I can. But eventually I want to blurt, "Look, it's not a male-female issue; it's about testosterone overload, and a person of any gender can have that."

> *I graduated from high school blissfully ignorant of how to broil a steak, remove grass stains, or compose a proper party invitation. I believed that I had succeeded in maturing into a young woman who was utterly unfit for becoming anyone's mother or wife.*

Granted this isn't a scientifically proven point, but what else could explain the fact that I find myself living, with my lesbian partner, in a gender-bent *Ozzie and Harriet* reality? How else to explain the fact that every time my partner and I get into a car she sits in the driver's seat and that I cook the dinners but she handles the barbecues? Or that while I chauffeur my sixteen-year-old daughter to and from endless pointe classes and spend hours hanging out rows of her pink tights to dry, my partner listens to the Red Sox game and cleans the gutters? How, I wonder, did I fail so miserably at my goal of becoming a liberated woman?

By age twelve, I had determined that being a traditional woman meant trading your goals and priorities for a man's. Marriage for women, it seemed to me, meant accepting dominion over the kitchen and laundry room, and forfeiting the right to pursue adventure and success outside. Case in point: my mother, after high school, enrolled in an elite college with dreams of traveling to Europe and studying history—but rather than graduate with a diploma, she left with a marriage license, and for years her dreams of Europe were reduced to drilling me on the verb *être* before French quizzes.

To avoid this fate, I began systematically to refuse to learn to do laundry or mop a floor. During a required home economics class, I sewed meandering seams on my yellow tennis dress. It was at about this time, too, when the tectonic plates of affection holding my parents in close proximity, touching but never quite joined, began to slide apart. This confirmed my suspicion that marriage and happiness were mutually exclusive concepts, especially for the woman, who gives up so much the day she says, "I do."

I carry an image of my parents from that time: They are frozen as statues, as if the two figures that top a wedding cake had repositioned themselves sixteen years later, refrozen at the close of the marriage. My father is caught mid-stride, as he climbs the steps from the back door of our suburban home to the kitchen. He is wearing his Brooks Brothers suit, minus the red-and-blue striped tie, which is balled up in one hand. His mouth is puckered slightly, as if for a kiss; but really he is about to utter the two syllables that pull us all into his rigid orbit: "I'm home."

My mother is standing at the kitchen counter, the handset of the phone pressed to her ear. The phone cord is draped around her like a beauty queen's sash. Her head is cocked to one side, lips slightly parted, and in the instant before she speaks, one might think she is being flirtatious or coy. Instead, she is apologizing. "Sorry," she tells her friend, "I've got to go."

"Sorry," she says to my father, to us.

"Sorry," she says, about everything.

From that moment to the actual divorce was a reverse courtship that would take a year or two. During that time, I suspect, my mother pretended not to notice my anti-marriage maneuvers, while secretly cheering me on. I graduated from high school blissfully ignorant of how to broil a steak, remove grass stains, or compose a proper party invitation. I believed that I had succeeded in maturing into a young woman who was utterly unfit for becoming anyone's mother or wife.

I was baffled, therefore, when my first few serious boyfriends, with whom I had unabashedly shared my objections to being Mrs. Anyone, persisted in bringing up the subject of marriage. The fact that nothing I said or did seemed to convince men I was unmarriageable may have been the reason I allowed myself to be swept off my feet by a tall, dark, handsome woman I met in the college cafeteria my first semester away from home.

Not long after, I called my mother from a pay phone in my dormitory with the news that I was gay. She paused. I waited nervously. "I'm glad you're in love," she said finally. "I'm only sorry you won't have children." This was 1982, before the lesbian baby boom, before *Will & Grace,* and back when a Boston marriage was something that would never be recorded by a clerk in City Hall. I managed not to say, "That's the point, Mom!"

Meanwhile, in my Feminism 101 class we were debating whether biology is destiny. I was opposed to the idea that a modern woman had to be slave to her reproductive capability, that just because one could have a child didn't mean she had to sublimate her other goals in favor of motherhood. But somehow I seemed unable to escape at least part of this fate. My next lover sat me down shortly into our relationship and announced that she wanted to have a baby.

At first I resisted. But eventually I gave in. Being a mother in an equal relationship, I reasoned, could be more radical than not being a mother at all. So when my partner gave birth, we tried to split the family duties down the middle. Confronted by the inherent inequality of the biological bond that nursing the baby would create, I purchased a device for adoptive mothers that lets women "breast-feed" with the help of a tiny tube laid alongside the breast and attached to a pouch of formula.

We traded off night feedings and diaper changings, and we divided the responsibility for earning an income. We agreed that I'd freelance from home so I could watch the baby while I worked. It was while I was typing at my word processor with the baby balanced on my lap that the idea of a division of labor based on male and female responsibilities crossed my mind. This time the concept seemed wildly appealing.

But before I could explore this idea, the relationship between my partner and me failed. At this point strict equality would have meant having our two-year-old daughter spend half the week in each of our apartments, which seemed unfair to her. Instead, I settled into the role of divorced father, seeing her on weekends and holidays and helping out with the finances as best I could.

Meanwhile, I fell in love again, this time with Chris, a woman who could drive a nail like nobody's business. She looked sexy with a tool belt slung across her hips, and after the devastation of my breakup, I welcomed the feeling of security that comes when someone you love seems able to fix anything: a stopped-up toilet, a leaking roof, a weary heart.

But I soon found that she also refused to stop and ask directions if we were lost, and she thought it perfectly natural that I should wash dishes and she should take out the trash. Still reeling from the ache of separation from my daughter's daily life, and the searing pain of my recent breakup, I found surprising comfort in the illusion that

I was sheltered by the rooms of our new home and by the more predictable tasks inside of it. I was—perhaps not unlike some traditional wives—content to let someone else handle the less wieldy problems that required power tools, steel-toed work boots, or, simply, exposure to the elements. No, it wasn't perfect. But at the time, it worked.

Then one day as we were driving (she at the wheel, of course) I heard her mutter in disgust at the car in front of us, "Women drivers!"

"That, of course, would include you," I pointed out. She rolled her eyes and shrugged.

Later, during an argument in which I was all emotion and had lost my grasp on logic, she spat, "You're acting like such a girl."

"You can't say that!" I sputtered. "You're one, too."

Being a lesbian, I now saw, hadn't shielded me from the sexism I once feared would suffocate me. Rather, I learned that gender roles aren't as simple as biology. Every successful relationship requires its own hard-won formula for accepting the people we are, and for pushing to outgrow limits.

Decades have passed since my parents split up. My mother has had her chance at a career of her own, and my father has had time to fall in love again and learn to love the people around him while letting them live their own lives.

And in the fourteen years since Chris and I have been together, I have learned that her sexist outbursts are as painful to her as they are to me. After all, in the world beyond our front lawn she is subject to the same preju-dice I am. We grapple with what it means to be a woman without being trapped in a stereotype. I have come to see that a clean floor really can be something to be proud of. But I also don't forget that I know, too, how to shingle a roof, milk a goat, and paddle a canoe through white water.

The other day, when my best friend, who has a special fondness for bestowing nicknames, called just as Chris and I were on our way to play tennis, she said, "You two are Venus and Serena today." I quickly corrected her: "Try Billie Jean and Bobby."

On the court that afternoon, Chris and I laughed at the absurd aptness of my remark. Joking aside, I did put an extra spin on the ball. After all, I didn't want to be accused of playing like a girl, and I really wanted to win.

The Day the House Blew Up

Ronald K. Fried

WE WENT OUT TO THE HOUSE LAST MONTH TO CELEBRATE Valentine's Day. But then the house exploded. The house that we always joked would be taken from us because of our outsize love for it literally blew up.

It was an easy house to love, built in 1830 on a tree-lined street in the heart of the unpretentious, austerely beautiful historic fishing village of Greenport on the North Fork of Long Island. We'd owned it for close to a decade.

> *Yes, we knew there was perhaps something inappropriate about our love for the house.*

We were inside the house when it exploded. The firefighters, the ambulance driver, the doctors and nurses in the ER, the insurance agent all agreed: We were lucky to be alive. It's a miracle, they said.

This was our twenty-first Valentine's Day together, and for fifteen of those years we've been married. Before I met Lorraine I hadn't taken Valentine's Day seriously since grammar school. But my fiercely intelligent, utterly modern wife, despite her abhorrence of cliché, observes holidays in a pleasantly sentimental way. Valentine's Day, St. Patrick's Day, Halloween, and all the rest are occasions for the baking of frosted cookies and, on Valentine's Day, the creation of handmade cards.

This sense of occasion connects her to the best parts of her childhood near Pittsburgh.

Our Valentine's Day ritual is simple. I cook dinner for Lorraine, and we split a bottle of champagne. We always try to arrange our schedules so that we can be in Greenport for the holiday, and I can make a wintertime barbecue, preferably in a backyard filled with snow. This year everything was working out. A huge snowstorm was forecast, and we were planning to prolong our weekend until the day after Valentine's Day, a Tuesday.

When we walked into the house late that Friday night, we smelled the familiar mix of ancient wood and mildew, and heard the centuries-old creak of the front door and the endearingly crooked pine floor. I said, as we both often did, "We're so lucky to own this house."

And that was true. The house was perfect in its simple way: clapboard siding, original wide-plank floorboards, handblown glass in the sidelights, a modern kitchen and bathrooms revamped a few years back. But it was also the way the house seemed to hold the light throughout the day no matter what the season.

Late that Saturday afternoon, we sat in the living room with friends. One, an architect, asked that we not turn on the lights after the sun had set so we could watch the lilac-colored twilight linger on the walls. Frederick Law Olmsted himself could not have sited the house better, we all agreed.

Martin Amis said in an interview, or maybe in one of his books, that couples without children are funny. Okay,

I admit it: my wife and I are funny. But at least we know it. So, yes, we knew there was perhaps something inappropriate about our love for the house.

What was more suspect—to us, at least—was the love we had developed for our next-door neighbors' cat Speckles, a calico with beige and white highlights in her black fur. We started making friends with Speckles as soon as we moved into the house. The neighbors, Bob and Debbie Allen, told us their cat's story. Speckles was a stray that Bob's mother had taken in. Soon we started taking her in as well, and Speckles began spending nearly as much time in our house as theirs.

Who wants to listen to a middle-aged man describe the wonders of the cat he loves but doesn't even own? I'll add only that I wouldn't have noticed Speckles if my wife had not taught me, besides much else, to love animals. She loved Speckles first, but then I fell, hard. Harder, perhaps.

Amis is right: couples without children are funny.

On Valentine's Day morning, I slept past nine. I was awakened by the sound of Lorraine chatting downstairs with the man from the gas company, who had come to fill the propane tanks that hung on the outer wall of the house and fed the kitchen stove.

Coming downstairs, I smelled what I thought was the scent of cooking tomatoes and garlic, and I wondered why Lorraine was preparing dinner. The smell was gas, Lorraine said; probably just residue from the delivery. But she was concerned. I boiled water for my coffee, no problem. Lorraine reread the notice the gas company had left, debating whether or not to call. She went into the dining room to see if the birds hopping on the snow in the garden were tufted titmice.

I turned away from the stove. And then the house blew up, a pulsing boom and pressure against my face, like the wave of sound you feel if you sit up close at a big rock concert. I thought: This is it, I'm going to die.

It was a surprisingly calm moment, almost as if I were finally finding out how a story ended, the story of my life. There was a brief moment of recognition: Oh, this is how it ends. How unexpected. I felt a great sadness, of course. How sad, I am going to die. But no panic, really. And then I didn't die. I was forced to conclude that I was alive and ambulatory.

I walked into the backyard shouting Lorraine's name, and I was astonished to see that the back wall of the house had preceded me there. Broken window frames and shattered glass were spread out on the snow. A few seconds later Lorraine followed me. Though she had been closer to the explosion than I was—directly above it, we later discovered—she had dashed into the kitchen to find me or what was left of me.

We hugged each other and reported the amazing news: we were alive. We said what everyone says at moments like this: I love you. I love you, darling. I love you with all my heart.

And then we went back inside to get the fire extinguisher. But the fire behind the stove, where once the kitchen wall had been, was not the only fire. There was fire in the basement. Probably the propane had leaked under the crawl space in the kitchen and then, because it is a heavy gas, filled the basement, which was below the dining room. It's likely that the electric water heater down there sparked on, causing the explosion. Or so we reasoned later.

The wooden planks in the dining room had exploded upward toward my wife, and the dining room chairs slid into the basement. Lorraine's hair was singed, her nose was cut, there was a huge bump on her head, and she had more bruises than she knew. But she was alive.

Standing in the backyard we saw that the blast had blown out our neighbors' windows. But it had not killed us, even though we were right on top of it. Why? Perhaps because we were at the epicenter of the blast, a friend later speculated.

"Speckles is in there," Lorraine said, looking into our second-story bedroom, which we could see clearly because the back wall of the house no longer existed. "Speckles is dead."

Speckles had joined me in the bedroom as I slept, and had been sitting on the red farm chair in the upstairs hall the last time I saw her.

Speckles dead? This news hit me much harder than the destruction of our house.

I love my wife for her brave and heroic heart, so I should not have been surprised to see her charge into the house in her bare, snow-covered feet to look for Speckles.

I did not follow Lorraine, owing to either good judgment or lack of physical courage, I'm not sure which. I was trapped in the backyard for maybe ten minutes. I couldn't get out through the driveway because the walls of our house had collapsed and blocked the way. I tried to climb over the picket fence, but it was too high.

I later learned that Lorraine had searched for the cat briefly before leaving the house through its nonexistent front wall. She then pushed past a policeman to get into our neighbors' yard, where she was able to help me over the fence that separated the two properties. Together we walked through our neighbors' house to the safety of the street. Lorraine had tried her best to find Speckles, she reported, but with no luck.

From the street we watched as flames began to engulf the house. But the loss of Speckles weighed on us. Oscar Wilde warned that we destroy what we love, and had it not been for our perhaps misplaced but entirely heartfelt love of that cat, I told myself, Speckles would not have been visiting with us that morning. And she would be alive still.

But she was. She was alive.

A second tank of gas caught fire. As the orange flames and black smoke bellowed toward the heavens, Speckles jumped out of the ruins and scampered down the street. "Speckles! Speckles!" we cheered.

"She's alive," we said. "She's alive!" I hugged the Allens' son, Teddy, and gave him a kiss on his stubbly cheek, and Lorraine hugged and kissed their daughter, Susie.

A great sadness had been lifted from our hearts. Our house was gone, but we were alive, and our love for each other—the love of a married couple who had put up with each other for twenty years—would survive. Though we accused ourselves of indulging in a foolish love for a cat, that love had not destroyed her.

I still believe Martin Amis was right: couples without children are funny.

But at that moment we were not funny. On this Valentine's Day I knew what grown-up love was, or at least I knew one of the things love *does*.

It tells us what matters.

UPDATE: *Ron and his wife, Lorraine Kreahling, are planning to rebuild their home in Greenport, New York.*

Two Decembers: Loss and Redemption

Anne Marie Feld

ON THE AFTERNOON MY MOTHER DIED, SHE LEFT WORK early. Her day as a computer programmer at Chase Manhattan Bank had skidded to an abrupt stop courtesy of a systemwide computer failure, and all the employees got the afternoon off. It was late December. My sixteenth birthday. Gray, snowless, cold enough to make the lawn crunch underfoot, but close enough to Christmas to make a few uncrowded hours seem like a gift. Or in my mother's case, a curse.

> *I convinced myself that Dave was a con man planning an elaborate sting to separate me from my down payment on our house. The year we had spent together was the setup for the graft.*

Rather than enjoying some last-minute shopping or hitting the couch, she methodically cleared her desk, drove the Honda home, fired up a pot of Turkish coffee, and hanged herself in our garage.

Twenty years later my father insists that she wouldn't have died that day if the systems hadn't gone down. He might be right. Work gave my mother a structure that sealed the madness inside, if only for small chunks of time. Idleness brought trouble.

My memories of my mother all have her working at something: cooking, staying up all night scraping wallpaper, poring over fat textbooks to get her master's degree. In home movies my sister and I, long-limbed and small-bodied, dance and do gymnastics in the foreground while my mother lurks in the background, washing dishes or zooming diagonally through the frame on her way somewhere else.

Though my mother worked full time, my sister and I never lifted a finger in that house. It was spotless, without the piles of clutter and tides of dust that mark my own house.

My mother's madness seeped in so quietly that my father, an optimist to the end, was able to ignore it, believing that it would get better on its own. In our house, questions about what we did and how we felt went unasked. Or if asked, unanswered. My sister and I ate alone in our bedrooms beside flickering black-and-white televisions.

I wasn't told about my mother's two earlier attempts at suicide and would never have guessed. In my mind, suicidal people raved and ranted. Madwomen were locked in attics, where they would moan and rattle chains. Occasionally they set fire to country estates. They certainly weren't grocery shopping or dropping the kids off at the community pool on their way to the office.

From fielding calls on the yellow rotary-dial phone in the kitchen, I knew that my mother saw a therapist, a woman named Barbara, whom she tried to pawn off as a friend. I knew better. My mother didn't have friends.

When I was fourteen, my mother started sleeping on the living room floor and wearing a dark gray ski hat with three white stripes. She seemed to drink nothing but gritty coffee and red wine poured from gallon bottles stored under the kitchen sink. She would send me into the pizzeria to pick up our pie, convinced that the men spinning crusts were talking about her behind her back.

As I limped along in my teenage bubble, very little of this registered as alarming. This was how all families were. As my mother's madness amplified, she came to believe that our house was bugged and that her boss was trying to hurt her. But as long as there was a computer program to write or a carpet to vacuum, she could be counted on to do it and do it well.

In her insistence upon getting things done, on living an ordered life, my mother managed to miss out on the nourishing aspects of family life and life in general: laughing at silly things, lying spooned on the couch with your beloveds, sharing good food, the tactile delight of giggling children crawling all over you. Without this, family life is an endless series of menial tasks: counters and noses to wipe, dishes and bodies to wash, whites and colors to fold, again and again in soul-sucking succession.

On the morning of the day my mother died, I headed toward the door to catch the 7:10 bus to school. My mother and twelve-year-old sister were just waking up in their sleeping spot on the gray carpet in the living room. They sang "Happy Birthday" to me, my mother's beautiful, low singing voice frosted with my sister's tinny soprano.

Eight hours later I stepped off the Bluebird bus, looking forward to an afternoon of *One Life to Live* and *All My Children,* and was disappointed to see my mother's car in the driveway. I dropped my knapsack on the window seat, stroked the dog's dusty ears, and called, "Mommy?"

Her purse sat on the table. I checked all the rooms but found them empty. Then I opened the door to the garage and stopped breathing.

I shut the door, ran up the stairs and outside, and sat on the cold concrete stoop, looking up the street. House after split-level house stretched along the curved road with one thing in common: no one was home. All of the parents in my neighborhood worked, and since I had taken the early bus home from school, the kids were still gone as well.

I sat hunched over my legs, arms circling my shins, as my heart slowed. Finally I stood up, opened the screen door, went back into the house, and dialed 911.

In the days that followed, my father, sister, and I sloshed through a sea of awkwardness. The wife of a friend of my father's bought me a dress to wear to the funeral, a maroon velvet Gunny Sax monstrosity with puffed sleeves and lace trim.

Regular funerals are hard enough; the funeral of a suicide tests even the most socially skilled. When all the robotic thank-you-for-comings had been finished, my sister tried to open the coffin when no one was looking. My father stopped her just as she was about to lift the lid. "I just wanted to see her," she explained, almost inaudibly.

Other details needed handling, providing my first, metallic taste of the kind of chores that come with adulthood. For the first time in my life, a formal party had been planned for my birthday at a local catering hall. The party favors—clear Lucite boxes filled with Hershey's Kisses, decorated with pink and silver hearts—sat in bags in the garage, waiting.

But there would be no party. I picked up the phone and said, over and over, "I'm sorry, my Sweet Sixteen is canceled." By the time I was done, cold sweat ran down my wrist, wetting my sleeve. I didn't cry.

On the day the party was to be held, I stood in Loehmann's with my father. My mother's dress for the occasion, a gray wool sheath with long sleeves, lay on the counter. The clerk told my father that the garment couldn't be returned. My father looked at the clerk and said very quietly, "But she died." They took the dress back.

And as soon as I could, I fled. First to college, then to a place as far from Long Island as I could manage: San Francisco. Every night I would shimmy into a short black dress, tights, and platform boots and belly up to small, scarred stages, staring at would-be Kurt Cobains or boys in porkpie hats wailing Louis Armstrong covers, or nodding my head to the beat as shaved-bald DJs spun in corners of warehouses while hundreds of people raved, shaking water bottles over their heads until the sun shot weak rays through dirty skylights.

My rent was $365. I had some savings; work seemed optional, as did stability. Over the next decade I would have ten apartments, thirteen jobs, and at least as many boyfriends. I met Dave at a film festival, while waiting in line to see a movie called *Better Than Sex*. We started seeing movies together, always picking films with *sex* in the title. Months after we had run out of movies about fornication with no signs of doing so ourselves, he finally kissed me under a lamppost outside his front door. I was wearing knee-high black leather boots. He was wearing sheepskin slippers.

He phoned every day. He listened. He smiled a lot. He told me I was beautiful. He made up rap songs about our love. He wanted to talk about everything, from politics to my period. He wanted children. He was, as my best friend's father said, "a good citizen."

We found a house together, a 1920s cottage on a street of Spanish Mediterranean houses in every color of the rainbow. We split the down payment fifty-fifty and started packing. Driving alone through a torrential downpour to sign the title for our house, I lost it. I didn't do stable.

I convinced myself that Dave was a con man planning an elaborate sting to separate me from my down payment. The year we had spent together was the setup for the graft. Now I was going to be out twenty-five thousand dollars and a boyfriend. It was a hop, skip, and a jump from there to standing at the side of the road, homeless and utterly alone, the victim of aiming too high.

My hands were shaking when I pulled up outside the title company. Dave was standing there, holding an umbrella, waiting to walk me the ten feet from the curb to the building. Eight months later, just back from our honeymoon, he carried me up our wonky front steps and across the threshold before collapsing from exertion on the blue sofa in our office. Another eight months after that, a plastic stick with a pink line told us that our remodeling plans were going to have to wait.

On my first visit, the ob-gyn calculated the baby's due date: my birthday. I was terrified that my day of personal infamy would be shared by the next generation of my family. Friends spun it beautifully: "It'll be healing. It'll give you back that day."

The contractions didn't hit hard until Christmas night, four days after I turned thirty-six. Fifty-six hours after the first tremors hit my abdomen, three hours after the epidural wore off, I pushed my daughter into the world.

I wasn't thinking about my mother. Or about my sister, who stayed at the head of the bed, cheering me on when I thought my body would rip in two. Or about Dave, who watched tearfully as Pascale poured out. I thought nothing, and just lay there, shocked by pain and exhaustion. But when they finally returned her raw, chickenlike body to me after bathing her, my first thought was that she looked like my mother.

UPDATE: *Anne and her husband recently had their second child, a boy.*

Part Five

Leaving

THE TIES THAT FRAY

The Chicken's in the Oven, My Husband's Out the Door

Theo Pauline Nestor

SOME MARRIAGES GRIND SLOWLY TO A HALT. OTHERS, like mine, explode midflight, a space shuttle torn asunder in the clear blue sky as the stunned crowd watches in disbelief. And the hazardous debris from the catastrophe just keeps raining down.

It was late September, still warm but past the last hot stretch of Indian summer. I had waited for a day cool enough to roast a chicken for my husband and two young daughters. When I put the five-pound chicken in the oven, a shower of

> When I took off my wedding rings, my finger had atrophied underneath in a manner that seems excessively symbolic. I protect this white band with my thumb like a wound.

fresh green herbs clinging to its breast, our marriage was still intact. By the time I pulled it out, my husband had left our house and driven away for good, his car stuffed with clothes slipping off their hangers.

It was my call to the bank to check our balance that caused the fatal blowup. Although my husband's destructive compulsions with money had threatened our marriage before, I believed those days were long behind us. But that afternoon, without even trying to, I discovered the truth: far from changing his ways, he had simply become more secretive. I confronted him. And that, as they say, was that.

So the roast chicken fed only one person that night: our nine-year-old daughter, Elizabeth. I couldn't eat, and our five-year-old, Grace, announced she wouldn't eat a real chicken, only chicken nuggets. I took the red box from the freezer, plucked out five tawny squares, heated them in the microwave, and placed them in front of Grace, who believed, as did her sister, that their father had gone downtown to meet a friend and that he and this friend were going on an impromptu car trip. "Dad will come home in a week," I told them. I didn't know what else to say.

I thought of my childhood friend Nancy, whose marriage had fallen apart a year earlier. I have three friends from childhood I am still close to; coincidentally, all four of us married around our thirtieth birthdays. For ten years we beat the odds. Then Nancy's marriage broke up, and now, with mine, our little group reflected that often-cited statistic: half of all marriages end in divorce.

At Nancy's wedding, the minister had briefly turned his attention from the newlyweds to address the group directly. "It is up to the community to hold a couple together," he had said in his commanding voice. "Each of you here is responsible for remembering for this couple the love that brought them together and the commitment they've made."

I took his words to heart, silently vowing to support Nancy and Terry, to remind Nancy of Terry's strengths someday when she might vent to me after a marital spat. Despite their vows and my support, despite ten years and two sons, their marriage couldn't be held together. And now, despite eleven years and two daughters, neither could mine.

The women I grew up with, like most women today, have tangible, marketable skills. One is an electrician, another a graphic artist, a third a nurse. Inside or outside a marriage, they can support themselves. I, too, am a well-educated woman with a decent work history, who actually made more money than my husband when we married. I prided myself on being self-sufficient. But we both wanted someone to be home with the kids, and we decided it would be me, so I stopped working and let him support us. And now I've ended up in the same vulnerable position I once thought was the fate only of women who married straight out of high school, with no job experience beyond summer gigs at the Dairy Queen.

Not that I would have done it differently. I have valued my time with our daughters more than any other experience I've had. But for a stay-at-home mom like me, divorce isn't just divorce. It's more like divorce plus being fired from a job, because you can no longer afford to keep your job at home, the one you gave up your career for. When I worked as an English professor at the community college, we called people like me displaced homemakers. I imagined legions of gingham-aproned Betty Crockers spinning perpetually, forever tracing their feather dusters across imaginary furniture, never ceasing to "make" the "home" that was no longer there. Now that my income has dwindled to child support and a meager "maintenance" check, I must leave this job and get a "real" one. I add up our expenses for a month and then subtract his contribution. The remaining total indicates that to keep the girls and myself out of debt, I will need to net a third more than the most I've ever made.

And divorce is its own job, with its course of study, its manuals. One of the many divorce books heaped on the floor beside my bed urges me to develop two stories about the breakup: a private one and a public one. I'm told that I should practice a few sentences that I can recite (in the grocery store, on the playground) without excessive emotion, a sort of campaign slogan for my divorce. And it does seem as if much of my daily work involves negotiating the snowy pass between my private and public self. Alone, I shriek into my pillow, and I shout "Bonehead!" through the closed car window as I drive past my ex's new apartment. In public, I am stoic, detached, nodding philosophically as a married mother from Elizabeth's soccer team tells me, "Your grief is like a house. One day you'll be in the room of sorrow and the next you might be in anger."

A humbled divorcée, I can only act as if all this is news to me.

"And oh, denial!" she adds. "That's a room, too—don't forget."

Eventually you have to tell everyone who hasn't heard through the grapevine. Some people get "the whole story" and some just get the abridged "we've separated" version.

The whole-story people are exhausting. At first it's all relief and adrenaline as you recount the moment you realized the shuttle was breaking apart. But then you are overwhelmed with dread as you come to understand

how many whole-story people there are in your life. Still
ahead are countless oh-my-gods and I'm-so-sorrys and
you-must-be-kiddings. You hear sympathetic and under-
standable questions coming at you, and your tongue
grows thick and unfamiliar forming all those words one
more time. You consider a form letter:

Dear Good Friend Who Deserves the Whole Story

I'm sorry this is coming to you as a form letter.
I'm sorry about a lot.
I'm just sorry.

Or perhaps there could be a Web site: www.whatthehell
happened.com, complete with a FAQ link.

Q. *What about the children?*
A. *They live with me but will stay with him every Friday*
   and every first, third, and fifth Thursday night as well as
   the first Saturday of every month. Yes, it's hard to
   remember which week it is.
Q. *Will reconciliation be possible?*
A. *No. If you read the whole story you will understand why.*
   (Use password to access the secure site.)
Q. *Are you okay?*
A. *No, I'm not. Thanks for asking.*
Q. *Is there anything we can do to help?*
A. *Yes. Click on the Send Money link below.*

When I took off my wedding rings, my finger had
atrophied underneath in a manner that seems excessively

symbolic. I protect this white band with my thumb like a wound. I look at other women's ring fingers: gold bands, simple solitaires, swirling clusters of diamonds. The fact that they've managed to keep those rings in place seems miraculous, a defiance of gravity. When I wore my rings, I was a different person, emboldened in the way one can be in a Halloween costume. I could laugh as loudly as I wanted and go out with dirty hair and sweatpants. I was married. Someone loved me, and it showed. I could refer to a husband in conversations with a new friend or a store clerk. They didn't care if I was married or not, but I did. My ring said, You can't touch me. It's like base in a game of tag. You're safe.

Now when I go to bed I turn the electric blanket to high and let the heat soak into my skin. Sometimes, lying here, I think of this divorce business as something like the flu. The feverish beginnings, as miserable and sweaty as they are, are somehow easier to get through (they are a blur, really) than the many half-well, half-sick days that follow, days when you're not sure what to do. You're too well to lie in bed watching TV but too sick to go out and do all the things well people are expected to do.

To fall asleep, I resort to the old routine of counting my blessings. I count my daughters over and over again. I count their health, their happiness, the gift of who they are.

I urge myself to find something else I am grateful for but can't. And then I realize there is something.

It's this rawness of spirit, the way the crust of my middle-age shell has been blown off me, and here I am, the real me. I am no longer the person who can pretend everything's okay. I can no longer think of myself as "safe" or protected. I know now it is up to me to hunt, to gather, and to keep shelter warm.

UPDATE: *Theo and her ex-husband work hard to successfully co-parent their two daughters. They share a lawnmower, sit beside each other at school functions, and occasionally even laugh when the other says something funny.*

Witness to a Wedding That Wasn't

Jennie Yabroff

THE INVITATION TO THE WEDDING SAID BLACK TIE. THAT afternoon I put on my black silk spaghetti-strap dress and a pearl necklace while my boyfriend searched for the cuff links for his tux. Brian and I were at that point in our relationship (together just under a year) when we liked to talk about weddings ("What did you think of the cake?" "Would you ever make your best man wear a kilt?") but weren't yet ready to talk about marriage. Still, I loved going to weddings—loved, most of all, engaging in catty repartee about the proceedings, the splendor, the amazing and ridiculous pledge of commitment to lifelong everything that felt so beyond me.

> "There's not going to be a wedding," the groom's mother said. She laughed. Then she stopped laughing.

Black town cars were double-parked in front of the hall. The day was hot and humid, with the threat of a storm, and I was glad to step into the cool foyer, where a man wearing white gloves told us cocktails were being served upstairs. I squeezed Brian's hand in anticipation of a drink.

We went up the stairs and joined the short entry line. By the door an older woman in a midnight blue velvet dress was talking to a couple in front of us. I stared at the diamonds around her neck, which were large and abundant. I realized that they were probably real, and that I had never seen so many real diamonds on a real person in real life. The woman had a soufflé of brown hair, lots of makeup, and a mobile, active face. "Welcome to my anniversary party," she said to the couple, and laughed.

I looked at Brian. He knew the bride from school, and I had met the couple only once. He looked as confused as I was, and I wondered if we were at the wrong event.

"Welcome," she said to us. "I don't know who you are, but please come in and enjoy my party. Have a drink." She introduced herself as the groom's mother.

"This is a beautiful space," I said. "Thank you so much for having us."

"Oh, you're welcome," she said. "You know there's not going to be a wedding."

The woman laughed, so I laughed, thinking she was already drunk. Then she stopped laughing. I stopped laughing, too.

"Are you serious?" I said.

She was serious. "But please come in," she said. "Have a drink, have dinner, enjoy the party."

"There's not going to be a wedding," I said to Brian, who seemed not have heard.

"Are you serious?" he said.

"There's not going to be a wedding," the groom's mother repeated, patiently. "A couple of hours ago he decided he just couldn't go through with it. Better now than tomorrow morning, I guess! But, really, please, enjoy yourselves. Come in and have a drink."

We made our way into the room, holding hands, staring at each other, neither of us certain what to say.

"What should we do?" I asked Brian.

A tuxedoed waiter approached, holding a tray. "Champagne?" he asked. "Watermelon margarita?"

Brian took two of the margaritas, which were pink with red balls of fresh watermelon floating in them, and handed me one. "I guess we should have a drink," he said.

We drank. We drank the margaritas, and then cocktails from the three open bars, and then champagne from a passing tray. We ate sushi from the long table where sushi chefs in kimonos rolled unagi and spider rolls, and then we moved on to the scallops and oysters and lobster ceviche from the raw bar, and pot stickers and chicken satay with four different dipping sauces. We balanced mini crab cakes and tiny beef Wellingtons and bite-size pigs in blankets on little plates and sipped our drinks.

"I knew it would never happen," an older man said to me as I placed a second helping of California rolls on my plate.

"I don't really know either of them," I said.

I went to find a bathroom and slipped on the marble steps.

A uniformed attendant looked my way. "I'm not drunk—it's just slippery," I explained, then I realized it made me sound drunk. I fixed my lipstick and wondered if there was a pay phone anywhere. I wanted to tell someone about this miraculous nonevent. But I didn't see a phone.

When I found Brian he was talking to the bride's two best friends, who would have been her bridesmaids had there been a wedding. I stood next to him, and he ran his fingers lightly down my back. We walked over to a balcony that looked down on the main floor. Tables had been set for the dinner, and a ten-piece band was setting up on a small stage. Brian said he thought it must be where they would have held the ceremony, and we agreed it would have been beautiful, with the high vaulted ceilings and marble columns and orchids everywhere.

We went downstairs, where the vocalist for the band had begun singing jazzy, love-affirming songs: Stevie Wonder, Kool and the Gang. A few older couples were moving around the dance floor, doing that sort of up-tempo waltz older couples do, adapting the steps they know to music they don't. We found our table, and a waiter came over to pour us wine.

As we waited for dinner Brian realized that none of the bride's other friends had come downstairs. Whole tables sat empty. Through the main doors I could see guests hailing cabs and ducking into waiting town cars. Brian said the bridesmaids had told him the bride's friends were meeting at a bar downtown. He thought we should go, too.

I wanted to stay. I wanted to dance and have dinner, which Brian had told me would be my choice between steak or a whole fish. I wanted to see what happened when it was time to cut the cake, if it would be cut discreetly in the kitchen and served as though it were any other dessert, or if the groom's mother would make a speech and thank everyone for coming to her son's aborted nuptials.

She had changed in my mind from an addled dipsomaniac to a mythic figure, stoic in the face of epic tragedy.

I had the feeling of being both witness to and participant in a rare spectacle, like a supernumerary in a Wagnerian opera. I imagined all of us guests this way, whispering among ourselves about the scandal: "He called it off at five o'clock! She was already in her gown!" the pitch rising, the pace increasing, until we came together as a group and stood, facing the audience, to sing our chorus: *"He called it off at five o'clock! She was already in her gown!"* Then the groom's mother would step to the front of the stage, and we would sweep around to the other side of the proscenium. Wearing a diamond-encrusted, horned Viking helmet, her massive breasts heaving beneath her blue velvet sheath, she'd raise a hand, finger pointed to the sky, and sing out, in a thundering mezzo-soprano, *"He changed his mind!"*

Brian said if I was still hungry I could have a chili dog at the bar. I said I didn't want a chili dog, I wanted a whole fish and free champagne. But the bride was his friend, so I put down my wineglass and followed him out of the room, past the empty, orchid-laden tables, away from the dancing couples and attentive waiters with bottles at the ready. We passed the groom's mother, and I took her hands and thanked her for the party. She looked at me blankly, and I wondered how much longer she would have to endure this, making jokes about her "anniversary party" and delivering her line about "better now than tomorrow morning" with the same smile and quick nod.

Out on the street the sky was swollen and gray, though it still wasn't quite dark, and I felt the moisture collect in my hair and on my exposed skin. In the cab on the way back downtown the air-conditioner made me shiver, so I opened my window to let in the warm, sticky breeze.

Around the table at the bar the couples talked, rehashing the stories of how we had found out the big news: "I thought his mom was joking." "I thought she was drunk." "No, no one knows where he is." "There's no way her family's paying for this now." "Sixty thousand dollars just to rent the hall!" "Did you see all the orchids?"

We agreed this situation was unprecedented in our experience, maybe because of the figures involved, which were repeated around the table: the number of hours before the wedding that the groom called it off (two), the amount of money spent on the event (several hundred thousand dollars, by most estimates).

Someone had called the hall and had a tier of the wedding cake sent down. We ate slices of cake and finished our beer. Then it was time to go. Brian and I walked back to his apartment, holding hands. My lipstick had worn off and my hair was frizzy from the humidity, though it still hadn't rained. Brian took off his jacket.

In his apartment we changed into T-shirts and lay together on the sofa, talking about the wedding. I thought of all the other couples we had seen that night and wondered if they were doing the same thing, cozy in their casual clothes, complicit in their happiness. The evening had afforded us all a reprieve: for one night, at least, we all had successful relationships. We had dressed up for each other and held hands, and at the end of the evening we were still together, while the bride and groom were not. We got to go home and take aspirin for our hangovers and decide to sleep in late and then lie together, conspiring, gossiping, reminiscing about the events of the last few hours. Already Brian and I were rehearsing the way we'd tell the story when we had brunch with another couple the next day, and it became the story we told every time we went out with another couple, for the rest of the summer and into fall, until I finally said we had to stop talking about it for a while.

UPDATE: *Jennie and Brian have attended nine weddings together since the events described in this essay, and she's happy to report that both bride and groom showed up at each of them.*

So Handsome, So Clever, So Gone

Martha Moffett

LOEFFLER WAS MY TROPHY INTELLECTUAL. WE MET AT a party, where he hovered around my conversational circle for a while and then came up to me and asked, "Are you with someone?"

"Yes," I said. I'd come with my office mate, another editor.

"Come home with me," he said.

I did. We sipped dry sherry on his porch until sunrise, and shortly thereafter he moved in to my small Florida home.

I began displaying him almost immediately, once I'd reviewed his credentials. They were just about right: Harvard, NEH grant, a fellow at Yale, two sabbaticals in Africa, where he labored at compiling a Chamba dictionary. One night I half-woke and mumbled some words, and he shook me awake: "You know what that is, don't you? It's Chamba."

I'd been the one with the job, the means, the power, and the will. And I suppose I liked that part of it. But over the long haul it wore me out.

But, no, I don't speak Chamba, not even in my sleep. There are only about twenty thousand Chamba speakers

264] MODERN LOVE

in the world. Maybe one day they'll use Loeffler's dictionary, if he ever completes it.

He has another unfinished book, on African motifs in *Finnegans Wake*. He's been writing this book for about twenty years, including the two years it took to put his notes on computer when he got his first PC.

Publish or perish did him in academically. He couldn't finish his work, so he couldn't publish it, which meant he couldn't get tenure, which meant, essentially, the end of his academic career, and along with it any reliable way of earning an income. Oh, he got a grant at one point and also had some money from the sale of his mother's house. But mostly he lived cheaply and was happy to be supported principally by others—by me, for example.

By the time I met Loeffler I'd already had a trophy husband, a man so tall and handsome and mannerly that I sometimes believed I married him just to confound my family, who long before had decided I was too stubborn and uncommunicative to attract a desirable man. That's the unspoken agenda in acquiring a trophy *anything,* to say to those who doubted you: Look, you were wrong.

After I separated from my trophy husband and was left with three children and no child support or alimony (my husband, too, had arranged to have no income), I procrastinated for a long time on initiating a divorce. For one thing, I knew the whole endeavor would fall on me; I'd have to pay the fees for us both and complete the paperwork, file everything, see it through.

But also I had the idea . . . well—I don't know why I'm embarrassed to admit this, but I had the idea that maybe I could sell him. This was back when I lived in

New York, and I imagined a wealthy Manhattan woman might spot him, a tall, handsome, well-spoken man, and think that, even as an escort, he was worth something. So she would ask me to divorce him, and I would say to her, "I'll sell him to you."

Just such a woman ran over his foot one day as he stood waiting for the light at Lexington and Fifty-ninth Street. She jumped out of her Lexus and apologized profusely, but unfortunately he did not get her name or phone number. I would have called her, definitely.

Trophy intellectuals also are not without selling points. For example, you never have to do any research. When I asked Loeffler a question—"How important is sequential order in narrative presentation?"—he gave me the answer.

Loeffler was best at small parties. At big parties he got lost. It was different with my trophy husband. His height caused him to stand out. I remember flirting with an average-size mathematician at a party. He asked me to point out my husband. When I did, he exclaimed enviously, "Oh, wouldn't he be the tallest man here?" And it seemed entirely natural for him to say that. It's the sort of thing that happens when you have a trophy husband.

With a trophy intellectual you sacrifice height for hair, or at least that was the case with Loeffler, whose thick hair grows from his forehead like a furious wind-whipped fern forest. And he has the other stuff, too: the piercing eyes, the knitted brow, the sudden rewarding laughter.

But with a trophy intellectual (or a trophy husband, for that matter) you also sacrifice basic competence and assistance in life's demands for raffish charm or good looks or a kind of precious companionship. And the play of power, in a trophy relationship, goes like this: you can *ask* your trophy to do something, but you cannot *expect*.

For example, I asked both my trophy husband and my trophy intellectual to take out the trash, and neither knew what I was talking about. I also asked both to get a job, but that suggestion went nowhere as well.

Decisions on entertaining, new clothes, major purchases (washing machines, vacuum cleaners), whether we could afford Europe this year—all this fell to me. The debit side of this much responsibility was that all of our negative experiences, acquisitions, and travel were my fault. On the credit side, of course, was that all positive results ended up in my column as well.

I loved dressing both of my trophies. My trophy husband had ties to die for and a collection of cashmere socks that I used to wash by hand. When we separated, there was a whole wardrobe of Saks Fifth Avenue shirts at the laundry that was lost to history because neither one of us would pick up the laundry—he too passive, I too stubborn.

He eventually wound up with a baby boomer who supported him with her great career and big salary while he made her breakfast, went out for the paper, ironed her clothes, packed her lunch: all those tasks I never could seem to get out of him. I could weep when I think of the care I lavished on his socks.

Dressing Loeffler was much harder. He wouldn't let me take him shopping. He bought his clothes at the Goodwill on Federal Highway and the Church Mouse in

Palm Beach. This meant he got the castoffs of the guys who went to St. Mark's and Harvard or Yale, so he was able to stay within his learned dress code.

Once we were all dressed up, standing in line for tickets at the Society of the Four Arts, a peculiarly Palm Beach institution. If you're not a member, you can't buy tickets. But if you're standing at the box office, appropriately dressed, and there are unused members' tickets, you are allowed to purchase them. We were there because Loeffler was in love with Frederica von Stade.

I was happy about Loeffler's eccentric crushes. They were always appropriate for a trophy intellectual. He also adored Jamaica Kincaid and Jeanette Winterson. Some women feel threatened if their men exhibit any outward-directed passion. But I felt our relationship was enriched by these passions. Loeffler's passions were bread and wine to me.

But coming up with appropriate dress for this concert was proving to be a problem. After going through boxes and boxes at Goodwill, Loeffler finally found a ten-dollar tux, and I discovered I fit into my youngest daughter's prom dress.

We looked good. Rather, we looked good up close. From a distance, you could see that the crotch of Loeffler's tux pants fell at about knee level.

When the von Stade concert was over, a woman sidled up to Loeffler and asked him a question. Soon he was arguing, his usual style of conversation. I moved a bit closer, curious to know what they were saying. Oh, no, she was arguing that everybody's reality is equally valid and that therefore there is no reality.

I knew what Loeffler thought of that.

He looked over and inclined his head, which meant that he was ready to leave and wanted me to drag him away. I went over and said in a loud voice, "Your plane is at eight in the morning. If you have any packing left to do, you'd better do it tonight."

He looked surprised, as if a stranger had told him that he had been elected to some office. "Me?" he seemed to say, although the tickets were in his jacket pocket.

He bowed to the Palm Beach woman, and we left, possibly looking more ridiculous as we moved farther away.

And the next day there would be a farewell at the door, me still in my nightgown, Loeffler in his Church Mouse good suit and fresh white shirt, shaved and shining, on his way to Oaxaca, Mexico, to observe the Day of the Dead. And from that day on he would be dead to me as, in Oaxaca, he would fall in love with someone else, and they would run away together, and it would be left to me to gather his notes and manuscripts and mail them off to him.

In such a relationship one is always the dreamer, and it falls to the other to be the practical party. With my two trophies I'd always been stuck in the role of the practical party. I'd been the one with the job, the means, the power, and the will. And I suppose I liked that part of it. But over the long haul it wore me out.

What I'm looking for now is someone useful, a working man, a classic, the low-cut jeans. If he's not a plumber, he'll work at the power company or maybe BellSouth.

He'll be someone I can watch football and basketball with—ice hockey, even. No upkeep, no display, no occasions. Just a man who's hardworking, dependable, loyal, and in possession of necessary skills.

Two mounted heads on my wall are enough.

A Reincarnation, and Just When I Didn't Need One

Robin Hemley

A WOMAN WITH A LOPSIDED SMILE APPROACHED ME AFTER class the day my marriage ended. She had dark hair in a pageboy cut and ever-scanning eyes, as though reading some invisible TelePrompTer. "Professor Hemley," she said, almost too quietly for me to hear. "May I speak with you?"

I didn't want to speak with her. I wanted to flee, to take care of what needed taking care of, to start packing, compartmentalizing, rationalizing my way into a new life.

"Of course," I said. "What's on your mind?"

"I read your memoir about your sister, Nola," she said. "It made me remember. I'm pretty sure I'm her reincarnation."

> *"We have met over many lifetimes, entwined, loving, doomed," she wrote. "Please do not run from me."*

My sister, eleven years older than I, had died in 1973 at the age of twenty-five of a prescription drug overdose. A schizophrenic. She was much more than that, of course—people too often become known by their diagnoses, by the category that most easily sums them up.

I've always resisted this. I hadn't written a book about schizophrenia. I had written about a brilliant young woman who had been fascinated by the supernatural and obsessed with God from a young age, a woman with a lovely singing voice whom I loved, and later feared when she sank into her sickness.

Toward the end of her life, she tried to strangle me, and ever after I had been phobic around people with mental illness. But even if that weren't the case, I still did not want to be confronted with the reincarnation of my sister, or someone who thought she was, on the day my marriage was breaking up. It was hard enough to process the death of my marriage without having to concern myself with the rebirth of my sister.

"What makes you think that?" I said, gathering my papers and placing them in my satchel.

Her scanning stopped and she looked at me directly. "I just know I am," she said. "By the way," she added, handing me a sheet from Disabled Student Services. "Here's this. I might need some extra time to complete tests and assignments." By law, I couldn't ask anything about her disability, nor could anyone at DSS tell me anything.

"Okay, then."

I went home to do my packing, but I felt strange when I entered the house. Several decades ago a bomb was developed, the neutron bomb, that leaves buildings standing but people dead. That afternoon, it was as if the place had been hit with such a bomb; the structure was standing but lifeless.

It's often said that when you face death, your life flashes before you. When your marriage dies, scenes both happy and sad play themselves out at odd moments. On Wimbledon mornings, my wife liked to eat strawberries and cream as she watched the tennis. An Anglophile, she admired British traditions, the reserve and humor of the people, and was addicted to certain BBC comedies (not Benny Hill) and dramas such as *EastEnders*.

Not that that matters to anyone else, but it was knowledge I had of her, something I could expect within our singular marriage that now suddenly made no difference to my life anymore. And I made no difference in her life anymore, she told me.

A couple of weeks earlier, sitting together silently in the living room, a sob had escaped from her—the saddest, most bereft sound I'd ever heard. It was the sound of her realizing, as I had much sooner, that our twelve-year marriage was over. That I was the cause of that sound remains to this day almost unbearable to me.

I hurriedly packed, as though fearing my immunity to the bomb would soon wear off. But before I left, I turned on my computer and quickly checked my e-mail messages. There were several from someone calling herself Janey Butterfly.

One read: *We have met over many lifetimes, entwined, loving, doomed. Please do not run from me. We must talk soon.*

I thought of deleting the message, but then figured I had better keep it, even though I had had recent occasion to regret not deleting e-mail. My wife had discovered e-mail messages between me and the woman I had fallen in love with, and that's why I was moving out.

Not my brightest moment, but what I regret now, more than the stupidity of leaving love notes virtually lying around, was the additional pain I caused her because I was too much of a coward to admit what had happened before she found out for herself.

A few days later, at school, I received another e-mail message, this one from a "friend" of "Janey Butterfly."

You have not answered any of Janey Butterfly's e-mails, it said. *You are heartless and cruel, and these actions have not gone unnoticed! The friends of Janey Butterfly, myself included, think you're a meanie. You are going to be sorry.*

No need for that e-mail message to make me sorry. I felt sorry all right.

I'm not one of those people who believe that every action of mine produces an equal and opposite reaction from heaven, hell, or the karmic forces of the universe, though the timing did strike me as a little too ironic.

I don't mean to be cruel, I wrote to Janey Butterfly's friend, *and I'm sorry if it strikes you that way. But it's inappropriate for you to write to me this way and I would like for you to stop, please.*

Shortly, I received a response. *Behind your "professional" distance lurks a monster. There is something inside you essentially untrustworthy.* This last bit she had paraphrased from my memoir.

Yes, there was something untrustworthy in me, but it wasn't for Janey Butterfly to point out to me. It was something for myself, for my wife—Janey Butterfly and her friends had no idea. Not about my current life, anyway.

The next day she didn't appear in class. A relief. I figured she must have dropped it. But the day after, she

reappeared and stared at me fiercely throughout the hour.
I went to my department chairman, who was sympathetic but said we couldn't remove a student unless she
was disruptive or caused harm. Well, wasn't she being
disruptive and causing harm? Oh, he meant in class. He
called up Disabled Student Services and didn't learn a
thing. But student services knew of the situation, from
the student's side at least. What was the student's side,
I wanted to know? Silence.

The e-mail messages continued. Every day, I would
receive at least one or two, each castigating me and telling
me how sorry I was going to be. One evening, I went to
my office in search of financial records I needed for my
divorce. It was after ten, and the campus was deserted, the
halls appropriately spooky and dark. As I sifted through
my papers, the phone rang. No one knew I was there. I let
it ring six times, then picked it up.

"It's me," she said. "I want to talk to you. Please stop
avoiding me."

"How did you know I was here?" I asked.

She ignored the question, said she loved me and that
we belonged together.

I told her that that wouldn't be happening. Trembling, I put the phone back in its cradle.

The next day, I went to my old house and spoke to
my wife. I warned her to be careful, that I was being
stalked by one of my students and that she might think
I still lived there. She listened, concerned, and thanked
me for letting her know. I asked her how she was doing.
She said she was fine. We had passed into a cordial, if formal, stage.

I called the university's lawyer and spoke to her. She told me she would speak to Disabled Student Services on my behalf. She also suggested we meet with the campus police—we might need to obtain a restraining order to keep the student away from me. So, I met with the campus police and the lawyer several times over the next few days. I showed them the collected e-mails, and they shook their heads. My department chairman called me in to see him. "Disabled Student Services called," he said. "They wanted me to ask you if you've had a physical relationship with this student. She's suggesting you have."

Never, I told him. But I saw doubt flicker across his face. He knew I was getting a divorce. He knew why. He was not my friend, but my supervisor. His voice became distant, professional.

After three months of continuing harassment I finally received a restraining order. My student was not allowed within a football-field length of my third-floor office, which meant in effect that if she wanted to get anywhere near the English department, she'd have to hover on a cloud outside. The department chairman came to my office one day and asked if I'd show the student mercy and allow her at least to go to the English department offices. Of course I said yes.

Meanwhile, my divorce took on a sad life of its own, as divorces tend to do. At one point our court-ordered counselor told my wife and me that we were the most mature divorcing couple she had ever worked with. And it's true we were very well behaved. There were no threats or ugly outbursts, little in the way of arguing.

But our divorce was still the most painful thing I had ever been through.

The worst came when my wife announced her intention to take our daughters, ages nine and seven, and move back to her hometown, half a continent away. I'd expected and hoped to remain in my daughters' daily lives, but the next few short months would be my last, perhaps forever, of living in the same town as they.

In the middle of this awful time, close to the end of the term, I looked up from my office desk to see my student standing silently at my door, staring at me. How long she had been standing there, I couldn't tell. She did not look like the ghost of my sister. She did not look like the ghost of my marriage. She did not look like the faces of my lost daughters. But still, when she said, "Boo," I jumped.

UPDATE: *These events took place six years before the publication of this essay. In 2004, Robin was able to find a job not too far from his children and now sees them nearly every other weekend, on holidays, and in the summer. He has remarried and has another daughter. He is not, to his knowledge, presently being stalked.*

Losing Custody of My Hope

Katie Allison Granju

I'M A GOOD MOTHER. THIS IS NOT AN IDLE BOAST; I HAVE A signed certificate that says so. I earned this de facto mothering license by successfully completing four weeks of court-ordered parent classes. Why did a judge order me to do this? Was I a child abuser? Did I leave my children alone and go out to a bar? Was I on crack?

No, I got a divorce. After twelve years of marriage and three children, ages eleven, seven, and four, my college sweetheart and I broke up. In my view this was due to his chronic infidelity. If you asked him, he would recite a litany of my failings (none involving adultery). His lawyer actually once told the judge that

> There were heart-wrenching scenes, with the children clinging to me like baby monkeys as their father attempted to peel them off. Once, as I drove away, I looked in my mirror to see our seven-year-old chasing my car down the street wearing only her Hello Kitty nightgown.

my primary fault was that I hadn't been a very good housekeeper. The reality is we are both responsible for the unraveling of our marriage.

In the wake of our separation, I felt as if I might keel over and die from heartbreak. I rarely ate, slept, or ventured out. Eventually, however, I began to pull myself together, thinking the worst was surely over. But I was wrong.

Seven months into the separation I received a call from my lawyer. "Are you sitting down?" she asked. My husband, she explained, was seeking full custody of our children on the grounds that I was an "unfit mother."

An unfit mother? I was flabbergasted. For the past eleven years I'd taken care of our three healthy children without any complaint from my husband. But the oddity of the accusation also stung because, as a writer specializing in topics for parents, I consider fit mothering to be the core of my professional work. My articles on discipline and breast-feeding regularly appear in magazines, and I'm the author of a popular book on parent-child bonding and a frequent speaker on these issues.

My husband, a civil engineer, spent far less time with our children, which was fine: that was our deal. I understood the reality, even as I wished he'd been able to do more. That's why I was pleasantly surprised when, during our separation, he began devoting more time to the children.

We agreed they would spend one night a week and every other weekend at his new place, a small house he'd rented ten miles from mine. For the first time since becoming a mother at twenty-three, I could regularly have a child-free night out with friends, and I began to think his stepped-up fathering might be the silver lining in the dark clouds that had taken up residence over our family. But the children didn't want to stay overnight with Daddy in an unfamiliar house. They love their father and enjoyed going to his house for the day, but our two youngest children in particular balked at sleeping there.

Despite my assurances that it would be fun to go with Daddy and, ultimately, my firm insistence that they had to go, there were heart-wrenching scenes, with the children clinging to me like baby monkeys as their father attempted to peel them off. Once, as I drove away, I looked in my mirror to see our seven-year-old chasing my car down the street wearing only her Hello Kitty nightgown.

My husband was understandably hurt by their behavior, and frankly it was hard on me, too. No mother feels good about leaving her children where they don't want to be, even if that place is their father's house. Still, I did what I had to do, and we were finding our way, or so I thought. I never saw the custody suit coming.

After recovering somewhat from the shock of my lawyer's call, I drove to my husband's office.

"Say it to my face," I demanded.

He just looked at me.

"Tell me to my face that you believe I'm a bad mother."

He looked away and said he didn't think I was a bad mother per se, just that he believed he could do a better job as the "primary caregiver."

I blinked. *Primary caregiver?* Turns out this was just the start of his new vocabulary.

The children were "too attached" to me, he went on, claiming that it was my fault our two youngest children weren't comfortable staying with him. He'd been reading up on "parental alienation syndrome," which he believed might apply in his case. But finally, after more outraged prodding from me, he got to the bottom line. His lawyer had advised him that to get what he wanted in the divorce, he would need to take a hard line on custody because that's what mattered most to me.

"Fathers have rights, too, you know," he added, apropos of nothing as I'd never suggested that they didn't.

For the next year, my husband's bid for custody tore through my life, shredding most of what I thought I'd known about the man I'd loved for so long. To him everything I did to retain custody was somehow part of my plot to interfere with his rights as a father, and even the most mundane aspects of my life became evidence of my alleged shortcomings as a mother.

Terrified that I would mess up and lose my children, I began to censor what I said to them, afraid they'd accidentally say something to their father that might prove damaging when taken out of context. I stopped drinking the occasional beer, lest I be labeled an alcoholic. I ceased having dinner dates with male friends to avoid being branded a child-neglecting slut.

But the more I struggled to prove I was a good mother, the worse I became. I snapped at my children for little things, and I became hypercritical of his fathering, which wasn't fair to him or good for the children. I'd always been happy to send the children to a friend's house overnight; now I couldn't bear their absence. I'd pace the house and often fall asleep across one of their beds, wrapped in their blankets. You want to see a mother become "too attached" to her children? Threaten to take them away.

My husband insisted that we undergo an independent custody evaluation, which would involve interviews and testing of me, him, and the children. Fearing this would further traumatize the children, I fought and lost that battle, and I had to cough up $1,500—my half of the evaluation retainer—to allow a stranger to evaluate my parental skills.

Just about anyone can call himself a custody evaluator. Most are psychologists or social workers, but many are simply professional custody evaluators with some background in one of the helping professions.

As the date of my first evaluation neared, I pondered how I could prove I was a good mother. I don't spank my children, but one divorced friend told me that her failure to use corporal punishment was noted in her evaluation, incredibly, as a "failure to assume an appropriate parental role."

I was a stay-at-home mother until the divorce pushed me into the full-time workforce, but in the court decisions I read, stay-at-home mothers were often described as "smothering" and "without boundaries," while working mothers lacked sufficient "quality time" with their children. It seemed there was no winning.

Then the day was upon me. How to dress, I wondered, to show I was neither smothering nor distant, maternal yet not frumpy? I settled on a pink twin set, pumps, and, yes, pearls.

Whether my choices made any impression on my evaluator, I couldn't tell. He was polite and professional as he administered the interminable Minnesota Multiphasic Personality Inventory and then the Rorschach test, in which I tried to stay away from seeing anything dark, violent, or sexual in the patterns. I figured trees, flowers, and butterflies would be safe bets, but when I looked to my evaluator for signs of approval he maintained a poker face.

Next stop on the custody-battle tour: the court-ordered child-rearing classes, required of all divorcing parents in my jurisdiction. I'd put off taking them even while my husband completed his, proudly waving his certificate at the judge, who admonished me to take the classes before our next hearing.

Not long after, I found myself in a dingy meeting room at our local family services agency with dozens of other women (and a few men). Leading us were two young social workers who would offer pearls of post-divorce wisdom such as "Always use 'I statements' when talking with your ex-spouse."

One skeptical mother finally asked, "Are either of you a parent?"

"Have you ever been divorced?" another asked.

"Has your husband ever beaten you?" a third wondered.

In each case the unsurprising answer was no.

A month later I was able to wave my "parenting diploma" at the judge. And afterward, eager to test out my new skills in using "I statements," I approached my soon-to-be-ex outside the court and said, "I feel very upset with you when you sue for full custody of our children and claim I'm a bad mother."

He turned on his heel and walked away.

My story doesn't yet have an ending, much less a happy one. Only days before our children were to be tested and interviewed by the custody evaluator, my ex and I agreed in court-ordered mediation to a plan in which he would take the kids exactly 37 percent of the time and I'd have them 63 percent. But only a few weeks into this arrangement he said he couldn't live with it, and now, six months later, he's considering taking the issue back to court.

After two years of hearings, mediation, classes, evaluations, counseling sessions, and thousands of dollars in legal fees, I no longer have faith that I'll ever be relieved of the fear of losing custody of my children. Instead I realize I must treat the situation like a chronic disease, something I must learn to live with and manage rather than get past.

And I've gone back to drinking.

How Could I Tell Him What I Knew?
How Could I Not?

Sara Pepitone

SHAKEN, I CALLED MY BOYFRIEND EARLY IN THE MORN-
ing on the day before Halloween. "I really think you
should clean out your gym locker today," I told him.
"We need to wash your stuff before the marathon."

"I still have a few days," he said.

"Do it today," I urged. "Seriously."

> *What I really wanted
> was to send him a
> warning without
> breaking any rules.*

After we hung up
I began to cry. Quietly,
but visibly. He hadn't
taken the hint. What was
I going to do now?

It was the second
week of my latest temp job, a short-term stint at the
same investment bank where I had previously worked as
a regular employee. For this assignment I was in a different division in a different building. And although it was
soothing, after my weeks of post–September 11 couch
confinement, to be surrounded by activity, phones, and
chatter, I wasn't at all thrilled about the task at hand.

This division, employee relations, was a department
of smart women, mostly lawyers, who'd somehow found
themselves in the position of firing squad. While they

mechanically ran the evaluation numbers, sorted the reviews and data, vetted the prospects—all steps that helped the bank through the magnificent process of "downsizing"—I closed my eyes and ears. Among the names and statistics driving our labor were acquaintances and friends from my past life here. And, as with my boyfriend, there were some very close connections.

Fixed income, banking, technology—each area has its own employee relations representative you can call when you get a religious or pornographic e-mail, or when you accidentally have sex with your co-worker on a desk in front of a security camera. I specifically told the temp agency that I could not be part of any assignment related to the departments of equities or investment management, where my associations were closest. I'd passed another background check to get in here; it should have been clear that I was living with a current employee and was, in fact, on his benefits. Yet they decided to bring me in anyway. So, needing the work, I took it and hoped for the best.

I knew my boyfriend would need his gym stuff to survive the marathon that weekend, his first. He'd become a bit superstitious and required the routine of wearing certain clothes, socks, sneakers, even eating certain pre-running meals—pasta with farmers' market arugula, tomatoes, criminis, garlic, olive oil, and Parmesan. I wanted as much of that as possible to be in place for the race, and when he lost access to his locker the next day, which was how these things happened, he'd never have time to break in the new shoes.

I called his assistant and begged her to make sure he emptied his locker.

She laughed but promised she would. "You really want to do his laundry," she joked.

What I really wanted was to send him a warning without breaking any rules.

We met when I was full time at the bank; he started on my desk the week I took a securities exam and got a license I would end up needing only for the next six months. It was cold and gray—hockey season—when he returned from a Tahoe ski trip, tan and smiling, happily beginning his new career as an investment manager. We started making small talk about the movie *Sliding Doors,* and he didn't flinch when I told him Blythe Danner was Gwyneth Paltrow's dad; he merely smiled and said, "Mom."

Right, of course. I'm not usually so flustered around the bald ones.

Soon after, we stayed out too late and danced in a bar now closed and nearly kissed in Father Demo Square. "We work together," I protested, stopping him. "And you're too short."

Well, we did kiss. And so on. Mostly we went out, stayed up late, struggled to get into work, and ate Joe's Pizza. We didn't fight, though we did break glasses in bars (I, accidentally) and throw shoes in the street (he, comically).

By the time we moved in together, eighteen months later, the desk had changed, the bank had changed, and his mood was graying. I bounced from job to job while he stood still, both suffering from different strands of the same disease: not knowing the right direction to go.

We floated along like this until that late October morning when Claudine approached my desk offering me a stack of red folders. "Who can take these?" she asked.

"What area?" I asked.

"Equities."

I shook my head no. I didn't want to see those folders.

Anyone who'd ever had any employee-relations contact had a red folder. If you had an exit interview, you had a red folder; if you called to say your boss mentioned liking you in short skirts, you each had a red folder; if you were on the list of prospective terminations, you had a red folder. Red folders never leave employee relations.

If you graduated from "termination prospect" to "termination," you got a blue folder. Blue folders contain general information about benefits continuation and job searching and specifics about severance and investments, along with questions such as: *Do you have a gym locker? Is it empty? Where is the key?*

Employee relations support staffers (me) created blue folders the day before the ax was scheduled to fall.

"I'll take them," offered Rod, a friend from departments past. Claudine walked away as Rod flipped through the stack. We'd been in this situation before, and Rod knew the stakes; like me, he had knowledge beyond data. He paused: a match. He looked at me and nodded. Who? I wondered. But I knew; Rod's eyes were serious and steady. I didn't even notice the tears until I was safely in the bathroom, cursing.

Though I'd feared this moment, I hadn't actually imagined it. But now this was really happening, and I had not a clue what to do. Call him? Run away? Throw up? I didn't even know what I was allowed to do.

"You can't tell him," Claudine said as I stood in her office. "He'll find out tomorrow. Are you going to see him tonight?"

I tried to imagine a scenario that would keep him away from home, but I couldn't. "I probably will," I admitted.

"You can't tell him," she said again.

Would he forgive me if I didn't tell him?

Claudine told me to go home, as if he wouldn't question that, my leaving work in the middle of the day. I needed a plan.

How could I tell him? "Hey, you know how you're kind of sick of finance? Great news, you don't have to go in there anymore!"

How could I not tell him? Even if I were the kind of girl who kept her mouth shut, which I wasn't, this could not be buried, and if I tried to bury it I knew it would be worse if he found out later that I'd known.

If I tell him now, I thought, he could clean out his desk and print out anything he might need. But he also could lose his severance and have a black mark on his National Association of Securities Dealers forms. If I tell him later, he might think of things he would have done if he had known and hate me.

I was on the couch when he opened the door. Normally if he saw me there wet with tears he'd think I was watching *Felicity* on the WB, but today I had already declined an afternoon coffee and called him three times about the locker. I didn't have to say a thing.

"When?" he asked.

"Tomorrow," I cried. "I'm so sorry."

"In the morning?"

"Probably."

"Who else?"

I told him the names, hoping it would make it easier, but I couldn't stop crying. "I should have told you to grab stuff from your desk."

He sat next to me on the couch and hugged me. Then he got up and started pacing the apartment. "What should I do?"

"You can't really do anything," I sobbed. And neither could I, then.

Weeks later, when his days consisted mostly of sighting celebrities and reading *Theodore Rex* at the Greenwich Avenue Starbucks, I was actually able to have his brokerage account released from firm control so he could play and day-trade, but he wasn't up for it.

The morning after he figured out his fate, he went in early and waited. In employee relations they pulled back the blue folder of one of his peers, someone he genuinely respected. Yikes, that one would have lessened the blow. Then they debated postponing the announcement until the afternoon.

My phone rang. "What's going on?" he asked.

My heart was breaking for him. "It's still a go," I said.

And then it went, and he was sent over to my building for his exit interview. Afterward, Claudine got me so I could walk him out, but he didn't want coffee and he didn't want to talk about it and he didn't even want to see me. And he really didn't want me to tell anyone that I knew before he knew.

And the depression, confusion, and sleeplessness that followed the so-called mutual agreement that ended his employment could not be remedied by poached salmon wraps with tzatziki or spaghetti and meatballs or even a plan to move to Los Angeles.

Being with me was no help, either. If anything, it was worse, as my employee-relations assignment continued through his severance and didn't end until I rejected a full-time offer. My landing a job in another department while he continued to flounder only increased the distance between us. By the time I quit the place for good it was nearly a year into his seemingly permanent vacation, and by then his life needed more drastic measures—he, too, had to downsize before he could rebuild himself. So he gave our relationship a blue folder all its own, and we went our separate ways.

And finally it was Halloween again, years later. The sun was as bright as the costumed kids running down Court Street. "How are you?" we asked each other, a chance meeting in front of a bakery. He was tan and smiling once again, happily beginning his new career.

Paradise Lost (Domestic Division)

Terry Martin Hekker

AWHILE BACK, AT A BABY SHOWER FOR A NIECE, I OVER-heard the expectant mother being asked if she intended to return to work after the baby was born. The answer, which rocked me, was, "Yes, because I don't want to end up like Aunt Terry."

That would be me.

In the continuing case of *Full-Time Homemaker v. Working Mother,* I offer myself as Exhibit A. Because more than a quarter-century ago I wrote an Op-Ed article for the *New York Times* on the satisfaction of being a full-time housewife in the new age of the liberated woman. I wrote it from my heart, thoroughly convinced that home-making and raising my children was the most challenging and reward-ing job I could ever want.

> *I knew our first anniversary would be paper, but never expected the fortieth would be papers, sixteen of them meticulously detailing my faults and flaws, the reason our marriage, according to him, was over.*

"I come from a long line of women," I wrote, "most of them more Edith Bunker than Betty Friedan, who never knew they were unfulfilled. I can't testify that they were happy, but they were cheerful. They took pride in a clean, comfortable home and satisfaction in serving a good meal because no one had explained that the only work worth doing is that for which you get paid."

I wasn't advocating that mothers forgo careers to stay home with their children; I was simply defending my choice as a valid one. The mantra of the age may have been "Do your own thing," but as a full-time home-maker, that didn't seem to mean me.

The column morphed into a book titled *Ever Since Adam and Eve,* followed by a national tour on which I, however briefly, became the authority on homemaking as a viable choice for women. I ultimately told my story on *Today* and to Dinah Shore, Charlie Rose, and even to Oprah, when she was the host of a local TV show in Baltimore.

In subsequent years I lectured on the rewards of homemaking and housewifery. While others tried to make the case that women like me were parasites and little more than legalized prostitutes, I spoke to rapt audiences about the importance of being there for your children as they grew up, of the satisfactions of "making a home," preparing family meals, and supporting your hardworking husband.

So I was predictably stunned and devastated when, on our fortieth wedding anniversary, my husband presented me with a divorce. I knew our first anniversary would be paper, but I never expected the fortieth would be papers, sixteen of them meticulously detailing my faults and flaws, the reason our marriage, according to him, was over.

We had been married by a bishop, with a blessing from the pope, in a country church filled with honeysuckle and hope. Five children and six grandchildren later we were divorced by a third-rate judge in a suburban courthouse reeking of dust and despair.

Our long marriage had its full share of love, complications, illnesses, joy, and stress. Near the end we were in a dismal period, with my husband in treatment for alcoholism. And although I had made more than my share of mistakes, I never expected to be served with divorce papers. I was stunned to find myself, at this stage of life, marooned. And it was small comfort that I wasn't alone. There were many other confused women of my age and circumstance, who'd been married just as long, sharing my situation.

I was in my teens when I first read Dickens's *Great Expectations,* with the tale of Miss Havisham, who, stood up by her groom-to-be, spent decades in her yellowing wedding gown, sitting at her cobweb-covered bridal banquet table, consumed with plotting revenge. I felt then that to be left waiting at the altar with a church full of people must be the most crushing thing that could happen to a woman.

I was wrong. No jilted bride could feel as embarrassed and humiliated as a woman in her sixties discarded by her husband. I was confused and scared, and the pain of being tossed aside by the love of my life made bitterness unavoidable. In those first few bewildering months, as

I staggered and wailed though my life, I made Miss Havisham look like a good sport.

Sitting around my kitchen with two friends who had also been dumped by their husbands, I figured out that among the three of us we'd been married 110 years. We'd been faithful wives, good mothers, cooks, and house-keepers who'd married in the fifties, when "dress for suc-cess" meant a wedding gown and when "wife" was a tenured position.

Turns out we had a lot in common with our outdated kitchen appliances. Like them we were serviceable, low-maintenance, front loading, self-cleaning, and (relatively) frost-free. Also like them we had warranties that had run out. Our husbands sought sleeker models with features we lacked, who could execute tasks we'd either never learned or couldn't perform without laughing.

Like most loyal wives of our generation, we'd con-templated eventual widowhood but never thought we'd end up divorced. And *divorced* doesn't begin to describe the pain of this process. *Canceled* is more like it. It began with my credit cards, then my health insurance and checkbook, until, finally, like a used postage stamp, I felt canceled, too.

I faced frightening losses and was overwhelmed by the injustice of it all. He got to take his girlfriend to Cancun, while I got to sell my engagement ring to pay the roofer. When I filed my first nonjoint tax return, it triggered the shocking notification that I had become eli-gible for food stamps.

The judge had awarded me alimony that was less than I was used to getting for household expenses, and now

I had to use that money to pay bills I'd never seen before: mortgage, taxes, insurance, and car payments. And that princely sum was awarded for only four years, the judge suggesting that I go for job training when I turned sixty-seven. Not only was I unprepared for divorce itself, I was utterly lacking in skills to deal with the brutal aftermath.

I read about the young mothers of today—educated, employed, self-sufficient—who drop out of the work-force when they have children, and I worry and wonder. Perhaps it is the right choice for them. Maybe they'll be fine. But the fragility of modern marriage suggests that at least half of them may not be.

Regrettably, women whose husbands are devoted to their families and are good providers must nevertheless face the specter of future abandonment. Surely the seeds of this wariness must have been planted, even if they can't believe it could ever happen to them. Many have witnessed their own mothers jettisoned by their own fathers and seen divorced friends trying to rear children with marginal financial and emotional support.

These young mothers are often torn between wanting to be home with their children and the statistical possibility of future calamity, aware that one of the most poverty-stricken groups in today's society are divorced older women. The feminine and sexual revolutions of the last few decades have had their shining victories, but have they, in the end, made things any easier for mothers?

I cringe when I think of that line from my Op-Ed article about the lineage of women I'd come from and belonged to who were able to find fulfillment as homemakers "because no one had explained" to us "that the only work worth doing is that for which you get paid." For a divorced mother, the harsh reality is that the work for which you do get paid is the only work that will keep you afloat.

These days couples face complex negotiations over work, family, child care, and housekeeping. I see my children dealing with these issues in their marriages, and I understand the stresses and frustrations. It becomes evident that where traditional marriage through the centuries had been a partnership based on mutual dependency, modern marriage demands greater self-sufficiency.

While today's young women know from the start they'll face thorny decisions regarding careers, marriage, and children, those of us who married in the fifties anticipated lives similar to our mothers' and grandmothers'. Then we watched with bewilderment as all the rules changed, and the goalposts were moved.

If I had it to do over again, I'd still marry the man I married and have my children: they are my treasure and a powerful support system for me and for one another. But I would have used the years after my youngest started school to further my education. I could have amassed two doctorates using the time and energy I gave to charitable and community causes and been better able to support myself.

But in a lucky twist, my community involvement resulted in my being appointed to fill a vacancy on our village board. I had been serving as titular deputy mayor of my hometown (Nyack, New York) when my husband left me. Several weeks later the mayor chose not to run again, because of failing health, and I was elected to succeed him, becoming the first female mayor.

I held office for six years, a challenging, full-time job that paid a whopping annual salary of eight thousand dollars. But it consumed me and gave me someplace to go every day and most nights, and as such it saved my sanity. Now, mostly retired except for some part-time work, I am kept on my toes by twelve amazing grandchildren.

My anachronistic book was written while I was in a successful marriage that I expected would go on forever. Sadly, it now has little relevance for modern women, except perhaps as a cautionary tale—never its intended purpose. So I couldn't imagine writing a sequel. But my friend Elaine did come up with a perfect title: *Disregard First Book*.

UPDATE: *After the publication of this essay, Terry found herself in much the same position she was in more than twenty-five years before—appearing yet again on the* Today *show, being asked to lecture about her cautionary tale of full-time motherhood, and being urged to write that second book,* Disregard First Book, *which she is indeed currently writing.*

A Leap of Faith

Renee Watabe

A LOT OF PEOPLE THINK I WAS BRAINWASHED. HOW ELSE to explain why I would allow Reverend Moon of the Unification Church to choose my spouse? Most people regard the choice of a life partner as a deeply personal decision, perhaps the most important decision anyone has the opportunity to make, and if you give up that choice you must be out of your mind. From the outside looking in, this evaluation makes perfect sense.

> *Was I brainwashed? Eighteen years later, on the verge of divorce, I still find the Reverend Moon's vision a beautiful one.*

Me, I like to look at things once, twice, again and again. When I was a little girl, my father, a chemical engineer, told me if you chew a piece of bland bread over and over, holding it in your mouth, it eventually becomes sweet. He was trying to explain to me about the breakdown of the molecules into glucose and such.

But what sticks in my mind is the deeper meaning I saw in what he'd said: how anything, any experience, conversation, scene observed, or moment reflected upon, is like that bland piece of bread. Look at it a while, chew it, hold it, and it becomes sweet and satisfying. There are hidden surprises and hidden flavors residing in everything and everybody.

So how did I find myself on a spring day in 1987, sitting on a bench by a pond in Central Park with a complete stranger, licking a vanilla ice cream cone, watching the toy sailboats racing by, and discussing our future together as husband and wife?

I'd met him only an hour or two earlier. He, like me, was a member of the Unification Church and had been invited to the grand ballroom of the New Yorker hotel, where Sun Myung Moon was to perform a matchmaking ceremony, pairing a thousand brides with a thousand grooms.

"Love your enemy," he preached, in echo of Jesus.

As we saw it, the path to world peace was through a coupling of the historically polarized: black and white, East and West, Jewish and Muslim. So many nations and religions are historical enemies. We "Moonies" were willing to sacrifice personal choice to spin gold out of the raw silk of ourselves, to help create world harmony through family harmony.

"I put you together not for your own happiness," stated our spiritual leader, "but for the beautiful children your marriages will produce." Children whose very existence would challenge established notions of racism.

With me, Reverend Moon was preaching to the choir: I was the product of an intercultural marriage myself. Back in the 1950s, my white, Kansas-born mother had married my Chinese father, who hailed from Shanghai. When they were wed, their marriage was illegal in most of the southern states. But my mother and father loved each other, and their racially blended relationship was a model for me.

So when Reverend Moon asked for those of us who wanted an international marriage to stand, I stepped forward. It wasn't long before he approached me, grasped the sleeve of my dress, and tugged me to the middle of the room. I glanced up at the serious face of a handsome young man whom I later learned was born in Japan. We bowed briefly in silence, and went off to get acquainted.

In a room just off of the grand ballroom, I looked at the young man next to me, born halfway around the world from my American hometown. In a sense, I didn't care who he was or what he looked like, only that he was willing, with me, to enter into this commitment to an ideal.

The first words he spoke to me were, "I never want to break this."

"Neither do I," I answered.

He liked to draw. So did I.

He liked to read good books. So did I.

He was a man. I was a woman.

So far, so good.

I had the feeling that God was living in this space between us, and that God, like a baby or a tender plant, needed our care and attendance in order to thrive. There was an undeniable sense of holiness about the whole endeavor.

As is customary, following our engagement and marriage ceremony, several years passed before we consummated our marriage. We were sent on separate church missions: I to South Korea, he to the American Midwest. We understood that a union built upon a foundation of celibacy would purify us for married life and allow us to dedicate our hearts to God and mankind first, spouse and family second.

Was I brainwashed? I sit here writing this, eighteen years and three children later, on the verge of divorce. Did he and I finally fail after all we'd been through? We certainly haven't turned out to be the ideal picture-perfect family we set out to be. Even so, I still find Reverend Moon's vision a beautiful one, this path remarkable, this project admirable. It's just that my husband and I didn't know how hard and gritty the path would be.

Yet I honestly don't think I was more brainwashed than any young bride who, starry-eyed, says yes to the man of her choosing. The one she met at work, or in a coffee shop, or on a blind date, or in art class. Marriage under any circumstances requires a leap of faith no matter who you are or how your paths may have crossed. My husband and I ate our ice cream, took a chance, and leapt.

It was difficult from the start, of course. But we soldiered on. After all, why should achieving a peaceful marriage be any easier than creating a peaceful world? So years passed, our children were born. One was diagnosed with cancer at age one, and for two straight years fought for his life, and we fought with him—a hardship, I'm told, that either binds a husband and wife closer together or tears them apart. With us it did neither.

Initially I attributed our relationship's ongoing strife and my husband's overall remoteness and anger to "cultural misunderstandings." Then I shifted into the mode of telling myself, "If only I were a better wife." Whatever the case, I didn't allow myself to consider breaking my wedding vows. My tradition-laden double whammy of being both Asian and religious made the idea of divorce extremely distasteful. Add to that the motto of our movement—"Live for the sake of others"—and any suffering I might incur from the agreement was rendered inconsequential.

I prayed. I read *Fascinating Womanhood,* which my Christian friends guaranteed would yield the desired result: a happy hubby. In my attempts to be a "domestic goddess" I got my hair done, bought pretty lingerie, read the Bible, and prayed harder. After consulting a spiritualist, I prepared a meal and offered it to the presumably angry ancestors of my even angrier husband by throwing it into the Hudson River. None of it worked.

Finally I came to understand what was missing. The religious call to "love your enemy" included loving that enemy as you would love yourself, and I didn't love myself. In all the sacrificing I'd done for marriage, children, and world peace, I'd lost a sense of who I was and what I wanted.

And so I deliberately set out to recapture that sense: I began to draw, to paint, and to write. I started having conversations with people from decades past, significant friends from the days before my celibacy and arranged marriage.

I got in touch with a dear old friend who was gay. He was successful, doing work he loved, and, most important, he was in love.

"He fills a need in me that is so deep," he said of his lover. "If he didn't exist, I'd have had to dream him up just to go on."

These words intoxicated me. I wanted that for myself.

One evening I removed my wedding rings in front of my husband, held them up, and made my declaration. "We need to do something," I said. "We should try counseling. Something . . . please."

I placed the rings on top of our bedroom dresser.

"When this marriage is a genuine marriage of heart," I continued, "I will put them back on."

But he wouldn't discuss the unhappiness of our marriage, and we never made it to counseling. The rings never made it back to my finger.

Eventually I fell in love with someone else, whose heart miraculously chose me in return. And this experience felt more scriptural, holy, and biblical than all the dogma I had tried to live up to for so many years. It was a revelation and it made me wonder, How could I simply have given all this power away?

People marry for all kinds of reasons other than love: to please their families, to satisfy economic demands, to submit to the guidelines of their religious faith. Cults do indeed come in all shapes and sizes. You don't need to become a "Moonie" to lose yourself; nearly any club, political party, or organized religion has the necessary ingredients.

And, of course, marriages dissolve for all kinds of reasons, too, even those that begin with love. But in one measure my marriage was an undeniable success: my husband and I were blessed with three loving children who are happy, healthy, and wise beyond their years.

Concerned about how our children were handling the separation and impending divorce, I sat down the other day with my twelve-year-old daughter. I meant to reassure her, but it was she who reassured me.

"Maybe God put you and Daddy together to have the three of us," she said. "And maybe now it's okay for you not to be married. Just look at how happy you are these days."

A marriage can end; perhaps it even can be doomed from the start. But it's impossible for me to look at my children and regret the chance my husband and I took, that jump into the unknown we made on that beautiful spring day, sitting by the pond in Central Park.

Part Six

Bound

FAMILY TIES

Beyond Divorce and Even Death, a Promise Kept

Jennifer R. Just

IT'S DONE: I'VE FINALLY FINISHED MOVING MY EX-HUSBAND'S belongings back into the large, cluttered farmhouse we used to share. He won't be coming back, but his shirts once again weigh down the closet rack, his boxes of household gadgets and financial files clog the attic and basement, and the furniture that wouldn't fit into the house now fills the third bay of the car barn.

Three years ago our marriage was ending. Corey and I had "outgrown" each other, shorthand for the malaise that had entered our marriage and despite our best efforts wouldn't leave. We were still friends; we didn't have big fights. All in all we'd had a pretty good marriage, and so we'd spent a lot of time discussing the necessity of divorcing.

> *It was hard to know how much to bring back of a man I had begun to extricate from my life.*

We had our boys to consider—Evan, nine, and Cameron, thirteen—along with eighteen years of shared memories. And the idea of living apart unsettled us. When you've lived most of your adult life with someone else, you don't know what you can and can't do on your own anymore, what you can and can't live without.

Neither of us, however, seemed able to muster enough imagination to see a happy future together. We were less husband and wife than tenants living in the same house.

Although we had a good partnership when it came to raising our children, we didn't share much of anything else and didn't want to. But when we did decide to end our marriage, we did so with one caveat.

One night, in discussing what might happen after the split, Corey and I found ourselves promising that we'd always watch each other's backs. He had an especially concrete reason to worry: he had multiple sclerosis. Although the disease had progressed slowly, its unpredictability meant he could slide further downhill at any time.

"Listen," I told him. "Worse comes to worst, we move you back here. You just come back."

I don't know why it was so easy for me to promise to hold a space for him in my life and for him to promise the same. Maybe we had decided we could keep some parts of our wedding vows after all.

When we finally did separate, Corey bought a little beach house twenty minutes away in West Haven, Connecticut, that seemed to say so much about what he wanted and what he'd chosen to leave behind. He'd always been a minimalist (in contrast with my penchant for cleaning out tag sales and relatives' attics), and his new place, a clean-lined Cape, reflected his aesthetic. It had few surfaces to crowd with family memorabilia, a lot of room for his books, and the view of the water he'd always wanted.

I was happy for him, and I was happy for me, too, that once again I could be my messy and complicated self without apology. Even the kids seemed happier. Now they reveled in the time he was carving out for them: entire weekends and weeknights when it was just him and the boys.

Last Fourth of July, Cameron, Evan, and I were on our way back from a trip to Long Island when we decided to call Corey. His beach had a spectacular view of our region's fireworks, an immense parabola of light running up and down the coasts of Connecticut and New York.

He was thrilled to hear from us; he was missing the boys, he said, and by coincidence was marinating way too much chicken. So we dropped by for dinner, and when darkness fell, we walked down to the beach for the show.

Instantly Corey and I fell into our old patterns with our sons, joking with them as we always had, making up stories, and laughing as we rarely did with anyone.

But when the noise and light subsided, it was time to go home, which for us of course meant separate homes. We shared a history and children, but what we had did not quite add up to a marriage. And that was okay. That night we'd found a way of being together that worked for us and our kids.

The next Saturday, I dropped off the boys to spend a whole week with their dad, and then I took them again for dinner the next Monday night.

Wednesday was Parents' Day at the boys' camp, and Corey was supposed to join me there, but he never came.

I figured something had come up and decided not to bother him. But when I got home, I found ten voice mail messages waiting. The first was from Corey's sister, crying, asking me to call her right away.

Corey's parents, I thought. Something's happened to his parents.

The second message, however, was from the West Haven Police, saying they needed to speak to me immediately. I didn't have to play any of the other messages. I never have.

Corey had died the morning before, alone in his little house, of a heart ailment no one knew he had.

In the sleepless nights that followed, questions tormented me: If we'd still been living in the same house, would I have been able to save him? Had divorce really been necessary? Might we have found a way back to our marriage after enough (too much) time being single?

I easily could have spent my waking hours obsessing over such questions, but I had to take care of our sons. And soon I realized I had to keep my promise to Corey.

True, I'd promised to move him back in with us if his health failed, but this wasn't exactly what I'd bargained for. For starters, in the original plan he was alive, and my agonized decisions about what to keep or toss were to have been his to make, he who never agonized about anything. Second, it was hard to know how much to bring back of a man I had begun to extricate from my life. I'd been unraveling the threads of our joined lives, but now I was faced with having to pick up some of those stitches and weave the tapestry back together.

Back up on the wall went the family photos I'd taken down when Corey moved out. I reserved one bookshelf for his books, so the boys would know what he read. His CDs, too, got their own shelf near the stereo. I felt I had to restore his presence in our house. How else to show that he was once here? That he is, in some measure, still here?

There are hours of videotape, and someday I will edit them. But will I tell our sons the true story of our life (there are uneasy harbingers of the demise of our marriage in certain exchanges on those tapes), or will I decide to create a more easily digested version? This, too, is up to me and me alone.

Moving him home also involved closing up his beach house, dealing with his financial accounts, tracking down the far-flung friends who had no way of knowing he was gone, and otherwise wiping his life clean.

I thought it would be easier to incorporate his life back into ours if I took him home gradually, in carloads, over a period of weeks. And it was good I took the time and did it alone, because while packing I found things he might have preferred to keep boxed up: evidence of the girlfriend he hadn't yet introduced to the boys, X-rated gifts from office pals.

Archivist that I am by nature, I considered each item for its possible historical value. Did it say anything significant about who Corey was? His girlfriend, after all, had been a big part of his life; it wasn't right to expunge all evidence of her existence.

Last month I made my final trip to Corey's house to clean it before the new owners took possession. I scrubbed the bathroom, the refrigerator, the floors, and the walls with an uncharacteristic thoroughness that would have made Corey laugh.

I sat one last time in the upstairs hall where he died and, as in the past, tried to imagine what he might have seen in his last moments. I like to think that he chose to fix his eye on an image to take with him as he went from this place to the next. If so, his eye might easily have caught the black-and-white photo just outside his office of our boys, then four and seven, dressed as pirates, eyes glaring at the photographer as if to say: *Come at us with everything you have. We're ready.*

Of course they were just playing at it then.

I hope Corey was able to take that image with him. As much as I am keeping, I like to think he kept something, too.

I finished. Wiped the pared fingernails from the bathroom sink and silvery hairs from the shower. Rinsed a few errant parsley leaves from the vegetable crisper. Packed the handful of items I'd somehow missed: a flyswatter, hangers, socks.

I brought them back to our home, full to bursting with what was left of my ex-husband.

It has been a heartbreak and an honor to be Corey's "one," to have been, despite the failure of our marriage, the most important person in his life.

Yes, we were heading into our separate futures. Yes, he had a girlfriend who would probably have met the boys in due time. Yet in the end I was the one who went to sweep the corners clean, to save what was precious, and to close the door on his life. Don't we all hope that when our time comes, we will have one such person left who will know what to do and feel privileged to do it?

Ten months after Corey's death, the boys are moving on admirably with their lives, having perhaps inherited their father's levelheadedness in such matters. And I have kept the promise I made to Corey back when we both thought he would live long enough to become infirm: I have brought him home.

UPDATE: *Eight months after Corey died, Jennifer's best friend, Philip Horvitz, also died, also of a heart arrhythmia, while flying from New York City to San Francisco. Because he was gay and unattached, and because his family lived farther away than she did, Jennifer found herself wrapping up Philip's life in much the same way she had done for Corey.*

Eight months later, Jennifer's longtime college boyfriend Jonathan Wayne died, in his sleep, of a heart attack. They were due to see each other for the first time in twenty years in May 2006, at their twenty-fifth Brown University reunion.

And three months after that, Jennifer experienced a heart arrhythmia of her own that sent her to the hospital. Doctors recommended a catheter ablation to find and destroy the tissue that was causing her heart to malfunction. In a procedure that lasted two and a half hours, the cardiologist fixed her heart, which has been beating steadily ever since.

When Mr. Reliable Becomes Mr. Needy

Katherine Tanney

MY MOTHER LIVED A SHORT DRIVE FROM THE NURSING home where, early last year, my father died. Yet she was not with him at the end, nor did she know that her three daughters were in town, gathered around his bedside. As his ability to draw breath slowly ebbed, it is probable that she was at home watching HBO, reading a novel, or fixing herself a snack. They were married forty-seven years—"all wonderful," to quote my mother, who apparently wasn't counting the last five, when her husband, at sixty-three, became ill with Alzheimer's, her world disintegrated, and nothing between them was ever wonderful again.

> *Magazines were full of articles about couples dealing heroically with Alzheimer's. You and me against the world. How many marriages are based on some form of this sentiment, and what happens when the world unexpectedly scores a coup?*

That's the ending. Concise, cold. Yet what does an ending say, really, about a life, a marriage? My mother's complaints began six years ago, when she told my sisters and me over the phone that our father was being "mean" to her and "impossible to deal with." He left the burner on in the kitchen. He needed help figuring out which end of his shirt to pull over his head. At 2:00 a.m., he shaved and dressed, then went to the curb for the morning paper, waking my mother to complain when it wasn't there. Worst of all, she said, was his stubborn insistence that nothing was the matter with him.

It is not hard for me to imagine their arguments during this period. My mother always reacted to things that frightened her by going on the attack or running away, and my father could be quite stubborn, even vindictive. The thing was, when my sisters and I observed our father firsthand, we saw none of the paranoia or belligerence she described. To us, he simply appeared a lot needier than before, more forgetful, and disconcertingly unaware that his perceptions no longer corresponded to reality.

It should be said that "needy" and "impossible" always had been my mother's signature traits, while my father was Mr. Reliable, Mr. Self-Control. He calmly took us to McDonald's on nights she was too busy slamming doors or breaking beloved objects to prepare dinner. On other occasions, when we went out as a family, he dutifully came around the car to open her door and gave the waiter her order as she sat and posed.

"The lady will have . . ." he always began.

My parents had big plans for their golden years, plans they both understood from the earliest days of their marriage. My father was tall and handsome, watchful and quiet, from a broken, modest home. My mother was outspoken and creative, furious and impulsive, from a wealthy, accomplished family. The longer they stayed married, the closer they came to her inheritance and their helium dreams of owning a retirement home in Aspen or a pied-à-terre in Paris or Manhattan. This is what my parents were about. They believed that money was for the exclusive purpose of giving themselves pleasurable experiences. Rarely did they contribute to charities, political causes, or even to the public television and radio stations they enjoyed. Their money supported pricey restaurants and performing arts box offices, makers of costly apparel, home furnishings, fine art, and fancy cars.

But then the Alzheimer's was diagnosed, which had not been in my mother's plan, and her response was to shut down. To our suggestion that she find a support group, she said, "I called. It's for widows, not people with living spouses."

To our recommendation that she find a therapist, she complained, "If they really cared, they wouldn't charge."

When we urged her to get someone to help her out, she said, "I can't have strangers in my house."

Rather than educate herself about the disease and how to handle it, she assigned my father chores to complete in the garden and around the house, as though disciplined work could restore order to their lives. Instead he'd wander away, get on a bus—he had lost his driving privileges by then—and turn up hours later in a cab, leaving the clueless driver to deal with my mother's foul state.

Those were the final days for them, when the flood of loving words my mother issued for her husband were in sobbing past tense, as though he had already passed away.

The man she was living with she considered a stranger she had to drive to the doctor and keep a constant eye on, but with whom a good conversation was no longer possible.

I often wondered how other spouses coped. Magazines were full of articles about couples dealing heroically with Alzheimer's, families coming together to care for the afflicted member. *You and me against the world.* How many marriages are based on some form of this sentiment, and what happens when the world unexpectedly scores a coup?

My father, who had always defended the worst of my mother's words and deeds, was now dependent upon the one who had depended upon him the most. In the absence of anyone my mother could blame for this betrayal, she blamed him. When my sisters and I learned from her that our father was roaming the city on foot without money or food or water, and that she refused to go get him when he called from pay phones in dangerous neighborhoods, lost and disoriented, it was finally agreed that for his own good he should be moved away from her.

So began my parents' separate journeys, still tumultuous because of my mother's increasingly erratic decision making. She developed an unprecedented fear of spending money that led to my father being moved six times in the final four and a half years of his life.

First he lived with my sister, who employed private help to attend to him when she was at work. When his condition worsened, we moved him to an assisted-living center, where his eventual incontinence triggered a rate hike my mother refused to pay. We found another place. Then, claiming she had come to the end of his money and citing a sudden desire to be with her beloved until the end, my mother announced her intention to discontinue paying again.

"I'm going to take care of him myself," she said. He'd been gone almost three years by then, during which she'd seen him only twice, when he could still walk, still speak. Despite our objections and explanations about his advanced condition, she moved him back home, where he lasted only three days before he got hurt, forcing her to call 911.

"I wash my hands of him," she told the hospital social worker on the phone. "I'm not paying another penny."

There are many things I've left out: walks my orphaned father and I shared; laughs we had; the entrance of lawyers into our lives, with their legalese and bills; the volley of angry communications between mother and daughters; scenes from the homes where Alzheimer's patients live together in a cuckoo's nest of monotony. I gave my father a big stuffed animal with a bell in its tail. He liked the feel of the fur under his fingers. I bought him a ball, and we played catch, which he was exceptionally good at. He enjoyed being touched and talked to.

At approximately the same time that my mother washed her hands of my father, she came into her inheritance. After his death, she continued to live in their five-bedroom, split-level canyon home, complete with deck, hot tub, and state-of-the-art kitchen. The kind of architecturally interesting house you might see in a magazine, all right angles and vertical thrust, it was worth more than a million dollars. Somewhere in that house, presumably in a tasteful urn, she kept my father's ashes. My sisters and

I had paid the crematorium bill, but when my mother found out about his death she insisted on paying what was owed and keeping his ashes with her. After all, it was his trouble she couldn't deal with, and now that he was no longer trouble she wanted him back.

I was not on speaking terms with my mother when my father died, and neither were my sisters. In a message she left me after he went, she told me I would die "alone and penniless"—for abandoning her, I presume, just as she had abandoned my father. And then, six months later, right before she was scheduled for bypass surgery, my mother had a heart attack.

I took my time getting out to see her, partly because she was unconscious and not expected to pull through and partly because I suspected my presence would offer little in the way of comfort. But when I finally got there, the sight of my mother—every bit as helpless and desiccated as my father had been—rendered the past newly irrelevant, and we ended our years of discord on a grace note. She died five weeks later.

It is hard for me to accept this wrenching example of familial dissolution handed to me midway through my own bumpy life. What is the moral? Who is the villain? Shouldn't we all, after so many years with my mother, have known what she was and wasn't capable of? And is it possible my father might have condoned her behavior, or at least forgiven it, if he'd been able to think straight? "Shoot me now," I imagine him saying at the outset, had he been able to see what was coming and what it would cost.

Did my parents have a "wonderful" marriage? Of course they didn't. Nor was it so bad. They had a marriage.

My father had a death. It should have been better, but such is the nature of survival and love. Last week, one of my dogs found a weakling of a bird in the grass and killed it slowly, expertly prolonging its life to keep it a toy for as long as possible. Watching through the window, I was torn apart and enlightened.

I used to think the final moment of life was the moment of truth, and I worried about it. I attempted bizarre feats of imagination, such as trying to will my own death during a moment of exquisite happiness. "Now," I coaxed the universe, my eyes shut, my breath on hold, "take me now." Because I knew all too well what tends to follow exquisite happiness, and I desperately wanted the universe to make an exception for me.

Dedicated to Two Women, Only One of Them Alive

Brendan Halpin

MY WIFE IS ABOUT TO DIE. AS I LEAVE THE HOSPICE to pick up our daughter at school, I tell Kirsten I love her. She is bald, gaunt, jaundiced, and slipping in and out of consciousness. It takes a lot of effort for her to speak. "I love you," I tell her, and she surfaces briefly and rasps "I love you, too." It's the last thing she will ever say to me.

I take our seven-year-old daughter, Rowen, from school to the hospice for a brief visit, and later that night, I go back alone and sit by Kirsten's bed with her parents and sister. Kirsten is unconscious, rasping and moaning with every breath. Sometimes there

> *She said the only thing that would make dying unbearable was thinking that Rowen and I would be unhappy forever.*

is a long pause between her breaths, and though it's become clear to me that prayer is ineffective, each time this long pause happens I just pray that she's dead because I can't stand for her to be alive like this.

I fall asleep holding her hand, and I wake up at one in the morning. I tell Kirsten's family I have to leave, because Kirsten and I agreed in advance that it was important for me to be with Rowen at bedtime and in the morning. I kiss Kirsten goodbye, and five hours later, it's Kirsten's parents and sister, and not me, who are with her, singing, as she dies. I know I did what Kirsten wanted, but still. We were together for fourteen years. I wish I had been there.

Weeks later, I have a dream. Kirsten, Rowen, and I are in the same mall where Kirsten and I went walking to try to get her contractions restarted on the frigid January day when Rowen was born. There's a bookstore on the third floor, and Kirsten and I take escalators all the way up. Suddenly I realize that I don't know where our daughter is. "Where's Rowen?" I ask Kirsten, beginning to panic. She is unfazed. "I guess she's still down by the bathrooms."

"Well, I have to go get her," I say, and as I get into the elevator, I see Kirsten heading into the bookstore. On the ground floor, I get off the elevator and find Rowen. I throw my arms around her and wake up. I'm at home, in my bed, where I need to be, with the living and not the dead. I am annoyed with my subconscious for choosing the mall as a metaphor, though I am comforted by the idea of the afterlife as a bookstore. If that's true, I'm sure Kirsten is content.

Of course, I don't really believe that's where she is. But she's certainly not here. Oh, I have some of her ashes with us in Boston, and, since I gave out baggies of ashes like party favors at her funeral, she's in the ocean, and in Georgia, Virginia, Pennsylvania, Illinois, and California. I will never again hear the ZZ Top song "I'm Bad, I'm Nationwide" without thinking of Kirsten.

But while some people talk about feeling the presence of their loved ones after their death, that's not the case for me. Kirsten is bad, she's nationwide, and she's completely gone. I can get through the days on automatic pilot. But at night, when I'm not crying, I'm furious: that my daughter will never have anything but a seven-year-old's knowledge of her mother; that so many evil, humorless clods are still living while my whip-smart wife with the razor wit is not. My daughter lives in the moment, makes me laugh, and gives me a reason to get out of bed in the morning. But now even the most mundane parenting decision becomes fraught with significance, because it reminds me I have to make every decision on my own: nobody else to consult, commiserate with, or blame.

I need a distraction, so I fixate on the idea of getting a date. Kirsten half seriously told me I could start dating after two years, and it's been only five months. But she also told me that the only thing that would make dying unbearable was thinking that Rowen and I would be unhappy forever. "You have to be happy," she told me. "You have to." I think it might make me happy to have a date, so I decide the serious instruction to be happy trumps the half-serious dating timetable.

I spend a week going through the humiliating process of creating an online personal ad. I write a desperate, needy, excessively long response to a woman who has a snarky sense of humor and bears a somewhat disturbing resemblance to Kirsten. Mercifully, she doesn't write me back. I then spend a couple of weeks exchanging e-mails with an attractive single mom. The e-mails lead to a phone call in which she talks about how difficult it is to date, and I get scared and don't ask her out because I realize I don't even really know what dating is. I met Kirsten in college; I've never dated as a real adult. It appears that it's terrifying and stressful. The hell with it.

Another month goes by, making seven since Kirsten died, and I've given up on getting a date anytime soon. I do, however, sometimes have nice conversations with a teacher at Rowen's school—a single parent like me— who is outside doing bus duty at drop-off. I think she's cool and smart and sexy, and she confirms all three when she tells me that she is going to Ladies' Rock and Roll Camp over April vacation. I am convinced that someone as alluring and joyful as she is could never be interested in anyone as awkward and depressed as me, but these morning conversations do feel flirtatious, and when she comes back from rock camp and gives me the lyrics to the song she wrote, I think, Am I crazy, or does she *like* me like me? I give her a copy of my novel, but I don't inscribe it because I'm paralyzed trying to think of what to write.

She e-mails me to tell me she likes the novel, and then our e-mails become phone calls, and we spend hours on the phone every night. I start mixing CDs for her. My friends say that's cute, and aren't we just like a couple of teenagers. I tell them that two single parents trying to date is a lot like two teenagers trying to date, except that the people preventing us from leaving the house at night are much smaller.

Eventually we both get some babysitting and we have a date. It's a walk in the park, which quickly turns into sitting in the park, and before long I am kissing a woman other than my wife. It feels good, and I don't feel guilty.

The phone calls continue, and we have a couple of "family dates," where Rowen and I get together with Suzanne and her two kids, and after one of those dates, Rowen says to me, "Are you going to get married again?"

"Uh, I don't know," I say. "I mean, maybe someday."

"Well, you know," she says, "this business can't go on forever."

"This business with Suzanne?"

"No," she says to me in that you-are-so-dumb-I-can't-believe-it tone with which all parents are familiar. "This business of not having a wife."

Late one night, after agonizing about it for days—*Do I really?* Yeah. *Is it time?* Maybe. *Will I scare her off?* Probably not, but maybe. *Am I really sure?* Yeah—I tell Suzanne that I love her.

"What did you say? You're mumbling."

I repeat myself, trying my best to articulate and project. "I love you."

I feel relieved and happy, but also guilty. For fourteen years those words belonged only to Kirsten. But now, they also belong to Suzanne.

And so, for the first time in my life, I find myself in love with two women at the same time. If both were alive, this would constitute a pretty serious problem. But here's the thing: I'm down here in the mall, and Kirsten is up in the bookstore. It would be a stupid waste of time for me to stand here on the ground floor staring longingly at the bookstore when I've found somebody to go to the Orange Julius with.

A month later, I am invited to the wedding of a former student. Suzanne agrees to be my date, and we get all dressed up—she looks breathtaking—and we drive to the church. We sit with a group of my former students, and they hug me. They are laughing and joking, and I feel proud to be with Suzanne, proud to be invited to this wedding, and happy to see so many people who have been so important to me.

But when the bride and groom arrive at the altar, I feel my chest tightening, my heart racing, and my tear ducts itching. I feel like jumping out of my skin, running from the church to save myself. I actually don't know why until the bride and groom are saying their vows, and suddenly I am back in a different church ten years ago, swearing to Kirsten and God and a church full of people that I will love and honor her in sickness and in health until death do us part. I was only twenty-six and didn't understand, didn't believe that the sickness and death parts of those vows would come true so horribly soon.

The bride and groom walk out arm in arm, the happy music plays, the attendants stream down the aisle with big, goofy smiles on their faces, and I'm lurched back into the present, surrounded again by people I love, holding the hand of one of the women I love, the one who's here and looking concerned at me right now.

Suzanne gives my hand a squeeze. "Are you okay, sweetie?"

"Yeah," I say. "I think so."

UPDATE: *One week after this essay was published, Brendan proposed to Suzanne. They bought a new house together in April of 2005 and were married in July of 2005. They live with their children, Casey, Rowen, and Kylie, in Jamaica Plain, Massachusetts.*

Looking at My Father, Inside and Out

Kerry Reilly

IT IS NEARLY MIDNIGHT WHEN I GET HOME FROM MY WAITRESS job. I've been out of college for two years and have moved back into my mother's home in Islip, New York, for the summer to save money for graduate school. When I walk in the back door, my mother is at the kitchen table with a cup of coffee and a cigarette. "Jane called," she says. "She wants you to call her. I think she's in trouble."

> *I half expect Jane to say, "Your father loves you very much." And maybe some stubborn part of me does believe it is impossible for a father not to love his children.*

Jane is my father's second wife, the woman he began having an affair with a week after my mother moved out nine years ago with my three siblings and me. I wonder if my father is drunk and throwing things across the room as he did when I was a child. He could even be throwing Jane across the room.

Immediately I start to worry about Michael, their son, my five-year-old half brother. Where is he in the midst of this trouble? Under the covers holding very still? Or with Buck, his older brother? Maybe they're both on the roof where my sister Meegan and I used to go when hell broke loose.

I dial Jane's number, and she picks up the phone on half a ring. She is drunk and whispering. She wants me to come get her at the end of the driveway as soon as I can. I hang up the phone, and my mother looks at me. I'm scared. I have not been in this type of hurricane for quite some time.

In another ten years my father will be dead from alcoholism, and Jane will be sober, and we'll all be survivors of some kind, but I don't know that now. All I know is he's capable of doing great damage.

Maybe my mother should have said, "Don't go" or "Call the police." Or maybe she at least should have said, "I'll go with you," though her spending any time in the car with Jane, her replacement, would be hard to imagine. Yet the look on my mother's face is not bitterness but resignation and concern for this unlikely sort-of sister who knows all too well what it is like to live with my father.

I drive the dark roads to his house. When I reach the driveway, there is Jane in bare feet, her nightgown blowing in the wind, a bottle of Scotch in her hand. She is only five feet tall and weighs maybe ninety pounds, and the bottle looks enormous in her grip.

Jane must have been desperate to have called me. She and I have never been close. I'm not sure I've ever seen her sober. The first time my siblings and I met her, nine years before, she said, her voice slurred, "Your father loves you very much."

What the hell do you know? I wanted to say. It was the

middle of a winter afternoon. My father had told us that Jane lived in Mexico for several years, and I thought maybe her strange speech was due to a Spanish accent.

Jane gets in the car, swigs what is left of the Scotch. As she talks in her drunken way, we drive to nowhere in particular, sometimes stopping at dead-ends that over-look the Great South Bay.

"Michael is my beautiful little boy," she tells me. "It doesn't make him a sissy to need to go to the hospital. He knocked his head on the coffee table and cut his eyelid, and there was so much blood, but your father wouldn't let him go to the hospital. He's hit his head so many times, and your father just says, 'He's not a sissy. He's not going to grow up to be a pretty boy like Buck. He's going to be a hockey player, and hockey players don't care about scars.'"

I listen to this horror in silence.

"But Kerry, am I wrong? Is it wrong to want to take him to be checked out? Now your father won't talk to me. Did he used to give your mother the silent treatment? Buck got home and saw Michael's eye and said, 'I don't care what Peter says. We're taking him to the hospital. He needs stitches, Mom.' So after your father went to sleep, we walked up the road to Tom's, and Tom drove us to the emergency room, and they stitched up Michael, and now your father won't talk to me. Tom said, 'Thank God you brought him in because if you hadn't he would have had a lazy eye for the rest of his life, and actually he still might.'"

My father was a successful negligence lawyer, of all things. I don't know what his problems were besides alcoholism; no one ever will. My mother used to tell us his mother never held him when he was a child.

I have a picture of my father as a four- or five-year-old boy. In the picture he looks shy; his face is gentle. He wears shorts with suspenders and leans against a fence. My half-brother Michael and I have his blond hair, fair skin, and knobby knees.

I saw my father cry only once. I was in fifth grade, and I had been sitting at my desk, drawing a map of the United States for school. It was very late, but I had to finish my homework; everyone else in the house was asleep.

"The Great Lakes look like a palm tree," I said to my father as I shifted in my chair.

"I never would have thought of that," he said.

I heard something in his voice, so I looked up and saw there were tears in his eyes.

That's when he told me that he loved our family very much, but that he was going to be moving out for a while. He said he had been a bad boy. I had never liked the Scotch-and-Dial-soap smell of him and would hesitate even to hold his hand while we crossed the street. But he seemed to like my map, and he looked so sad, so I put my hand on his arm and said, "It's okay, Dad. Really."

But soon after, he was living at home again, backing me into the full dish rack while pounding my chest repeatedly with his fist. I don't remember what had set him off. Maybe he'd found a gum wrapper of mine on the lawn that I'd failed to put in the garbage can.

The next day in gym class I changed in the bathroom stall because I was worried that the teacher would see the bruise. When my father got home from work that evening, my mother must have pulled him aside because he came right over to me, pulled down the neck of my T-shirt, stared at the bruise for a moment, and then walked away, looking sad about what he had done. Once again my impulse was to reassure him: *It's okay,* I wanted to yell. *It's okay.*

But Meegan, who is three years older than I, saw things more clearly. One evening she made clay ornaments for the Christmas tree. She had baked them and painted them in bright detail. And then my father came in and whacked the cookie sheets into the air, and the ornaments flew against the walls and floor, shattering.

As my mother knelt to gather the pieces, Meegan bolted from the kitchen into the dark of the garage, where she ran straight into the blade of the yellow snow-plow, which was up on blocks, knocking it over with a loud crash. The blade gashed her leg open, but still she kept running. I took off after her down the dark road, my heart shaking. And when I caught up with her, we didn't take the road because we feared each set of head-lights could be our father looking for us. Instead we walked behind hedges, through yards, for a mile to her friend Jillian's.

Meegan was brave enough to tell Jillian's parents what had happened that night and other nights. I sat there hardly breathing, feeling there was something wrong about Meegan telling. It took me years to realize the wrong thing was that Jillian's parents did nothing. Just as our neighbors did nothing when we showed up at their place one evening after Dad sucker-punched Meegan in the head. Just as my friend Amanda's parents did nothing when we showed up late one night in our pajamas with similar tales. They listened intently, patiently, then drove us to the end of our driveway and watched as we walked up to our house and in the front door.

Jane wants a cigarette, so I drive to the 7-Eleven. She gets out of the car in her nightgown.

"Jane, I'll get them," I say, opening my door. "You're in your pajamas. They won't let you in there without shoes."

"All right," she says.

Back in the car she smokes cigarette after cigarette as I tell her that nothing has changed since I lived with my father. But I sense she doesn't want to hear this. Her guard is creeping up; she is slightly more sober, talking less freely.

I half expect her to say, "Your father loves you very much." And maybe some stubborn part of me does believe it is impossible for a father not to love his children, even the ones with eyes he has left bloodied, even the ones who are bruised and limping, even the ones who have had to do mental gymnastics to try to understand themselves and him.

"Don't pull in the driveway," Jane says to me. "I don't want Peter to hear the car."

I stop in the road, and she gets out. I know it will not be okay for her to be back in that house with my father, yet I don't stop her. And she knows it will not be okay, yet there she goes, up the driveway. In her sleeveless nightgown and bare feet Jane looks like a little girl walking into that unlit jack-o'-lantern of a house.

Researching Jenna, Discovering Myself

Brian Goedde

WHY DO YOU THINK JENNA LEFT ME?" I ASKED FRIENDS and family, pen and paper in hand. I admit it looked silly, and it felt silly, too. But my psychotherapist had urged me to start writing down my conversations with people about what had happened with Jenna (instead of, as she put it, "just letting the wheels spin"), and I had decided to follow her advice. Enough with the endless whimpering. Time for some hard-nosed research.

Of course I also hoped I might find an answer. I certainly wasn't having much luck staring at my ceiling night after night, sleepless and distraught. And Jenna had proved to be a poor source of information since she'd stopped returning my calls.

> *The way things had been going with Jenna before she left me, I'd thought Tom and I were on the path to becoming in-laws. Now we were nothing.*

I didn't think any of my interviewees knew Jenna better than I did; she and I had been together almost ten years. But still there was a Jenna I didn't know: namely the Jenna who left me so suddenly over the phone that warm afternoon in March. This Jenna, I hypothesized, must be the composite of the imaginings of all these other people.

Flipping open my steno pad, I first posed my question to a friend of mine with whom I'd quickly started an affair after Jenna left. She was in her kitchen, perched on a stool, smoking a Marlboro in her green bathrobe.

"Oh, Brian," she said, "why do you want to torture yourself?"

"It's not torture," I said. "It'll be good for me."

"Is it something about beating a dead horse?"

I urged her to say something. She and Jenna didn't like each other too much, but I'd always felt they were a lot alike.

My rebound lover took a drag on her cigarette and said, "I think it has to do with the age difference between when you started out and now. You were nineteen when you got together. Over time she developed needs and desires, needs that maybe she didn't even know she was having. And whether or not she told you about these needs, you weren't fulfilling them."

Scribbling down her thoughts, I tried to think of a good follow-up question, as a good researcher would do, but I realized I'd been hoping she'd say something more like "I don't know, I don't care, let's mess around." Instead she had concluded that Jenna had left because of my inadequacy. And did this mean that she, too, was anticipating my inadequacy? Suddenly hurt, I ended the interview.

Next I asked Cynthea, Jenna's favorite professor in college, who'd become a good friend of us both. It was at a party; she wore a colorful blouse that looked like it had been shredded and sewn back together. I pulled her onto the front porch so we could be alone for my interview.

"She left you for her own reasons," Cynthea said. "I think she had a lot of small unhappinesses, the most recent being that she felt unsupported when her dad died. She felt he abandoned her, and she decided that you abandoned her, too. She had a big catharsis, and you were a part of that."

She looked away from me. "I also think she wanted someone to stand up to her and fight her more. But that's probably projection. That's why I leave men; they don't stand up to me."

I winced at the thought that in Cynthea's mind I was no better than her two ex-husbands, but she was right, I think, about Jenna's dad, who had died, suddenly, four months earlier. This wasn't the father who raised her but the estranged, alcoholic, misanthropic father whom her mother had left when Jenna was two, taking Jenna with her. When he died, Jenna was visibly upset but soon stopped talking about it. They weren't close, Jenna would say, adding that it was more of a relief to her that he was in "a better place."

The subject of his death didn't come up again until she called me to say that losing her father had turned her whole world upside down, and that I was no longer in it. I figured I needed to take my research deeper, closer to her family, so my next interview was with Jenna's stepfather, Tom.

When I asked him why he thought Jenna had left me, he said simply, "I don't know."

We were standing on the sidewalk in front of my house. He'd stopped by after work to pick up some things Jenna had left behind and didn't want to retrieve herself: artwork, books, printmaking supplies.

I stood there waiting, pen to paper, until he said again, "I don't know."

"I don't know. I don't know," I repeated, writing it down. I shouldn't have mocked him—Tom had been consoling to me in the past—but today his rushed and dismissive response irked me. I looked up from my notepad and said, "That's it?"

"I'm probably going to answer every question like that," he replied.

I started to write that down, too: "Probablyanswer-every—"

"We've all been in relationships," he finally said, interrupting, "and we all know that no one around you knows the answer." He paused as I wrote silently. "And the corollary is, no two people in any relationship know what's going on in that relationship."

This seemed very wise to me, and I told him so. I had always liked Tom. But as we put Jenna's stuff in his car, his statement lingered between us and became extremely troubling to me. In rapid succession I wondered about my relationship with Jenna, about his relationship with Jenna, and about my relationship with him.

Before Tom drove off, we shook hands and wished each other well. The way things had been going with Jenna before she left me, I'd thought he and I were on the path to becoming in-laws. Now we were nothing. This much we could know for sure.

My mother was the last person I needed to speak with for my research project. That requires some background information.

When I was eight years old my mother divorced my

father and left us in Seattle, moving across the country to start a new life. For two years I was an emotional wreck, but finally I got on with the business of growing up. I saw her for Christmases and summers, got along great with her new family in Virginia, and fit in perfectly with my new stepfamily in Seattle. I never resolved my feelings about my mother leaving, but I decided they would be unresolvable. Everyone's got issues with parents, I decided. Life isn't fair. Deal with it.

In my first visit to a psychotherapist after Jenna left, while I was in my spinning-out-of-control phase, my deft counselor identified this trauma deep in my emotional life, and I erupted, first with tears and then with an overwhelming feeling of clarity. I was having, I realized, the same reactions I'd had as an eight-year-old: grief-stricken, lying awake at night wondering why she'd left, wanting to do anything to get her back.

I wrote my mother, telling her of my realizations, and she told me it was high time for her to pay me a visit "to work some things out."

Weeks later, over our steak-and-salad dinners in the restaurant next to her hotel, my mother told me what it had been like for her to leave me, my sister, and my father. She talked about how necessary it was for her to "rebuild" herself, how it was a decision she hated having made, but the life she had been living was something she had hated more.

I was surprised to feel uninterested in these monologues. For so many years I had wondered why she'd left, but now I realized I didn't care. The point, for me, was that she *had*. All I actually needed was to tell her that her leaving had "really screwed me up for a really long time."

She looked up from her plate and nodded.

I didn't get to ask my mother why she thought Jenna had left me until I was driving her back to the airport two days later. I handed her my notepad and pen and told her about my research.

"You want me to write down what I think?" she said, incredulously.

Yes, I told her; it was part of my psychotherapy.

She was quiet for a moment, then she wrote: "She had too much pressure (master's degree and family of origin problems). Communication broke down because of pressure."

She stopped writing and spoke out loud about how you can't have too much pressure from family issues if you're going to have a successful relationship. You have to "really sweep the floor," she said; it was all a part of being "on the ball," not only in your relationship but in your life.

"But you'll see," she said. "In your next relationship, you'll have learned."

I glanced at my dashboard. The "low gas" light was on. Damn. I tried to remember how many miles I had before it would run out. I tried to remember how many miles it was to the airport. I pictured myself trying to flag down a cab on the highway as my mother missed her plane. Damn, *damn!*

At the next exit I apologized and pulled off the highway.

"That's fine," my mother said, waving off my apology.

But when I got back in the car after pumping gas, the first thing she said was, "Never let it get below a quarter tank."

"Okay, Mom."

"Maybe you're not quite ready for that next relationship," she said, laughing.

I laughed too, but it stung. "*Okay,* Mom," I said.

And she was right about me, of course, but not because I'd failed to maintain at least a quarter-tank of gas in the car. It wasn't about that, just as her talk about sweeping the floor wasn't about Jenna and her father but about me and her, just as the friends I'd interviewed had been talking less about us than about themselves, and just as my research hadn't led to the discovery of a Jenna I didn't know but of a me I didn't know how to approach.

When we arrived at the airport, I walked my mother into the terminal and hugged her goodbye. Then I returned to my car and my life, content, this time, to be left behind.

Father and Daughter: One Final Connection

Ellen Pall

WHEN MY FATHER WAS FAIRLY WELL ALONG INTO THE dementia of Alzheimer's—not as far as he was to go, but four or five years in—he developed a taste for looking attentively at trees. At the time I was not aware that this is a common pleasure for Alzheimer's patients, some of whom are known to enter a Zenlike state of meditation before them.

In my ignorance I speculated as to what the allure of looking at trees might be for my father. All he could say about it, or would say, was, "Look," pointing out the window (or, in better weather, up from a chaise longue)

> *Watching my father's illness progress was watching him move inward to some secret native core.*

at the gently moving branches of an oak or maple. And repeat somewhat urgently, "Look!"

And I would look, sometimes standing and coming around to his side to please him, because he seemed to want me to share the exact perspective on the thirty-foot pine outside his kitchen that had caught his attention. I would nod my agreement and wonder if perhaps, because he had grown up on the prairies of Canada, trees of this size still held a fascination for him.

I wondered if he was thinking of these mature trees, so much taller than when he had bought this house thirty-five years before, as symbolic of his own accomplishments in life, of his having come to patriarchy atop a hill of achievements.

He was in his early eighties when his memory started to go; by now he was heading fast toward ninety. I suspected that when we were together, he thought a lot about his being my father; the knowledge that I was his daughter stayed with him almost to the end.

One time he gestured at a statue he owned of a parent—a tall, curving leaflike parent, cast in metal—sheltering a small leaflike metal child. He tried, I thought, to acknowledge the switch in caretaking that had come about between us, by pointing first from metal parent to metal child, then from metal child to metal parent, then from himself to me, until tears spilled out of both of our eyes.

So I thought that trees might seem like families to him, and that the tall, grown-up trees perhaps were fathers.

My father was a man of great intellect who devoted his life to scientific invention. Among other achievements, he founded a thriving company and was awarded the National Medal of Technology.

No one influenced me more than he did (unless it was the ghost of my mother, who died when I was seven). I tried to please him all my life. But we had been close only when I was a very little girl.

He liked little children. When my siblings and I were small, he would toss us up in the air, let us climb over and tickle him. Very young children diverted and cheered him, bringing out an otherwise dormant silly side. When I was quite tiny, he would have me sit on his back and give him "massages" whose only efficacious element, he later admitted, was the weight of my small body on his spine.

At bedtime he patted my middle—what we called tummy rubbles—and told me the continuing adventures of a very foolish traveling ostrich. After he learned to play the guitar, he would sing folk songs to me before I went to sleep: "The Riddle Song," "The Foggy, Foggy Dew," "All the Pretty Little Horses." During some part of my mother's long stays in the hospital, he occasionally let me sleep in his bed, whether because I asked to or because my warmth and company comforted him. None of this was even slightly sexual; it was only warm and loving and kind.

But with my mother's death—maybe even before, as its looming shadow crept inescapably over our little family— he started to draw away from me. Perhaps I reminded him too much of my mother.

By the time I was ten or eleven (he had remarried quickly, when I was eight), formality had entered into our relationship, and I seemed no longer to have anything to offer him by way of cheer or ease. He was busier than ever anyhow, working on, among other things, the development of a blood filter that might have prolonged my mother's life. It would take more than twenty years of work to bring it to market.

All these years, he and I were not close. I desperately wished to be. But I saw him as cold and removed, uninterested in personal life. We shared a slightly whimsical sense of humor that occasionally lightened an hour or two between us, and he was certainly steady, fatherly, good, and very generous to me in many ways. But I would never have said we were close.

Until he got Alzheimer's.

Few friends came to visit my father once he began to fail. Innocent as Alzheimer's victims are, a stigma still attaches to this disease, to any kind of dementia. In the case of my high-achieving, cerebral father, those who knew him also turned their eyes from the spectacle of a gifted man's great fall.

People are said to die of "complications" of Alzheimer's, but "simplifications" might be closer to the truth. Watching my father's illness progress was watching him move inward to some secret, native core, past layer upon layer of socialization, education, religious training, life experience, physical skill, personal habit.

First he was forgetful, and when his children told him so (he had asked us to tell him; he didn't want to end as his father had: with Alzheimer's), he denied it. We hoped his forgetfulness was the result of stress: my stepmother had just died after a lengthy and miserable battle with Parkinson's.

But our father's memory did not improve. Instead, a new, crafty side of him emerged, shrewdly determined not to let show any sign that he was losing his wits. This was followed by a period when his forgetfulness would annoy him. He would sometimes strike his knee in irritation as yet another word or name eluded him, another whole concept. Sometimes he would laugh at these lapses. Once or twice he joked rather desperately, "I'm getting stupid."

Then there was a long period of paranoia. He feared that a child passing through his yard might be a target of enemy soldiers. (His own home now unfamiliar to him, he seemed to think he was in the army.)

When the nurses and aides we eventually hired to stay with him tried to groom or feed him, he sometimes lashed out at them, confused as to why unfamiliar hands should take such liberties. He hid his watch, lest it be stolen. He went into someone else's house, thinking it was his own. He struck out angrily even at family members.

Then this period passed and, with the help of small doses of medication, he became more content, more compliant. When I visited him now, I would bring CDs for us to listen to. Cecilia Bartoli could move him to tears. A recording of a rhapsodic Georges Enesco composition was "the most beautiful music" he had ever heard. He beat his hands in time, conducting. Sometimes he hummed along.

Meanwhile language deserted him. He spoke at length, but in words no one recognized, a gibberish that came to him with remarkable ease, as if he were Sid Caesar pretending to speak French. We knew he was telling a joke when his voice rose animatedly and his breathing quickened. We laughed when he laughed. Once in a long while, piercingly, he said something that made sense about his own condition.

"Is there any hope?" he asked me once.

Of course, of course.

It interested and touched me very much that to his end—once the angry phase was finished—he was courtly and affectionate toward his aides. Early on he had given up eating dinner alone at the end of the long, polished table in his dining room and gone to join the aide and housekeeper at the more convivial round table in the kitchen.

One of his last coherent remarks, spoken long after he ceased to be able to walk or even stand and support his own dwindling weight, was to offer to help a nursing aide perched on a chair to adjust the curtains over a pair of French doors. He always offered me half his food.

Sometimes he greeted me as if my appearance were the most wonderful surprise anyone could have imagined, as if we had met by chance in a desert on the other side of the world. In the gravityless reaches of his swirling, upside-down mind, he had become the kind, good little boy he must once have been on the prairies of Canada. And I was close to him now. At last I had the chance to help him—he needed me—and I helped him, and we were close. The symmetry of it: my childhood, forty years of constraint, his childhood.

Now my father is dead, my mother is dead, and I am next in line. Now in the summer, when I see trees lighted by sun, moving in the wind, I am amazed at their beauty. Some of their leaves wink like coins, some wave like hands. Sometimes a whole branch sighs and bows, like a courtier. Look. Look!

A Devotion That Eclipsed the Family

Caroline Miller

MY SISTER E-MAILED ME THE DEATH NOTICE FROM the *Seattle Times* with just this cryptic note: "Make sure you read all the way to the bottom."

The subject was Roy Maus, seventy-five, a former Boeing executive and passionate sports fisherman who had died peacefully on board his boat, the *Sanlino,* at Shilshole Bay Marina. His Boeing career was recapped, as were his favorite fishing destinations, from the San Juan Islands to the Skagit River.

> *Roy loved my father with a confidence I found stunning. The man I admired but never felt quite comfortable around was somehow transformed in his telling: lively, funny, loyal, adventurous.*

At the end, following a list of his survivors—sisters, sons, grandchildren, nieces, nephews, and cousins—was this sentence: "Roy was preceded in death by his daughter Susan, mother Johanna, father Roy and his best friend John Bixby."

John Bixby was my father. And he had "preceded" Roy—his colleague at Boeing, his fishing partner, and eventually my mother's nemesis—in death by more than fourteen years. It had been almost that long since I had talked to Roy. But there he was after all these years—after his own death—claiming my father in print. I was shocked. And thrilled. And relieved that my mother wasn't alive to read it.

Roy was a phantom figure when I was growing up in the Seattle suburbs, my father coexisting with three women—my mother, my sister, and me—in a house that had a rowboat suspended from the garage ceiling and a basement full of fishing gear. I loved to poke around in my father's stuff, when he wasn't there of course.

The elegant, tensile rods and reels. The clownishly big rubber hip boots. The faded wooden oars, with their clanky oarlocks hanging like heavy bracelets. The battered tackle boxes filled with tiny, fanciful feathered lures, with shiny, lethal-looking hooks gleaming under them. And, until he found out that my sister and I had discovered them, his stash of *Playboy*s.

My father's first few boats sat on trailers in the driveway. As the years went by, they got bigger; by the time I was in college, he had a slip at Shilshole a few docks over from Roy's. The two buddies abetted each other in more and more ambitious forays. They were up in Canada salmon fishing, in Alaska in pursuit of steelhead, in New Zealand after trout.

Going through the files in my father's basement office after his funeral, I found dozens of photographs of those trips with Roy. The images were all so alike, there was virtually no way to distinguish one trip from another, except for the date stamps on the back and the advancing gray in their hair.

There was Roy, grinning into the sun, in a red plaid woollen jacket and baseball cap, holding up a fish, his fingers tucked under the gills. My father in weathered khaki, holding up his fish. There was the catch, four or five salmon, spread on the dock or the grass, arranged from largest to smallest. My father in the stern, in a director's chair, holding a drink. Roy at the stern, in a matching chair, holding a drink. My father at the wheel, with a beer. Roy at the wheel, with a beer.

The only other pictures they took were of sunsets.

I didn't get to know Roy myself until 1990, when my father, after a campaign of several years, was losing his battle with colon cancer. Roy was suddenly a big presence at the hospital, charming and genial, telling me stories about the exploits he and my father had shared, at Boeing and on the boat, or stepping outside, with my mother and sister, for a cigarette.

He was affectionate and chivalrous, steering my mother protectively to lunch and walking her to the car. And he was a great deal more forthcoming than my father, who never had been much of a storyteller, at least not at home. Roy's company was oddly seductive, and it wasn't just because he animated the hours of enforced awkwardness in antiseptic hallways and waiting rooms. As my mother, my sister, and I huddled around my father's hospital bed, I felt my distance from him as acutely as I did my closeness. Roy seemed to feel the way I wanted to feel, thought I should feel.

Roy loved my father with a confidence I found stunning. The man I admired but never felt quite comfortable around was somehow transformed in his telling: lively, funny, loyal, adventurous.

In part, I think, he wanted me to know, as my father was wasting away, that my father had been more than the conscientious but emotionally absent man I grew up with, who quietly anesthetized himself with drink every evening and took little active interest in his daughters' lives. Unless, that is, my mother collared him and assigned him some duty: a father-daughter banquet, a school science project, teaching us to drive.

Roy wanted me to know that he and my father weren't just a couple of guys boozing it up out on a boat, safely out of range of reproving wives. He wanted me to know that he not only loved my father but knew him, knew him better than any of the rest of us did, including my mother.

Among the things we didn't know, Roy confided in one of our hallway tête-à-têtes, was that my father had had a mistress for more than ten years. She worked at Boeing, Roy said, and everyone who knew them had expected my father to leave my mother and marry her. Eventually, when he didn't, she gave up on him and ended the relationship. But she had been to the hospital recently, he said, to visit my dad.

Roy delivered this information with odd urgency, as if he had decided that someone in the family must know who this dying man really was, and he had chosen me for the mission. He seemed to trust, in sharing this secret, that I wouldn't think less of my father for being a philanderer, or confront him on his deathbed. Or discuss it with my mother.

Roy was right: I never did. And whether he intended it or not, his revelations made me feel oddly less desolate, grateful to know that my father had enjoyed a greater passion than was evident in our domestic life, even if that passion excluded us.

Those revelations allowed me to reimagine, in retrospect, the narrative of our family, with my father a more complex and exciting character. A man with a double life—triple, if you count fishing. I had spent my teenage years plotting my escape from a family life so carefully, cautiously choreographed I could barely breathe. Suddenly it appeared that I was not the only one who had been dying to get out; my father had actually beaten me to it. It was something we had in common.

My father died in January 1991; the first gulf war began the day of his funeral. It was only fitting, I thought, because in those last few weeks in the hospital he seemed to have withdrawn into the television over his bed, into CNN's coverage of the countdown to war. He found it harder and harder, it seemed to me, to take his eyes off the screen and engage with us.

The last time I visited, as I left the room, I turned; he smiled wanly and stretched out his hand. I returned the smile and the gesture. And that, it turned out, was goodbye.

After my father's death Roy started calling me in New York with some regularity, mostly to commiserate about our mutual loss. At first I was glad to hear his voice. The immediacy of his suffering and his desire to share it with me made me feel chosen in a way my father had never made me feel. But since Roy's principal solace was the bottle, he'd call me late at night, when he had been drinking alone on the boat, and leave sloppy messages on my voice mail. After a few months I stopped returning his calls. He stopped calling.

It was my father's wish, to my mother's sorrow, that his ashes be scattered at sea, rather than interred, next to her, in the memorial garden at the church. She saw it, not erroneously, as an acknowledgment of just how limited her claim to him had been, despite forty-eight years of marriage. It was a symbolic defeat, particularly because the person designated to scatter the ashes was Roy.

When it was warm enough for Roy to take the boat out, he and my mother agreed that she would drive over to the marina with the urn containing the ashes. Roy would meet her at eleven in the parking lot, and she would, as much as it pained her, hand them over. She couldn't take the ashes down to his boat, where he was living, because the dock was gated, and she didn't have a key.

On the appointed day, she picked up the urn at church and drove out to Shilshole. She sat on a bench in the parking lot with the ashes and waited for Roy to come get them. No sign of him. After a half-hour she went to the pay phone and called his number on the boat. No answer. She waited some more. She called again. She checked to make sure his car was in the lot; it was there. He had stood her up.

I imagine, as she did, that Roy had had a particularly long night communing with my father's ghost and a bottle of Scotch, and was sleeping it off. Or, as my sister thought, that he just couldn't face it.

Either way, there was my mother, sitting on the bench on a mild spring day, a once-lovely blonde with sensibly cropped colorless hair, faded blue eyes, a touch of lipstick her only makeup, tears streaming down her face. And I imagine, too, that I know what was upsetting her most: the knowledge that of all of us who mourned my father, Roy was the only one certain of his love and loyalty.

For the rest of us the pain was more complex: a mixture of what we had lost and what we'd never had.

At Sixteen, I Gave Him Up. Could We Try Again?

Meredith Hall

THE CALL CAME IN MAY.

"Hello," the woman said. "My name is Ann Hurd. I work with the New Hampshire courts. I want you to sit down. Your son is looking for you."

> **We blurted out every thought that came, our conversation leaping as we tried to reconstruct the lost years.**

I had been hoping for this call for twenty-one years, and it came like a dream into an ordinary spring day.

"We will take this very slowly," she said. "This can cause enormous problems for both the child and the birth mother."

"But I'm ready now. I've been waiting for years."

"First you will write letters for a while, through me. It is devastating to the child to experience a second abandonment."

"I could never abandon him again."

"But it happens a lot," she said.

"Where is he?"

"I can't tell you that yet."

"Can you tell me his name?" I felt myself separate from my voice.

"His name," she said, "is Ron."

This sound was electric. My son had a name!

"Your son," Ann told me, "is extraordinary. Ron is a spectacular young man."

Three weeks later, a letter finally came through Ann. There was a picture enclosed, my first sight of my lost child. It was blurred and gray, but here was Ron—serious, a strong jaw, intelligent eyes.

Dear Meredith, he wrote. *I don't know what to say. I don't know how to do this. Ron.*

His handwriting was slanted along the page, hurried. I carried his note in my pocket, reading it again and again as I stared at his photograph.

Ann called and said, "Write back to him right away. He is very scared. Ask him some questions."

Dear Ron. My name is Meredith Hall. I live in East Booth-bay on the coast of Maine. I have a son, Morgan, who is 10. And a son named Zachary, who is 7. We keep sheep and chickens and big gardens. Tell me about your family. Tell me about your room. Tell me about what you like to do. I want you to know that I have always loved you.

Ann edited our letters for revealing details. They came to us blacked out:

My name is Meredith————. I live in————on the coast of————.

My name is Ron————. I grew up on a farm in———— —in southern————. My mother and father,———— and————, are very loving and supportive.

Our ghost lives slowly took shape. Five months later, Ann arranged for us to meet.

It was 10:00 a.m., October 18. Ron drove slowly along my dirt road. He glanced at me quickly as I stood waiting on the porch steps. I could see blond hair, curls. He turned off the engine, got out of the car, looked at me, and our eyes locked. He was thin, athletic, handsome. My son. He was not a child. He was a young man, wearing jeans, a striped sweater, and soft old loafers. He came toward me, his shoes crunching on the stone path. His teeth were brilliant white, with a space in the front. My father had a space like that. I moved toward him. Every day, for twenty-one years, I had played this scene. I had never known what to do, and I did not know now. I was breaking with joy, and with grief, too, because here he was a grown man, here I was nearly forty—all those years lost forever. I reached for him, held him in to me, a stranger, my son, this beautiful, radiant, terrified, smiling son.

We did not hold each other long because we were shy, strangers to each other. We walked to the railing of the porch and stood, three feet between us, facing the river, looking out over the coast of Maine. I could not find the question that would start our life together. What I wanted to ask was, Have you felt my love each day? Have you felt me missing you? Have you known how sorry I am? Have you been loved? Have you been happy? Will you forgive me?

All I could come up with was, "Do you like UNH?"

"Yes." His first word to me. His voice was soft and deep.

"What year are you?"

"Well, I'm working my way through so I have another two years."

His body was taut, as if he were ready to fight something off. His face was open, his eyes enormous, blue, set wide apart. He had a scar across his chin. He was very serious. He turned to me and smiled suddenly. He had deep dimples. My brother had those dimples. We smiled, then turned to the ocean again in overwhelmed silence.

"Do you want to go for a walk?" I asked. I felt deep happiness, which stirred old sorrow into wild confusion.

We walked down the dirt road to the river, blurting out every thought that came, our conversation leaping as we tried to reconstruct the lost years.

"This is the owl tree," I said. "Morgan and Zachary are my sons. Your brothers." I saw Ron tense for just a moment, then slip back into the rhythm of our walking. "They find owl pellets here and we dissect them."

Ron said, "My mother let me play hooky to go fishing with her."

My mother. I breathed. Of course. We were two mothers.

We sat on an old bench above the undulating seaweed, talking fast. I knew he would drive away that afternoon, and I didn't know if he would ever come again. He must have wondered if I would want him to come again. Sometimes, we found ourselves laughing. Twice, Ron said, "I've never told anyone this before."

We climbed back up the hill, and I showed him the downstairs of our homey little Cape.

"Do you want to see your brothers' rooms?" I asked.

"Yes," he said quietly.

He glanced quickly into their sunny rooms, at their toys and books, at his brothers' lives here with me, where they've been loved, safe, not given away. We went back down to the kitchen. Eating tuna sandwiches, we returned to our stories, the joy we felt right at that minute lying like a pond within our grief.

"Would you like me to tell you about your father?"

His hands stopped midair, a picture of our first day I will never forget, the image of his powerful hunger to belong.

"You look like him," I said. "I was sixteen, and he was a sophomore in college. We met at the beach. He came to see me after you were born, for five or six years, showing up, never asking any questions."

I watched him struggle to integrate this information into his twenty-one-year-old identity.

"It doesn't matter anyway," was all he could say.

He let me hug him goodbye at his car. He called on Wednesday and said he was coming on Sunday.

"Can the boys be there?" he asked.

I was overcome by his courage. It was the beginning of our new family.

I ached with guilt about my two young sons, understanding that I was asking them to take in stride the effects of my own enormous history. They never balked. When I told them they had a big brother, they immediately embraced him. They stood in front of Ron at that first meeting and grinned. They climbed on him, giggling. Like monkeys, they studied every inch of him, probing and touching, pulling off his socks and shoes, studying his toes and hands and back, comparing them with their own. They peered inside his mouth. Morgan draped his arm over Ron's shoulder while they sat on the couch; Zachary got in under Ron's arm. Ron came every Sunday, then for weekends, then for the summer. I was stunned by my sons' capacity to include him, to give him part of me.

And Ron took me to his family, too. "This is my mother, Rose," he said. "This is my other mother, Meredith." He did not call me Mom, or Mum, or Mumma, like Morgan and Zachary. He had a mother. He had a sister, Tammy, adopted when she was two. He had a father, Hank. Astonishingly, Rose and Hank welcomed me as if they were happy I had come into Ron's life. I felt as if I had stolen their son.

Those months were confusing, upheaving, yet laughter often filled the house. And we cried. We rested in our deep love for each other, then we would fly apart in despair or hurt. Some days we needed to be reassured that this was forever. Other days, we fought for our lives, the lives that had worked pretty well before. Sometimes we couldn't contain everything that had been lost.

I had never told my friends about this child. The grief and shame of losing him at sixteen had stayed with me all my life as a fiercely private sorrow. Now they argued with me, telling me that Morgan and Zachary should not have to pay the price of my history. "Are you telling me I should send this child away again?" I asked. Yes, they said. This isn't fair to your children. But an older friend disagreed, telling me, "This is your son. Don't listen to them. This is a miracle. It is a fairy tale with a happy ending."

Then it was October 18 again, our first anniversary. Our days had found rhythm. The upheaving emotions were quieting. My friend was right: this was a miracle, a fairy tale, though each day felt fragile, as if it all might disappear if we turned our backs. Still, our old lives receded, and our new family held together. I had my son. He had his mother.

To mark the day, I gave him my small clay owl, the only thing I had from those devastated years after he was born. "This is to remind you every day that this place in my life is forever," I said.

He gave me an acorn. "My renaissance," he said, his voice soft and hopeful.

There were no patterns for how to do this, how to hold each other safely and fully after a lifetime apart. We could not plot out the future. We were a family. We loved each other. We needed each other. That was our only map.

UPDATE: *Meredith and her two younger sons and Ron have remained close in the years since these events took place, seeing one another frequently despite living on opposite sides of the country.*

SANDRA BARRON is an assistant correspondent at the New York bureau of the *Tokyo Shimbun,* a Japanese daily newspaper. Her articles on health and relationships have appeared in *Marie Claire* and *Essence.* She won the Grand Prize in the 2001 Writer's Digest Annual Writing Contest for a feature she reported from Botswana, on young local volunteers working to educate their peers about HIV/AIDS.

JEAN BRAITHWAITE is an assistant professor of creative writing at the University of Texas–Pan American. She has published nonfiction and stories in *The Sun, Bayou,* and other literary magazines. She is currently completing a book-length memoir about being fat in America.

KEVIN CAHILLANE is a frequent contributor to the *New York Times* and an advertising copywriter. He lives in Summit, New Jersey, with his wife and three children.

VERONICA CHAMBERS is the author of *The Joy of Doing Things Badly: A Girl's Guide to Love, Life, and Foolish Bravery; When Did You Stop Loving Me* (aka *Miss Black America*); *Having It All?;* and *Mama's Girl.* She was formerly the culture writer for *Newsweek,* a senior associate editor at *Premiere,* and an executive editor at *Savoy.* Her writing has appeared in many magazines, including *Glamour, Vogue, Esquire,* the *New York Times*

Magazine, and *O, The Oprah Magazine.* You can read more about her work at www.veronicachambers.com.

LINDA DACKMAN lives in San Francisco, where she is public information director of the Exploratorium, a museum of science, art, and human perception. Dackman is the author of two books, *Upfront: Sex and the Post-Mastectomy Woman* and *Affirmations, Meditations, and Encouragements for Women Living with Breast Cancer.* She has published articles on an array of topics in publications ranging from *Art and Architecture* to *Vogue.* Dackman holds a BA from Brooklyn College and an MA from Washington University, St. Louis.

REBECCA ECKLER is one of Canada's most well-read journalists. She has a weekly parenting column in Canada's national newspaper, the *Globe and Mail.* She is the author of *Knocked Up* and *Wiped!* and a teen novel, *Dear Apple.*

STEPHEN ELLIOTT is the author of six books, including the political memoir *Looking Forward to It,* the novel *Happy Baby,* and the erotica collection *My Girlfriend Comes to the City and Beats Me Up.* He lives in San Francisco.

TREY ELLIS is a novelist, screenwriter, and essayist. His acclaimed first novel, *Platitudes,* was recently reissued by Northeastern University Press, along with his influential essay "The New Black Aesthetic." He is also the author of *Home Repairs* and *Right Here, Right Now,* which was a recipient of the American Book Award. His work for the screen includes the Emmy-nominated *The Tuskegee Airmen,* and *Good Fences,* starring Danny Glover and Whoopi Goldberg, which was shortlisted for the PEN award for Best Teleplay of the year. His essays have appeared in the *New York Times, Playboy,* the

Washington Post, and the *Los Angeles Times,* among others. He is a regular blogger on the HuffingtonPost.com and lives in Venice, California.

ANNE MARIE FELD lives in San Francisco with her husband and two children. Her weekly column chronicling her pregnancy and the birth of her daughter can be found on Babycenter.com.

RONALD K. FRIED has published two novels, *My Father's Fighter* and *Christmas in Paris 2002,* as well as one book of nonfiction, *Corner Men: Great Boxing Trainers.* His work as a TV producer has earned him five New York Emmy awards. He has just completed a new novel about the television industry.

STEVE FRIEDMAN is the author of *The Gentleman's Guide to Life* and, with former NBA player Jayson Williams, *Loose Balls: Easy Money, Hard Fouls, Cheap Laughs, and True Love in the NBA.* He has written for *Esquire, GQ, Outside, New York Magazine,* the *New York Times,* and the *Washington Post,* and his stories have appeared in *The Bastard on the Couch, Outside 25: Classic Tales and New Voices from the Frontiers of Adventure,* and, five times, in *The Best American Sports Writing.* A St. Louis native and graduate of Stanford University, he lives in Manhattan.

HELEN GERHARDT finished active drilling duty with the Army National Guard in May of 2006. She currently attends the MFA program in creative nonfiction at the University of Pittsburgh, where she is working on a book about her experiences as a bisexual woman in a highly conservative military transportation company. Her writing appears in a National Endowment for the Arts anthology of writing by veterans of Iraqi Freedom, titled *Operation Homecoming.*

BRIAN GOEDDE'S essays have appeared in *Resonance, Popular Music* (UK), and *Oakland's Urbanview,* among other places, and on Iowa Public Radio's *Weekend Edition*. He was a Richard Hugo House Writer-In-Residence in Seattle and will graduate from the University of Iowa Nonfiction Writing Program in May 2007.

TZIVIA GOVER is the author of *Mindful Moments for Stressful Days*. Her essays and articles have appeared in the *Boston Globe, Creative Nonfiction,* the *Christian Science Monitor,* and many more. She has published in more than a dozen anthologies, including, *Family: A Celebration* and *Home Stretch*. She received her MFA in creative nonfiction from Columbia University. She teaches poetry to adults and young adults in literacy classes. She lives in western Massachusetts with her partner of sixteen years and her teenage daughter.

KATIE ALLISON GRANJU is the author of *Attachment Parenting* and a contributor to several anthologies, including *It's a Boy: Women Writers on Raising Sons*. Her essays and articles have appeared in *Salon;* the *Chicago Tribune;* the *New York Times; Hip Mama; Brain, Child;* and others. She is a former producer with the Oxygen network and a current producer with an NBC/Gannett television affiliate. She lives with her three children, Henry, Jane, and Elliot, in Tennessee. She has a blog at www.katieallisongranju.com.

MEREDITH HALL'S work has appeared in the *New York Times* and in many journals and anthologies. She is the 2005 recipient of the fifty-thousand-dollar Gift of Freedom Award from A Room of Her Own Foundation, and the Maine Arts Commission's Individual Artist Fellowship. She won the Pushcart

Prize and was listed in Notables in *Best American Essays*. Her memoir, *Without a Map,* from which this piece was excerpted, will be published by Beacon Press in 2007. She teaches writing at the University of New Hampshire and lives in Maine.

BRENDAN HALPIN'S most recent novel, *Long Way Back,* was published in 2006, and his next, *Dear Catastrophe Waitress,* will be published later this year. He is also the author of *Donorboy,* a novel that received the Alex Award from the American Library Association; *It Takes a Worried Man,* a memoir of his late wife Kirsten's cancer diagnosis and treatment; and *Losing My Faculties,* a memoir of nine years of teaching.

TERRY MARTIN HEKKER is the author of *Ever Since Adam and Eve: The Satisfactions of Housewifery.* In the late seventies her work appeared in *TV Guide, McCall's,* and *Good Housekeeping,* and she lectured across the country on the "Occupation House-wife." She served as the first woman mayor of Nyack, New York, and is mother of five and grandmother of twelve. You may find her online at www.terrymartinhekker.com.

ROBIN HEMLEY is the author of seven books of fiction and non-fiction and has published stories and essays in the *New York Times,* the *Chicago Tribune, Southern Review, Prairie Schooner,* and others. His books include *Turning Life into Fiction; Nola: A Memoir of Faith, Art, and Madness;* and *Invented Eden: The Elusive, Disputed History of the Tasaday.* He is the director of the Nonfiction Writing Program at the University of Iowa and writes a column for *The Believer* on defunct literary journals.

ANN HOOD is the author of seven novels, including *Somewhere Off the Coast of Maine* and *Ruby;* a memoir, *Do Not Go Gentle:*

My Search for Miracles in a Cynical Time; and a collection of short stories, *An Ornithologist's Guide to Life.* Her essays and stories have appeared in *Tin House, Glimmer Train, The Paris Review, More, Traveler,* and *Bon Appetit.* She has won two Pushcart Prizes, an American Spiritual Writing Award, and is a recipient of the Paul Bowles Prize for Short Fiction. Her new novel, *The Knitting Circle,* will be published in January 2007 by W.W. Norton. She is currently working on a collection of essays, *Comfort: A Journey Through Grief.*

MINDY HUNG is an editor and writer in New York City. She has written for *Salon,* the *Winnipeg Free Press,* and the *New York Times.*

HEATHER L. HUNTER lives in New York City, where she works for a nonprofit organization in Harlem. Her blog, This Fish Needs a Bicycle, can be found on iVillage.com, where she also occasionally lends her voice to the iVillage Love Council.

JENNIFER R. JUST lives with her two sons, Cameron and Evan, in Woodbridge, Connecticut. She writes essays for newspapers, magazines, and the radio, and is currently working on a memoir. She also works part time at Whitlock's Book Barn in Bethany, Connecticut, which sells used and rare books.

HOWIE KAHN works at *GQ* magazine, where he checks facts, reports, and writes. Originally from suburban Detroit, Kahn graduated from the University of Michigan, where, in 2000, he won a Hopwood Award for excellence in nonfiction writing. In 2003, he earned an MFA in nonfiction writing from Sarah Lawrence College, where he originated and edited *For the Gathering,* the school's literary response to 9/11. Kahn's writing has appeared in *GQ, ARTnews,* the *New York Times,* and in the Goings on About Town section of *The New Yorker*. He is currently working on his first novel.

JEAN HANFF KORELITZ lives in Princeton, New Jersey, with her husband, the Irish poet Paul Muldoon, and their two children. She is the author of three novels, *The White Rose, The Sabbathday River,* and *A Jury of Her Peers,* as well as a novel for children, *Interference Powder,* and a collection of poems, *The Properties of Breath.* She has written for *Vogue, Real Simple, More, Organic Style,* the *New York Times,* and *Newsweek.* Currently, she is at work on a novel about Ivy League admissions.

CLAIRE SCOVELL LAZEBNIK co-wrote, with Dr. Lynn Koegel, *Overcoming Autism: Finding the Answers, Strategies, and Hope That Can Transform a Child's Life.* Her first novel, *Same As It Never Was,* was a national bestseller that was made into a movie for the ABC Family cable channel called *Hello Sister, Goodbye Life.* Her second novel, *Knitting Under the Influence,* was published under Warner Books' 5 Spot imprint in September 2006. She has a short story in the collection *American Girls About Town.* She lives in the Pacific Palisades with her husband and four children.

KIRSTEN ALLEN MAJOR was born in Milwaukee, Wisconsin, and educated at Emma Willard School in Troy, New York, and Carleton College in Northfield, Minnesota. She has an MFA from Cornell University. Her fiction and nonfiction have appeared in *Chelsea,* the *Berkeley Fiction Review, Popular Mechanics, Real Simple,* and *The Rake.*

MARK MCDEVITT was born in Dublin, but grew up in Sligo, in the northwest of Ireland. A graduate of University College Dublin, he moved to the United States in 1994. His work has appeared in the *Irish Independent,* the *Examiner, In Dublin, The Iconoclast,* the *Miami Herald,* the *New York Times,* and *Giant,* among others. He is the author of several screenplays, stage plays, and a short story collection. Less frequently, he works in the film industry as a cameraman.

CAROLYN MEGAN'S essays and short stories have appeared in several literary journals and magazines, including *The Kenyon Review, The Massachusetts Review, Crab Orchard Review, Bellevue Literary Review,* and *MS.* Currently she is working on *The Golden Handcuff,* a memoir that explores her decision to remain childless. She lives and writes in Maine.

CAROLINE MILLER, the former editor in chief of *New York* magazine, as well as *Seventeen* and *Lear's,* is a graduate of Stanford University. She and her husband, Eric Himmel, the editor in chief of Harry N. Abrams, have three children.

MARTHA MOFFETT, born in St. Clair County, Alabama, worked in publishing in New York City and now is a freelance writer in South Florida. She received a Yaddo Fellowship and two Florida State Council on the Arts grants, one for short fiction and one for playwriting. A novella of hers in the *Chattahoochee Review* was included in *Best American Mystery Stories 2000.*

LIZA MONROY is a twenty-six-year-old freelance journalist whose articles and essays have appeared in the *New York Times, Newsweek,* the *Village Voice, Time Out New York, Travel Savvy,* and several anthologies, including *Mexico: A Love Story.* She has lived, worked, and studied in Mexico, Italy, Holland, the Czech Republic, Greece, and Venezuela. She currently lives in New York, where she recently completed a novel and is at work on a memoir about how her marriage to her gay best friend helped her understand the meaning of devotion.

THEO PAULINE NESTOR teaches for the University of Washington extension program in Seattle. Her memoir, *How to Sleep Alone in a King-Size Bed*, is forthcoming from Crown.

HELAINE OLEN is a freelance writer whose work has appeared in the *New York Times*, the *Wall Street Journal*, the *Washington Post*, the *Los Angeles Times*, *Salon*, and a number of other newspapers, magazines, and Web sites. She is also an editor for *LiteraryMama.com*. She lives in New York with her husband and two sons.

FRANK PAIVA graduated from the Lakeside School in Seattle in June of 2005. He currently attends the Gallatin School of Individualized Study at New York University, where he is concentrating in theater and creative writing. His work regularly appears on MSN.com.

ELLEN PALL is the author of *Among the Ginzburgs*, *Slightly Abridged*, and other novels. As a journalist, she has written about the arts for the *New York Times Magazine*, the *New Yorker*, and the *Washington Post*. She is also the originator of DebbiesIdea.com, a literary Web site.

SARA PEPITONE is an assistant at an investment bank. She is also a freelance writer. Her work has appeared in *Fodor's Road Guides*, the *New York Observer*, *New York Runner*, the *New York Times*, *Time Out New York*, *The Shore Line Times*, and on the Bloomberg wire. She is working on a collection of short stories.

KERRY REILLY grew up on Long Island, backpacked on five continents, and has lived in England and in many places in the United States. She has taught writing at the universities of New Hampshire, Iowa, and Colorado, worked as a publicist for a Broadway theater, and decorated cakes at a bakery in Rhode Island. Reilly earned a Master of Fine Arts degree in nonfiction writing at the University of Iowa. Her essays, stories, and poems have appeared in the *New York Times, The Threepenny Review, The Gettysburg Review, Delmar,* and *Sentence.* She is currently working on a memoir.

RICHARD REISS is the senior vice president for University Advancement at Fairleigh Dickinson University in New Jersey. In the early 1990s he wrote a weekly humor column for the *Piscataway-Dunellen Review* called "Reiss' Pieces," for which he won a Best Writing award from the New Jersey Press Association. Currently, he is completing a MFA in creative writing at Fairleigh Dickinson University and is writing a book about his son.

BONNIE J. ROUGH has her MFA from the University of Iowa's Nonfiction Writing Program and was a winner of the Annie Dillard Award for Creative Nonfiction. Her essays have appeared recently in the *New York Times, Alaska Quarterly Review, The Bellingham Review, Ninth Letter,* and *Isotope: A Journal of Literary Nature and Science Writing.* She has been supported by grants from the University of Iowa, the Kappa Kappa Gamma Foundation, and the Mary Anderson Center for the Arts. Rough lives with her husband, Dan, in Minneapolis, where she teaches at the Loft Literary Center and is at work on two books of nonfiction: a collection of essays on flight and a family story about heredity.

DAN SAVAGE is the author of the internationally syndicated sex-advice column "Savage Love" and the editor of *The Stranger,* Seattle's weekly newspaper. His books include *The Commitment; Skipping Towards Gomorrah; Savage Love,* a collection of his advice columns; and *The Kid,* an award-winning memoir about adoption. His writing has appeared in the *New York Times Magazine,* the *New York Times, Rolling Stone, The Onion,* and other publications. He has also contributed numerous pieces to *This American Life* on NPR.

ABBY SHER is a performer and writer who lives in Brooklyn with her new husband. She can be seen onstage at the Magnet Theater and read on the pages of many major magazines. She is working on her first novel.

IRENE SHERLOCK is an administrator at Western Connecticut State University and an adjunct lecturer in the English department. She lives in Danbury, Connecticut. Her essays can be heard on WSHU *National Public Radio.*

LARRY SMITH is the founder and editor of *SMITH* magazine (smithmag.net), an interactive, online magazine that showcases the many forms of personal storytelling. He has been an editor at *Men's Journal, ESPN magazine, Yahoo! Internet Life, P.O.V.,* and *Might,* and editor in chief of the nightlife magazine *Egg.*

DEBORA SPAR is the Spangler Family Professor and senior associate dean at Harvard Business School, where she teaches courses on the politics of international business, comparative capitalism, and economic development. Spar has published numerous articles in academic and public policy journals, such as the *Harvard Business Review, Foreign Affairs,* and *The New England Journal of Medicine.* Her latest book is *The Baby Business: How Money, Science, and Politics Drive the Commerce of Conception.*

AUTUMN STEPHENS is the editor of two anthologies of personal essays: *The Secret Lives of Lawfully Wedded Wives* and *Roar Softly and Carry a Great Lipstick: 28 Women Writers on Life, Sex, and Survival.* She is the author of *Crusaders, Curmudgeons, and Completely Corsetless Ladies in the Otherwise Virtuous Victorian Era,* and several other books in the Wild Women series of women's history and humor from Conari Press. A former book reviewer for the *San Francisco Chronicle,* she currently conducts writing workshops for people with cancer. She lives in Berkeley, California, with her husband and two sons.

KATHERINE TANNEY writes a monthly column, "Please Don't Feed the Writers," for the *Austin American-Statesman,* about her take on literary events in Austin, Texas, where she has lived since 1996. She is also a DJ with a weekly music program, *Really Motional Music,* on Austin's community radio station. Her novel, *Carousel of Progress,* was published by Villard in 2001 and won top prize for a first novel from the Texas Institute of Letters. She has published poetry, short fiction, and reviews, and works as a freelance writer, editor, and occasional writing teacher.

AYELET WALDMAN is the author of *Love and Other Impossible Pursuits.* Her nonfiction has appeared in the *New York Times, Elle, The Guardian, Allure,* and *The Believer,* among other places. She lives in Berkeley, California, with her husband and four children.

Born in California and raised in New Jersey, **RENEE WATABE** studied fine arts in New York City during the early eighties, at the School of Visual Arts, Parsons School of Design, and The New School for Social Research. She makes her home in New Jersey with artist Tim Folzenlogen and her three children. She works as a patient advocate in a hospital emergency department and is working on a collection of stories about life-altering experiences. She joined the Unification Church in 1981 and remained an active member for twenty-one years.

JENNIE YABROFF writes about art and culture for the *New York Times, Newsday,* the *San Francisco Chronicle,* and *ARTnews.* She received her MFA in literary nonfiction from Columbia University, and lives in Manhattan with her boyfriend, Brian.

ACKNOWLEDGMENTS

At the *New York Times,* style editor Trip Gabriel conceived the "Modern Love" column and has overseen its editing and production with great skill and passion ever since. I thank him for including me in his plans and for being such a decent, smart, and steady editor and friend. Thanks also to his deputy Danielle Mattoon; to the Style copy editors for their provocative headlines and last-minute editorial saves; to David Chelsea, whose illustrations give the column its distinctive visual flair; to Michaela Williams and Linda Conte for their guidance with matters contractual and administrative; and to Lee Riffaterre and Alex Ward for their expertise both legal and navigational.

At Crown, Rachel Klayman expertly guided this project from proposal to finished book and proved to be wonderful company along the way. Thanks also to Steve Ross and Carrie Thornton for their invaluable support and enthusiasm.

At ICM, Amanda Urban knew yet again what to do, how, and when. I thank her for being there for me, instantly and always, with unparalleled advice and advocacy.

At home, Cathi Hanauer has been my silent partner in this work all along (meaning, of course, that she has *not* been silent). Her editorial instincts and acumen have helped shape this column from the beginning. My appreciation and love to her for that and all the rest.

ABOUT THE EDITOR

DANIEL JONES, who edits the weekly "Modern Love" column in the Sunday Styles section of the *New York Times*, is also the editor of *The Bastard on the Couch: 27 Men Try Really Hard to Explain Their Feelings About Love, Loss, Fatherhood, and Freedom* and the author of the novel *After Lucy*, which was a finalist for the Barnes & Noble Discover Award. His writing has appeared in the *New York Times, Elle, More, Redbook,* and elsewhere. He lives with his family in Massachusetts.